THE ECONOMIC THEORY OF DEVELOPING COUNTRIES' RISE

Explaining the Myth of Rapid Economic Growth in China

Yangsheng Zhong

Translated by Xiaohui Wang and Guangmin He

University Press of America,® Inc.
Lanham · Boulder · New York · Toronto · Plymouth, UK

Copyright © 2010 by
University Press of America,® Inc.
4501 Forbes Boulevard
Suite 200
Lanham, Maryland 20706
UPA Acquisitions Department (301) 459-3366

Estover Road
Plymouth PL6 7PY
United Kingdom

Library of Congress Control Number: 2010920187
ISBN: 978-0-7618-5078-6 (clothbound : alk. paper)
ISBN: 978-0-7618-5079-3 (paperback : alk. paper)
eISBN: 978-0-7618-5097-7

This English version has been translated and modified from the original Chinese book (sixth edition) published by the Party School Press of CPC Central Committee, Beijing, China, December, 2005 and by arrangement with Guangdong Economy Press, a division of Guangdong Publishing Group.

Contents

Contents

About the Author

Dr. ZHONG Yangsheng, born in Longchuan County, Guangdong Province, graduated with a college degree from the Department of Politics & History in South China Normal University in 1973, and earned a Master's degree in Philosophy from the Graduate School of Chinese Academy of Social Sciences in 1981. Through studying part-time he earned a Doctor's degree in Economics from the Department of Economics at Jinan University in 1998. Currently, he serves as a member of Guangdong Provincial Standing Committee of the CPC, the Executive Vice Governor of Guangdong Province, and also an Adjunct Professor of Economics at Jinan University, Guangzhou.

After he graduated from high school in June, 1968, ZHONG Yangsheng went back to his hometown and used to work as a teacher in a village school, then as the head of production brigade, and finally became the Secretary of the village's Party Branch. Upon finishing graduate studies in university, he worked as a faculty member in the Department of Politics & History and the department's Secretary of Party Branch at South China Normal University, and then as a researcher in the Chinese Academy of Social Sciences. In 1982, he was transferred to the Guangdong Provincial Committee of the CPC, acting as Division Chief, Deputy Director of the Policy Research Department. Meanwhile, he has served as Chief Secretary, and Vice General Secretary of a County Committee as well as Vice General Secretary of a City Committee and Mayor of a city for several years. After six years' service in the Guangdong Provincial Committee of CPC as a Standing Secretary and Director of Policy Research Department, he again became General Secretary of Jiangmen City Committee for five years. In 2000, he was appointed as a Standing Committee member of CPC and the Head of the Propaganda Department in the Guangdong Provincial Government, and later held the position of Executive Vice Governor since 2003.

His life of writing started in 1981 with *The Role and Position of Science in the Development of Society* published in 1985 by Hunan People's Publishing House. After that, he was the author of seven publications, five of which were awarded the best works or excellent prizes in scientific research on the national-level (two publications) or the provincial level. This book is his fifth publication and systematically illustrates his ideas on economics. In 1995, this book was published and was regarded as one of "The Top 10 Best Annual National Economic Reading". The proverb of the author is "Putting Practice as the First Priority; Taking People as the Foremost."

About the Book

From twelve perspectives, including: productivity development, resource environment, industrial development and construction, enterprise quality, technological progress and value systems, *The Economic Theory of Developing Countries' Rise: Explaining the Myth of Rapid Economic Growth in China* systematically discusses the problems, difficulties, advantages, choices and approaches that developing countries have encountered in the economical catching-up process. Following the main theme of economic growth and focusing on major economic issues in developing countries and regions, the book expounds the theoretical proposition of catching-up economic growth and development in a meaningful realistic sense.

One of the outstanding characteristics of the book is that the writer applies the methodology of historical materialism to the theoretical research of economic growth practice, underlining the concept of human need embedded in economical development, and insisting on the integration of theoretical logics and historical logics. Logically starting from human need and ending at the idea of "personal all-round development as the ultimate goal of economic growth", the book deeply analyzes important topics in the context of China's economic rise.

The writer firmly believes that economic growth should not be singled out from the economic system. He suggests that developing countries need to make good use of the later-developing advantages and to prevent them from turning to the later-developing disadvantages in the catching-up process. To realize the goal of high-speed and sustainable economic growth, the traditional orientations towards productive output value, amount, and speed have to be abandoned, and the idea of relying heavily on natural resources to push economic development should be changed. On the contrary, developing countries need to establish growth patterns oriented to effectiveness, quality, efficiency, and sustainability, and to optimize the use of natural, social, cultural and human resources.

The important and creative points of the book lie in the writer's in-depth discussion and analysis on criticizing defects of classic and modern Western economic growth theories, building economic growth theories with Chinese characteristics, and theoretically explaining the miracle of China's economic development.

Many of the scientific perspectives, thoughtful viewpoints, and reasonable suggestions make the book a masterpiece in economic growth theories with Chinese characteristics, and are highly valued by the policy-makers in local governments and the central government of China.

First published in 1995, the book was awarded as one of "the best ten books on economics" of the year since it was regarded as a book with "important theoretical breakthrough and creativity". Reprinted several times since then, the sixth edition of the book was elected as one of "the excellent original work on Humanities and Social Sciences" in April 2007, when the first country-wide selection of "Three One-Hundred" original works was held.

A Letter to English Readers

Hereby, I wish to express my gratitude to English readers, especially those from the U.S.A. and Europe, who have paid great attention to the economic rise of China and my book. It is a great pleasure of mine to have my book published in an English-speaking country.

With a Doctor's degree in Economics, I am both a Professor and an Advisor of doctoral students in the field of Economics. At the same time, serving as Executive Vice Governor of Guangdong Province, I have made contributions to the economic growth of Guangdong, the province with the largest economy in China. Guangdong's GDP has jumped into the top 25 in the world; economic theory played an important role during this growth process, and I was inspired to realize the immeasurable value of economics and theories. Thirty years ago, Guangdong Province was an underdeveloped agricultural province on the south coast of China, with a GDP of only 18.6 billion RMB. However, in 2007, the Guangdong's GDP has reached 3060.6 billion RMB, with an annual growth rate of 13.8%. Guangdong Province, the "experimental field" of China's economic reform and opening-up policies, is the epitome of modern China. Nowadays, with the GDP reaching 24 trillion RMB, China has become the fourth largest economy in the world, and is regarded as "a miracle of economic rise".

Due to the features of the times and practice, this book was regarded as "a theoretical breakthrough and innovative economic masterpiece, which probed into the mystery of developing countries' economic growth as well as the rules of economic take-off and modernization."[1] Therefore, it has been in the spotlight ever since its debut in 1994, receiving great attention from China's 1.3 billion people. After winning the prize of China's fifth "National Top 10 Economic Books" in 1995, there have been sixth editions published. In 2007, the sixth edition of the book won the prize of "National Humanity and Social Science Book of Excellence", and was regarded "Representative Book of Economic Growth with Distinct Chinese Characteristics."[2]

I sincerely hope that this book will become a channel through which

---

1. "Introduction to National Top 10 Economic Books", *Economic Daily* (Section of *Theory Weekly*), Beijing: April 29, 1996.
2. Han, Baojiang, *"Catching-up Economic Growth Theory* and China's experience", *World*, March, 2007.

American economic academia can better understand the theoretical route of China's rapid economic growth. Also, I hope that it could be a bridge to facilitate academic communications between China and the U.S.A.

Hereby, my gratitude first goes to the University Press of America. I also applaud the following scholars for their hard work on translating the book into English version: Professor Xiaohui Wang, Lingnan (University) College of Zhongshan (Sun Yat-sen) University (China), Ph.D. from the University of Minnesota; Dr. Guangming He, Chairman of Wu Chang Fa Association (Hong Kong), Adjunct Professor of England International Business School; and their associates. Meanwhile, thanks to the General Administration of Press and Publication of the People's Republic of China for the supporting policy of "making China's books global". I appreciate the efforts of the Guangdong Provincial Publishing Group which made this possible.

At last, I owe my gratitude to my wife Suzhen Zhong and mother Genglan Wang, who always love and support me.

Yangsheng Zhong
Guangzhou, China

January 2009

Preface by the Principal Translator

I would first like to express my gratitude to Dr. Yangsheng Zhong for insistently showing confidence in me as the appropriate translator to accomplish this English version. As a professor at one of the top business schools across China, I can say that *The Economic Theory of Developing Countries' Rise: Explaining the Myth of Rapid Economic Growth in China* has been a very influential and well selling book written on economics in China, and has received a lot of awards and accolades since it was first published in 1995. Most recently, in August 2009, Dr. Zhong and this book were selected and enrolled in the honorable book series – *100 Economist and their notable works impacting China's Economic Construction over the last 60 years.* Therefore, it is a pleasure for me, on both a professional and personally level, to present this book to the English speaking world.

The great economic development achievements of China within such a short period of time have surprised the world, and have also raised other developing countries' hopes for catching up with developed countries. Featured with traditional political economics and Chinese characteristics of socialism, this book is about the economics of developing countries' rise, based on the case of China and focuses on catching-up economic growth theory. Thus, the book is of interest to those who wish to know more about theories, practices, policies and causes of China's economic success.

It has been my job to translate the author's original thoughts and meanings as clear and precise as possible. It is my sincerest desire that readers find this English version both engaging and stimulating and that through it come to better understand the economic growth and development which China has undergone. However, translating a book, especially such kind of book, is arduous work. It is a very time-consuming project and also a very difficult job. Besides the tremendous cultural and historical differences between China and Western countries, in this project there are innumerable Chinese terms, phraseologies, wordings and concepts that have no equivalents in English. Hence, in many cases, I have had to be creative to make the most suitable translations. Should readers find any mistakes or errors in this English version, I sincerely ask for their forgiveness.

Lastly, I would like to extend my earnest thanks to the other translators, students and friends who helped me through the translation, refining, editing and finalizing process: Dr. Guangmin He, who, along with his associates in Hong Kong, provided a primary framework and the basic constructs for the whole book; Ms. Song Song from the World Bank (USA) greatly contributed to the first draft; Ms. Yuehua Xu, a Ph. D. student from the Chinese University of Hong Kong, made efforts on several chapters; Ms. Weiwei Wang, another Ph. D. student from Guangdong University of Foreign Studies, and a couple of master's students helped with one chapter and with checking index and notes as well as making the figures and tables; Mr. Michael Chang, a native English speaker from the USA and a current graduate student at Sun Yat-sen University, helped to proofread the draft. Their input and efforts were invaluable to me and I have been very fortunate to have had their support.

Xiaohui Wang
Professor & Ph. D.
Lingnan (University) College, Sun Yat-sen (Zhongshan) University
Guangzhou, China
Email: wangxiaohui28@hotmail.com

October 2009

Foreword

(Sixth Edition)

This is not a strict academic book, but an economic writing consolidating writer's thoughts on his past research experience and actual work experience. The birth of this book marks the great ambition of a new generation of Chinese communist. The author has integrated belief, theory and action into a body of knowledge. People working in research treat this book as an academic publication while people engaging in actual economic practices take this book as reference. Both types of readers enjoy reading this book. After being named as one of "The Best 10 Economics Readings" in 1995, continuously being published by the Guangdong Higher Education Publishing Company up to its fifth version in 2003. Now, the fifth version is almost sold out. Based on requests from readers, the publishing section of the Party School of CPC Central Committee deemed this book to have great value in scientifically executing social and economic development in China, and decided to publish a new version. Hence, they hoped that the writer could make some adjustments in the new version. This book was originally written during the author's study at the Party School of CPC Central Committee in 1994. As a member of the CPC, the author appreciates the kindness of the publishing section and has no choice but to publish it again.

The first version of this book was released almost ten years ago. During such a long period of time, there have been many changes in China and the global economy, especially when moving into the 21st century. Requesting the writer to make amendments is to make the book go parallel with time. Looking back on the economic development in China and the world over the past ten years, the beliefs and the basic judgments discussed in this book, including fundamental patterns, fundamental principles and fundamental viewpoints, are all correct. It also gives meaning to following generations for integrating theory and practice together.

Some meaningful points in this book may be summarized as follows: 1) from the late 1970s to the first 20 years of the 21st century, there has been a historical opportunity for developing countries and regions to actualize their goals of catching up; 2) human need remains as the highest principle of economic growth, and holistic personal development is the ultimate goal of economic development; 3) placing economic efficiency at the center, adjusting and improving the economic structure, and actualizing effective economic growth, all are important features of Chinese socialist economic growth; 4) industrial establishment is the core foundation for sustainable economic growth; capital and investment are the first motivators for economic take-off; technological improvement is the first motivator for modernized economic growth; needs are the guidelines for upgrading industries while resource constraint patterns are the settings of productivity, economic growth -- pattern of limiting resource environment; the basic regularity for technological improvement (uses and positions of pattern in innovation and dispersal); economic growth – pattern of mechanism constraints; and all other elements related to economic growth, like goals, directions, beliefs, strategies and tactics...etc. Moreover, applying the materialism theory into economics is a new research methodology to highlight the position and use of a nation in economic growth with focusing on the process of economic growth to find out issues in relation to solutions for economic growth, insisting on unification of theory and action; logic of theory and logic of history. This is a big difference compared with modernized economic research method, with actualizing how to prove the idea of scientific materialism -- a breakthrough from traditional research. One of the advantages of this book is "having a breakthrough and innovation in theory"(quoted in "Times Daily" on 29th April, 1996 in the description of "The Best 10 Economics Readings, 1995). In response to historical and social responsibility of the writer and the request of readers, a large amount of complementary information has been added into this new version with some adjustments to the not-so-clear points, and some proofreading on the use of words. An example is in the third section of chapter two, version five, initially stated as "productivity is the god of efficient economic growth" – a bit vague, this has been amended as "productivity is a critical point of efficient economic growth" which is more specific than the original one.

The author wants to take this opportunity to apologize to my readers about not putting in chapters about some influential issues into this book. The characteristics of economics are contemporariness, practicality and doing-goodness with functions of describing economic phenomenon, showing the operation of economics, predicting the trend of economic operation, and directly executing economics theory into society. Hence, I should include issues such as globalization, networking, and the application of knowledge into economic growth. Moreover, in this book I should have included references to my rich experiences gained from assisting a provincial supervisor on the routine economic activities of a big province, and my existing practical experience from the position of Party Secretary and strategic research. However, due to insufficient time, I have not done so but hope I can do much better in the future.

Lastly, the author wants to express my gratitude to the management and editorial board of the publishing section from the Communism Central Party School who have provided me with lots of support. And, of course, to all my comrades who have given me a hand together with my wife – Sunzhen Zhong, and to all those people who have always shown me care.

Yangsheng Zhong
Guangzhou, China

November 2005

Chapter One

Introduction: Meeting Human Need is the

Highest Principle of Economic Growth

Up to today, many economic theories have appeared that provide us with impressive insights that have opened our eyes. However, many of these theories are only concerned with things but people – a shortfall needed to be fine-tuned. These theories cover the increase of total economic volume, the changes in profit, the distribution of wealth and the relationship with economy. Or, we can say that these theories are more concerned with development and change production and productivity (where man is only treated as a material power), while the dominant role of people and the position of human need in economic growth is not emphasized sufficiently. Though Marxism has many insightful ideas concerning these aspects, many researchers are still not aware of them, not to mention able to make a further explanation of them. Tracing back the developmental history of human society, there is a definite truth in the idea of Marx that "we need to determine the most fundamental thing for human being which is also the first prerequisite of human history – people need to have clothing, food, shelter and other basic things before 'creating history'. Hence, the very first historical activity is to produce a material life for itself."[1] The development history of human beings and economy has indicated that social economy, including the process of socialist economic growth, actually is a man-focused process, with continuous development in productivity, process of social production and re-production, and the unceasing increase in social wealth and its quality. In fact, it is a process that therefore fulfills the growing material and spiritual need of people, and actualizes the value and holistic development of people in a society. Human need is demonstrated through the starting and ending points of the social economic growth process, with many conflicts hidden in this growth process. Also, as the proactive main body, the human need determines different stages of economic growth, developmental speeds, as well as industrial structures and directions. Therefore, historically, the human need becomes the highest principle of social economic growth. It is necessary to illustrate the process of economic growth from the perspective of human need, so as to have further studies and theories that support for establishing economic growth process and for developing a social economy in a correct way.

1.1　Human Need Determines the Driving Power for Economic Growth

We have to realize that human need determines the motivating power for economic growth from the beginning to end. It is fair to say that there are a variety of powers to drive economic growth, such as political powers with aims of achievement (developing countries aim to go beyond the developed countries; or, developed countries aim to actualize their great political power over others), fiscal- aimed power (the intention of increasing a large amount of income in governments, for instance, the local governments), profit-making power of enterprise (the aim of increasing profits from each enterprise for accumulating a great power for economic growth in a society), etc. However, no matter what kinds of aims they are, they need to have cohesiveness and integration which are based on human need – to drive survival, development and enjoyment of each individual by production and creation. Without the need and fulfillment of the need, no tools of satisfying human need will emerge to complete the exchange and the synergy among material, energy and information in the creation process of material and cultural products, for increasing material and cultural wealth in a society. Therefore Hegel stated in his book "*Philosophy of History*" that in order to fulfill the need of oneself, people have to interact with the external natural world through practices, so that they can have their needs fulfilled by conquering the natural world. The problem is that the opposing parties from the natural world have certain kinds of resistances. Hence, people must create various tools to combat these situations. With the invention of tools, there are productive and economic activities, and there is economic growth in a society. The driving forces for continuous production and economic activities in social economic growth come from the fulfillments of people's needs, and the creation of a higher level and a larger scale of the needs. Without stimulation from human need, no human production or economic activities could be conducted in a sustainable way.

The developmental history of human society has shown that the speeding-up of economic growth in a society is greatly attributed to growing human need – within the 10,000 years from New Stone Age to the beginning of B.C., human production had been doubled; from the beginning of B.C. to year 1,600, there was a 2.3 times increase in production volume; within the 300 years from year 1,600 to year 1,900, the increase was 2.2 times; and within the 90 years from 1,900 to year 1,990, the increase was more than 2 times. A French sociologist predicted that the wealth created within a 3-year period of today's production was almost equal to the wealth created in the 30 years at the beginning of the 20th century, the wealth in the 300 years prior to the Newton Age, and the wealth in the 3,000 years of Old Stone Age.[2] A Chinese scholar Zhu Ji claimed in his book of "On Global Economy" that the wealth value people create in one year nowadays was similar to the sum of value created over hundreds or thousands of years in the past. The Gross Domestic Product (GDP) produced globally in the year 2,000 was 31,336 billion US dollars which was 131 times of the year 1,500 (240 billion US dollars). Moving towards the 21st century, people only used about 3 days to create the sum of GDP for the whole year in the year 1,500. It is forecast that the time span of human economic activities would be further shortened, and the speed would be further increased, along with technological improvement. There are many factors that speed up economic development, among them the most important is the technological development and application factor. However, human need is a fundamental driving factor. If there are no needs to be satisfied in a society, nobody will spend the effort on technological development and application, not to mention the utilization of other production elements. Even though there is social production, no consumption will be created in a nation if there is not any need to be fulfilled. Hence, a direct motivation for developing production will be strong needs of people; otherwise, economic growth would be stagnated or lagged behind.

Surely, human need is of a definite value. However, it does not mean that all people's needs are in the core position to stimulate economic growth. The idea of Marx is that from a generic social economic perspective, human need refers to a relationship built between the needs of people (individuals, organizations and societies) and the external material world and the spiritual cultural phenomenon. It is the relationship that shows people actually or might utilize and consume the external material world and the spiritual cultural phenomenon. This can reflect how individuals, organizations and the whole society can obtain their social, material and spiritual living elements. As Marx said, this is a reflection of a society's ability to consume, and a new desire was created through the process of satisfying people's needs. On one hand, this process is subject to historical limitations of productivity and production relationships. On the other hand, it stimulates human beings to enhance productivity and economic growth. The needs referred here are men's economic needs but not those non-economic ones. Economic needs hereby refer to those needs that rely on labor products and social production to be satisfied, but can not be satisfied by ordinary materials, phenomenon and processes in the external world. It is these needs that create desire for satisfaction and consumption and are the starting and ending points of production activities that forge a great stimulation for productivity development and economic growth. According to the idea of Marx, without needs, production and economic growth can not appear, and hence there is no economic development. Marx said, "production creates appropriate targets for needs; distribution is based on certain patterns of a society; exchange is based on individual's needs to re-distribute what he has got from distribution; with consumption, products ultimately disintegrated from this cycle in a society and directly turned into targets and slaves for the enjoyment and fulfillment of individual's needs."[3] So, the starting and the ending points of production and economic growth perform simultaneously in the processes of production and economic growth; people are the focal point of unification and mobility of the production process with a core, natural and dynamic decisive function.

Why human economic need be in the core position with such a decisive function? The following figure illustrates the relationships between human beings as the proactive party and the exchange process of materials, energy and information in social production and consumption.

Figure 1.1

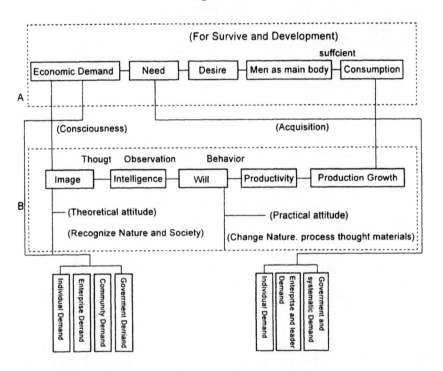

The Figure 1.1 shows the followings.

(1) The relations between people (the proactive party) and the other party of production and consumption are composed of a process A in which people create and satisfy their own needs for survival and development, and a process B in which people recognize and transform nature and society, and perform the exchange among material, energy and information. Processes A and B are two relative independent processes that are people dominated – and relay on people's abilities to know the nature, to conquer the nature, and to transform nature to satisfy one's needs. In other words, A and B are the processes of continually utilizing and developing the function of production, enlarging production and

re-production, and unceasingly increasing social material products, spiritual products and service products. There is a dual meaning in the nature of this kind of productivity: 1) relationship between people-dominated needs and the ability of oneself; 2) relationship between people-dominated needs and the external natural environment. These dual relationships are inter-dependent, antagonistic, and mutual-transferred. The only intermediary to actualize the process is the ability of the people in a nation, or the utilization of productivity.

(2) Ability of people in a nation, or the productivity, as an intermediary, uses human need as its own intermediary. Human beings are proactive animals with a physical structure and mental organization, and their survival and development rely on the consumption of material and cultural products. This kind of instinct and societal desire creates economic needs through the process of production, exchange, distribution and consumption. This motivates the development of social productivity and economic growth. On the other hand, the improvement of social productivity and economic growth, and the increase of different kinds of products in a society greatly depends on satisfying people's needs for survival and development. Otherwise, social production and economic growth will be hindered. Hence, we can see the central position of people's needs in the processes of production and consumption. Human need is both the starting point and the ending point of social production development and economic growth. With a spiral effect from these "two points", development of social production and economic growth will then be stimulated continually.

(3) Process A and process B form an open cycle system. There is not an everlastingly balance at the starting and ending points in this cycle system. As people need to survive and develop, they actively make use of their productivity to raise production, to create a large amount of material and spiritual wealth, and at the same time satisfy one's survival and developmental needs through production and consumption; and finally create a new self with a higher level of desire and stronger needs. Just as Marx said, "consumption creates new production needs which form an inner motivation in the concept of production"[4] to stimulate people to create new productivity, to enhance labor efficiency, and to enlarge social production and to speed up economic growth. That is to say the open cycle system is based on the actualization of production and continual economic growth with a core element of satisfying people's needs for survival and development in a society.

(4) In the open cycle system mentioned above, people's abilities are linked up with their needs, their choices, and their balance between the subjective (needs) and objective (production). People's abilities are referred to as the summation of physical and intellectual capabilities as producers. From chart 1.1, we can see that knowledge of nature and society is the prerequisite of

undergoing material and spiritual production; the broader the knowledge, the richer the concept and the higher the quality of the products will be. Glancing back at the history of science, human culture and development of economy – from primitive to ancient society, the role of people's physical abilities with productivity in a production process is more crucial. Moving into a modern society, especially a contemporary society, people's physical abilities are far outweighed by people's intellectual ability in the position and the function of production. Knowledge has become a much more important driving power in economic growth, which makes scientific technology the first productivity. Hence, from a perspective of international division and global economic competition, every country and region has to start from satisfying and enhancing the intellectual needs of people in their economic growth process with emphasis on education and scientific development. The needs of people in a nation is an internal driver for economic growth, the ability of people is an intermediary for actualizing economic growth, and education and scientific development are tools for economic growth. When integrating all these three elements, a direct motivation power for economic growth will be formed.

(5) Individual needs in a society and economic needs are the most fundamental needs and demands of a society. The needs and demands of enterprises, organizations and the government are originated from individuals' needs and demands. As a result, to satisfy people's needs of survival and the development of a nation actually means to satisfy individuals in a society. This is the aim of production in socialism as well as a belief in a capitalist market economy – "the customer is God". This can demonstrate that besides the consistent foundations and commonalities in the relationships, there are unique characteristics and distinctions. If enterprises, organizations, and the government disintegrate their needs from the needs of individuals in society, the economic behaviors in the society will fall apart from the human need and then hinder economic growth.

During the long period of the 20th century starting post-World War II to the 1990s, one significant feature that characterizes the growth of the global economy was "catching-up". The productivity of most industrialized countries had already caught up with that of the United States (based on the criteria of average income per capita of the wealthiest country in 1950) during the 1950s - 1960s. "Economic Miracles" were created by the "Four Little Dragons" in Asia and by Germany in Europe; tremendous economic development was also found in other countries. Japan and Germany have turned themselves into highly industrialized countries from the defeated countries of the 1950s. Later, they quickly caught up to the economic performance of the States. They have become giant economic nations, which rank as the second and third economic entities in the world, and are strong powers to compete against the States. China along with other socialist countries established after the two world wars were regarded as developing countries with economies lagging behind. A common mistake was found among China and other socialist countries – to politicalize the economy, and unilaterally pursue high growth speed, and ignore people's livelihood (needs) for a blind economic take-off until the late 1970s or even till the late 1980s respectively. Driven by this kind of goal, the government only sought for speedy economic growth while gradually isolating itself from the living needs of individuals and the survival needs of enterprises. As a result, economic growth was off the correct track, and a common behavioral preference was formed which showed: 1) preferring speed, unilaterally pursuing high growth speed, and treating it as an indicator for assessing the government performance; and 2) preferring centralization in a highly-intensive planned economy, only using administrative measures to align with economic resources, and the government directly participating in production and business activities.

Due to unilateral pursuit of high speed without giving consideration to economic efficiency, a great deal of waste occurred in economic resources and investment, and this made economic growth off the track. Consequently, there was a high economic growth but slow development, which was unable to satisfy the people's need in the long term and caused an economic downturn. Based on what we have learnt from China's experiences, speeding up economic reform and developing a market economy could shorten the economic gap, and could more efficiently utilize economic resources. Hence, China could go back to the highest principle of satisfying needs of people's survival and development. This is a great leap in history with success of reform as the economy has been motivated efficiently and people's lives have been improved.

1.2 Relationship between Human Need and the Process of Economic Growth

The relationship between human need and the process of economic growth is basically the subjective versus objective relationship. They are inter-dependent and have a mutual effect on each other. The proactive party is the human need. As human need is moving forward with advances, it can determine the scale of economic growth, the complexity of the products, and the adjustment and enhancement of the industrial structure. Most economic theories in the past were only concerned about the technical elements – the function of innovation in technology – without analyzing a deeper hidden meaning of the dynamic human need – the function of motivation derived from benefits. There is a need to investigate further about the highest principle of utilizing human need under the process of economic growth.

Now, let's take a look to see how human need can drive economic growth.

First, human need stimulates the scope of social production to become larger with an increasing number of economic departments, enriching the products produced, and with a broader foundation of economic growth. As mentioned previously that human need, social production and economic development are an open cycle system. People want to have their demands fulfilled; therefore, they engage in production and motivate economic growth to create wealth. In social production, fulfillment of demands will create new kinds of demands, and a greater motivation power will then appear for accelerating economic growth. History of social economic development has demonstrated that human need created different economic departments for development. Examples are: as people need to solve the problem of food, survival and physical health, departments of farming and catering will then appear; as people want to have better and more delicious food, tools and machinery of food processing emerge with the department of food processing; as people want to solve the problems of housing, departments of construction, and building materials, renovation services are established; as people need to solve the problems of transportation, to enhance social interaction, to improve channels of product exchange, and to enhance their speed of military protection, departments of transportation are created; as people need to solve the problems of technology, knowledge accumulation, and strengthen the ability of oneself, paper making and publishing technologies are invented; as people need to stay close together, to improve message transmission, to satisfy the needs of information exchange in production and in daily lives, tele-communication departments appear; as people want to pass their knowledge to their younger generation to improve their quality with developmental need satisfied, education and science technology departments are established; as people want to lead a full life with a variety of entertainment for enjoyment and art appreciation, art and cultural departments are created...etc. All in all, as long as there are demands to be fulfilled within actualization of social production, new economic departments with related social products will emerge. Moving along with the increase in production departments and social products, the scale of industries and volume of economic transactions will be greater, and economic growth will be faster. Although cognitive powers and production technologies are kinds of direct power for actualization, the original driver comes from formation of human needs for receiving benefits and the realization of economic results. Therefore, we can conclude that social economy is produced under demand satisfaction. People are the proactive party with demands created from their own image.

Second, human need stimulates adjustment, fine-tuning and upgrading of industry structure with product proliferation. Marx mentioned that "the formation of needs derives from the fact that human society produces the objective of need, and therefore produces demand itself."[5] Human need and social production form an open cycle system in which the actual process is: human need A → social production A (economic growth) → human need B → social production B (economic growth) → human need C, so on to infinity. In this process, human beings take production practice as an intermediary in which natural power is integrated with one's demands, so as to enlarge social production, satisfy the demands of one self, transform the quality of one self, and create a new born self under a new foundation. This kind of cycle makes demands diversify, develop and upgrade continuously in order to make social production adapt to industry structure.

So, how can human need motivate adjustment and improvement of industry structure within the open cycle system?

Let's take a look on need first. As we know, human need can be classified into different levels based on their importance. Marx, Engels and other scholars have conducted some kind of research on that. According to Engels, human need could be classified into three levels, these are, need of survival, need of enjoyment and need of development. A contemporary US psychologist Maslow stated that there were two distinct types of needs or instincts: 1) lower level needs or physiological needs - the needs or instincts that weaken as species evolve; 2) higher level needs or psychological needs - the potential needs that emerge as species evolve. Building on this foundation, he classified needs into five levels:

(1) Physiological needs of human beings, including food, oxygen, water, sleep, sex and other similar kinds of activities;

(2) Need of safety, including sense of security, sense of stability, sense of regularity within the environment of one self;

(3) Need of belonging, including love, and social interaction with people, like sentimental feelings;

(4) Need of esteem, like self-respect, self-esteem, integrity and sense of achievement; and;

(5) Need of self actualization, like realization of one's potential and utilization of one' abilities.

Maslow emphasized on the "primary subjective" needs – showing the trend of needs moved from a lower level into a higher level. This kind of classification is consistent with the idea of Engels – three levels of need in which both of them treat the development and the actualization of the values embedded in one self as the highest level of need. The evolution process of needs is linked up to the demand of products in other levels, and the level of itself too. The upward shift pattern of needs indicates that demand of economy moves parallel with human need from a lower level towards to a higher level. This forms a structure that directly influences social production and economic growth.

From here, we can see that human need is a channel for stimulating adjustment and upgrading industrial structure. Economic demands refer to the relationship between disposable income and variables with an ability of making payments. The function can be expressed in a formula: $C = C(Y)$ of which C on the left hand side of the equal sign represents consumption while C on the right hand side is variable and Y is income. $C = C(Y)$ means consumption is a variable of income. It tells us that if income is limited and can not satisfy all levels of needs, of course, people will spend their income on satisfying their physical needs first until there is an increase on income for utilizing some other higher levels of needs. Demands will then be shifted into a higher level of needs. Human need is based on the changing and upgrading structure of demand to lead the development of social production, to adjust, to enhance and to upgrade industry structure. According to some statistics, because the Engel Index[6] is too high, people with an average GDP per capita of US $300.00 or below usually only consume basic necessity goods. In this stage, people rely on farming and textile products. Correspondingly, farming and textile will develop as leading industries. When the average GDP per capita amounts to US $300.00 or more, the problem of satisfying basic necessity needs are solved; the focus of demand structure shifts from basic to non-basic living needs, especially durable consumer products. Hence, industry structure moves from farming and light industries into foundation industries processing raw material and manufacturing industries of durable consumer products. Therefore farming economies are transmitted into industrialized economies. The advanced development in farming and light industries with a great increase on labor productivity at this stage not only leads to a provision of basic living products, but also leads to capital accumulation and a surplus of labor that helps speed up the production development of basic industries and heavy industries and motivate production of non-living products. As there is a higher level of GDP with enrichment in consumer products, people want to satisfy spiritual needs with quality of living and a better living environment. People focus more on enjoyment, quality of one self, and actualization of their potential in various aspects. Hence, their life style will change tremendously with more diversified and proactive demands. This makes mass production with little choices change rapidly into diversified production with small volumes together with better before and after sales service. Therefore, the industry structure would be transformed from a rigid structure into a flexible structure, and social production would be highly automated, and with intellectual development and with the third industry replacing the first and the second industry, industrialized economies would change into a service economy. As needs of human beings are the focal point of self-development, some changes have already occurred in organizational structures and labor structures in developed countries – reducing the number of people in direct material production while increasing the number of technical and managerial people. In the United States, Japan, Europe, and many other developed countries, the ratio of labor structure is like this – manual staff: managerial staff: technical engineering staff = 1: 1: 1. Many developing countries in the world, including China, are moving towards this kind of structure. People start to disintegrate themselves from material production and engage themselves in management and scientific research, in technical development, in receiving education and training, in innovation and other kinds of intellectual development which are back to direct production processes. Under this trend, knowledge is the most important resource for economic growth which makes knowledge or information industry a leading industry as social and economic development relies heavily on information. As a result, the service industry is transforming into information industry.

People may wonder whether adjustment, enhancement and upgrading of industry structures are the results of technical revolution and development of productivity. It is undeniable that lots of evidence has proved that the speed of technical improvement varies among different industrial settings, departments, and therefore, productivity also varies among different industrial settings. Because of the differences in productivity, industry structure will be motivated towards a more advanced one. From a holistic point of view, better productivity can be obtained under changes of industry structure, that is, the productivity rate in the manufacturing industry is better than that of the farming industry; heavy industry is better than light industry; and the processing industry is better than the raw material industry. However, we cannot say that human need does not have a decisive effect in economic growth. When tracing back the development of scientific technology, the history of the invention and application of steam engines is a good example of this. In 120 B.C., a Greece scientist named Hero discovered that steam could produce mechanic power and invented a steam-driven machine. Unfortunately, this invention did not receive great attention in ancient times. The reason was that steam engines were aimed for mass production and laborers were concerned with their individual contributions to the production process. This kind of ignorance lasted until the 14th and 15th centuries. In the 15th century, though an Italian scientist Da Vinci had mentioned the use of steam engines, no positive feedback was received. This was because that period of time was only a budding time for capitalism. Later, British and French scholars also brought up a new proposal on steam engines in a manual labor workshop in the period of 1630 to 1690, yet still no attention was received. Not until the 18th century in Britain with the great developments of capitalism and the growing need of the textile industry did the application of steam engines became widely used; the first industry revolution then appeared during the mid of the 18th century and the 19th century. This made manufacturing the leading industry, replacing the traditional farming industry with the actualization of the first industry structural change. This demonstrates that human need possesses a driving force of economic development with the help of technology invention and application.

Based on the above, we can say that there is a pattern that human need drives the advancement of industry structure. No nation can escape from this rule of advancement. The 30 years before the opening-up policy of China, the needs of the people were ignored by only focusing on speeding up industrial development. China tried to copy the old story of Russia. While its heavy industries increased 90 times, light industries improved only 19 times; the ratio between light and heavy industries is 43.1 : 56.9 – imbalanced growth with heavy industries received too much attention while light industries were not well developed. The result was that the levels of needs were not followed in sequence

– from satisfying the basic needs to a higher level of living needs. There was a distance between heavy industries and consumption. This kind of expansion was not driven by consumption of product and it did not have an internal demand for industry structural change. It was only a repetitive cycle of having volume increased with a fault picture of enhancement without a real foundation of needs. This kind of development in heavy industries led to an insufficiency of basic necessity goods for people: needs were not fulfilled, products were not required, and ultimately productivity was idle. According to statistics, during the period from 1952 to 1979, investment in fundamental infrastructure in China amounted to 650 billion dollars with a fixed capital of 450 billion dollars; however, realized capital efficiency was only 300 billion dollars with a loss of 350 billion dollars (54.5 % of the total investment). Though China had tremendous economic growth of 8.4% which was seldom found in the world, there was a slow growth in improving people's lives with consumption only increasing 3.26%. This was due to a large part of growth isolated from human need and thus the growth could not realize the values in a society – inefficient growth. After having an opening-up policy in the late 1978, the Communism Party of China (CPC) followed the conceptual framework of emphasizing human need as their highest principle in economic development and brought the industry structure back to the right track. Starting in the year 1979, the speed of growth in light industries was faster than heavy industries; the Hofmann Coefficient[7] (the ratio of light industry to heavy industry) raised back and moved from less than 1 in earlier years to 51.5: 48.5 in 1981– a bit more than the level of 1. Until the year 1990, the level maintained around 1 with a gradual drop thereafter, and the initially closed situation of light and heavy industries was then opened up, reaching a balanced ratio between these two industries.[8] This was a fruitful result of the opening-up policy in China. Besides, it also established a material foundation for economic development, as well as a booming market to improve the livelihood of people. However, it was not the case for Russia. Though Russia used to be the second strongest country in the world with a high social productivity development level and strong national power, it did not solve the above problem well. In addition, there were some other critical issues in Russia, and the tragedy of national disintegration finally occurred. As leaders in political parties or in government, no one can violate the highest principles of economic growth in establishing industries and determining strategies for economic growth. It is the scientific decision that paves the way for sustainable growth. Otherwise, there will be severe undesirable consequences.

Development of human need not only stimulates growth and improvement of products, but also makes economy become continuous socialization and internationalization. Adjustment, enhancement and upgrading of industry structure are actually also factors in the increasement and advancement of products for human need, and drive the level of needs from a lower layer into a higher one. One of the fundamental needs of people is food, therefore, the farming industry is the first industry developed to fulfill this need. Moving along to the needs of enjoyment, the development of oneself and the actualization of self-values, and the utilization of individual talents in a society, second industry – industrial development and third industry appear with a large number of manufactured products and service products. Information products are also produced under the development of information industry. A climbing ladder of social products is then established under the upgrading needs of people in a nation – agriculture products (foods for survival) – manufactured products (productive and living goods) – service products (enjoyment and development items) – information products (spiritual and developmental tools). Social economy is also based on this ladder to develop: agriculture economy – industrial economy – service economy- information economy. Economic development creates a foundation for the utilization of material and spiritual elements that make people's all-rounded development come true. These two types of development are not comprehensive because a broader and more diversified social economy linkage is required. Marx claimed that "the holistic development of individuals (Die universalitat des individuums) does not come from prediction or imagination, but it is a generalization of linkage between practice and belief of individuals."[9] He also pointed out that this kind of generalization is formed under normal socialization and the existence of global market elements for equipping a proper foundation for a holistic development of individuals.[10] Openness can enrich innovation and other social economic linkages; labor diversification and co-operation within geographical regions and the world, and global market economic technology exchange can create generalized linkages to satisfy the need of holistic development. This is the highest level of actualization of oneself with holistic development. Under this type of developmental stage, people of a nation need to accommodate themselves into the whole world for unification with overcoming barriers of racism and enhancing mutual reliance among countries, and pushing to develop into a more advanced level. The formation of social economic production moves from a primitive economy into a country-based economy, an international economy, and a global economy. This aligns with and is motivated by the holistic development of people in a nation. Surely, the ladder-type development of economy is the result of technological advancement and development of productivity. From a dynamic point of view, needs are the force to drive technological advancement and development of productivity. These two aspects are only the channels to bridge the conflict found between human need and the external environment. Hence, the role of human need has a detrimental function. The advanced level of need development is to bridge the gap between countries without regional constraints, and strengthen international reliance and diversification with exchange in economic technology and cultural arts. As motivated by need development with a foundation of social productivity and speedy scientific development, modernized economy has transmitted itself from relying on natural resources and focusing on manufacturing industries into relying on information resources and focusing on service industry in an international economy. This kind of global economic development is the result of unceasing revolution of productivity and continuous motivation of human need. Without driving human need, social productivity will not be improved stage by stage with revolutionary transforms, the scale of improvement will not be that great, and the speed of changes will not be that fast. Only with needs of satisfaction and development of oneself, the pattern motivating social economic development will keep on moving forward.

1.3 Conflicts between Social Production and the Process of Economic Growth

Previous economic growth theories always focused on locating conflicts between social production and the process of economic growth while ignoring human need. Though economic conflicts have been found, but the internal hint and implication arisen from conflicts and related areas have not been aware of. This negatively affects people in controlling the process of economic growth and in finding solutions to the conflicts in which repetitive errors have occurred. This not only distorts human need, but also does not help to satisfy the need and development of one self. In order to further illustrate the highest principle of human need for economic growth, an in-depth analysis on the conflicts derived from human need and related areas in the process of economic growth is going to be described with theoretical explanation as a support.

The following chart shows the structure of all aspects driven from conflicts of human need.

Figure 1.2

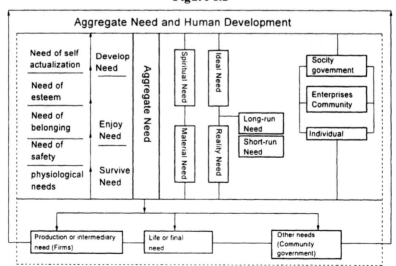

From the chart, we can see that the structure of human need is a complex dynamic system. No matter whether we look at the needs from a vertical or horizontal perspective, all levels of needs are inter-related with a final destination to satisfy people and their development. Changes in a group of needs or a kind of generic needs will connect with the needs of other levels, for example, a scenario will appear in the needs of material for survival – once the need of meat is satisfied, the need for staple foods will be reduced. The relationship exists not only in the same group of needs but also among different groups of needs. Under such a structure of needs, need for a certain kind of wealth drives some structural changes in other kinds of wealth. Needs always align with the developmental process of tools satisfying these needs. As a system of needs is opened, the foundation of its development is connected to production activities and a process of economic growth. Under this process, lots of changes are found in human living conditions and within human themselves, in new ways of exchange, and in concepts of consumption. Thus, new kinds of needs are produced unceasingly, making a breakthrough in the initial level of economic growth and pushing social economic growth to go further with conflicts arising again. Hence, economic growth brings about actual conflicts.

So, how can human need turn into actual conflicts in the process of economic growth?

(1) Conflicts between the needs of people and the abilities of utilizing needs drive a upward spiral shift of needs with adjustment, enhancement and upgrading of industry structure under an economic growth process. This reflects conflicts among speed, structure and efficiency in economic growth. It bears a consistent structure but with conflicts against each other. According to the chart of need structure, the pattern of upgrading needs illustrated by Lenin is correct.[11] It shows that needs move from a lower level of material survival need into a higher level of spiritual self-actualization needs – a continuous all-rounded development with complexity in needs. It also demonstrates that a larger scale of social reproduction will give rise to some possible conflicts between a production of needs and fulfillment of needs. Once the needs expand beyond the market demand, currency will be inflated as there is insufficient supply. This kind of inflated economic phenomenon happens when the sum of economic growth cannot catch up with the total demands or there is a lag in industry or product structure – insufficient supply or structural deficiency in supply with a shortage in the market. Market shortage forms a seller market where enterprises do not need to make any reform, innovation, adjustment or enhancement in their structures; and where products can be sold very easily with profits. Industrial structural adjustments, improvements and advancements will then be ignored – without improving product quality and economic efficiency but with a lag in industry enhancement.

(2) Material needs are contradictory to its spiritual needs. This makes conflicts between material production and spiritual production burst out. Material needs refer to satisfaction of needs derived from functions of commodities and labor services. This is the most basic, fundamental, and important need of human beings. There are two major categories of targets for this kind of need– commodities and services. Hence, materials not only include the efficient use of commodities and their values of satisfaction, but also efficiency in labor services, such as cosmetology, medical services, transportation, repairing etc. These kinds of needs are survival needs and developmental needs mentioned by Engels. Spiritual needs refer to non-commodities or non-labor services but involve sentimental feelings, friendship, mutual reliance and other kinds of psychological satisfaction, including utilization of one's innovation and enjoyment with results derived from cultural development. This is the first part of enjoyment and developmental needs brought up by Engels and the third to fifth levels of needs mentioned by Maslow's hierarchy of needs. Within these two aspects of needs, the first fundamental layer of needs is material needs while the second layer is spiritual ones. This tells us that the most important needs of human beings should be material needs. These two layers of needs are against each other but can be unified; they cannot go parallel with each other but can be compromised. As there is conflict between material and spiritual needs, material production is emphasized most of the time under social production and re-production while spiritual production is being ignored – industries are not aligned for social and spiritual development. This forces a nation with a socialist market economy to get hold of two things in its development – material production (material cultural establishment) and spiritual production (spiritual cultural establishment). The two have to be in harmony.

(3) Conflict is also found between actual and idealistic needs, which may also turn into further conflicts in the process of economic growth. Actual needs stand for the needs that can be satisfied by a certain level of productivity in a society, such as living needs, production needs and other similar kinds of needs. People realize that apart from strict spiritual needs, most of the needs must be fulfilled by the results of labor productivity. In *Strange Tales—Lao Shan Taoist*, there is a story of making a moon out of paper cuttings, and finding food in the moon - a legend that cannot be found in real social production. Hence, during certain periods of history, all needs with the foundation of actualization are "actual needs"; those cannot be satisfied by existing productivity levels but rely on further development in productivity are called "idealistic needs". These two kinds of needs are closely related to each other; no matter what, consideration has to be given to both of them. Without "actual needs", a nation will not have the foundation to realize people's needs. Without "idealistic needs", a nation will not have a soul for the future, and will lack motivation for production

development and economic growth. Having these two needs oppose each other in unification is a pattern which cannot be overlooked. The loss of unification between the two types of needs will be reflected through the ratio of accumulation and consumption when executing economic development strategy. If "actual needs" are over-emphasized, there will be more consumption and less saving, and then economic growth will not be boosted as it lacks resource and motivation. If "idealistic needs" are over-emphasized, there will be more savings and less consumption, and then it will affect the efficient growth of the economy as it reaches beyond what people can expect from meeting their basic needs.

(4) Individual needs, organizational needs and societal needs also form a kind of harmony with conflicts embedded inside. Individual needs are referred to as the needs for individual survival and development, mean individual reliance on materials and spiritual elements for living, and act as the foundations for collective needs and societal needs. Organizational needs refer to certain channels (economy linkage, firstly) linked up closely together to have some collective activities (production activities, firstly) for a mutual goal (unit of social economy, like unit of enterprises) to fulfill needs in production and living. Societal needs are those productions with all members in the society engaged in the fulfillment of living and production needs. The needs of all levels of the government and the whole nation belong to this type. The composition of these three kinds of needs form conflicts in unity that are reflected in social production and economic growth process. Specifically, if individual needs are over-emphasized, the other two needs will be affected. As these two kinds of needs are usually public facilities, social production accumulation (including education and technology) and military protection, social production and social security will be affected in the long run. On the other hand, if these two types of needs are over emphasized while individual needs are ignored, high consciousness with the enthusiasm of individuals for organizations or the society will be lost. All in all, three kinds of needs have to be in harmony in order to avoid lagging in social production and economic growth.

(5) A structural conflict is found among living needs, production needs and other kinds of needs, which also influence social production and economic growth. Living needs are the needs of laborers' production and re-production to survive and develop, which is demonstrated as the final needs of making payments in the market for survival and development. Production needs are the needs of enterprises or production units in a society for undergoing production investment and expansion of re-production which is expressed as an ability of monetary investment. Other kinds of needs are the needs for maintaining daily operations from organizations and the governments; under the system of socialism, they include the needs of public administration consumption and the needs of major investment projects for social economic development. Therefore,

three kinds of needs can be simplified as a conflict between ultimate needs and intermediary needs. This was mentioned by Marx as conflicts of section I and sections II in the social re-production process, and was mainly built upon human need which had a mechanism of conflict. If human need is overlooked during the process of social production and economy enhancement, no further understanding and handling can be obtained about these different kinds of conflicts. Hence, a proper ratio of actual intermediary or ultimate needs will not be arranged; strategy and decision will be made inappropriately without achieving goals such as reasonable relations between Section I and Section II in social production and economic growth.

(6) Judging human need from the whole process, there is another conflict in unity existing between the actual demands with current payment ability and the potential needs with future payment ability. There are some differences between a socialist market economy and a capitalist market economy. In a socialist market economy, there is a public system for labor distribution which bears a principle of mutual wealth; the ability of fulfilling needs from social productivity for a large number of people in a society is much greater. There is a greater tension of needs and demands as these things are quite close to each other. However, in a capitalist market economy, the ability of fulfilling needs only serves a small number of people, while pressure is put on the needs of masses of people and tension on a smaller multitude as well. Needs and demands are far apart from each other. Hence, the driving force for social production and economic growth under needs and demands of people in a socialist market economy is much greater than that of a capitalist market economy, which is where a socialist market economy has a comparative advantage over a capitalist market economy. These two kinds of market systems possess conflicts of needs and demands in social production and economic growth. If needs and demands are put in an equal position, the issue of overheating will appear which offers no benefit to the structural adjustment and improvement of economic efficiency. However, under a capitalist market economy, investment organizations are usually private enterprises with a wide gap between needs and demands. This makes investors treat needs and demands separately in a strict manner. This will pose a constraint on investment and when demands are under constraints another issue will come up – supply is greater than demand with a risk of "surplus".

Chapter Two

Development of Productivity:

the Nature of Economic Growth

The process of economic growth is an eternally advancing one with the formation, development and solution of two basic contradictions. One is the contradiction between demand and capacity to fulfill it; the other is the contradiction between man as the subjective and nature as the objective. The essence of this dynamic process is the material, energy and information exchange process between man's ability and nature. The accumulation of wealth is the result of productivity development, and the material and spiritual guarantee to fulfill the needs of human beings. Therefore, German economist Friedrich List (1789~1846) criticized the economic growth theory of Adam Smith[12], the founder of British Classical Economics, saying that he had put too much emphasis upon wealth itself: "the productivity of wealth is much more important than wealth itself; it can not only guarantee the accumulation and increasing of wealth, but also compensate the loss of wealth."[13] From the materialist perspective, social economic growth is surely a dynamic process that accumulates and increases social wealth via efficient usage of various resources and technologies, so as to diversify the products, ensure the quality, and improve people's living standards. However, from a more profound angle, the inner reason of material wealth accumulation, including socialism wealth accumulation is, after all, the development of productivity. Only when productivity is developed can the basic question be solved as to using what sources to create and how to create social wealth.

2.1 Productivity is the Ultimate Decisive Power of the Economic Growth Process

Growth of a society's wealth and improvement of people's living conditions are the results of the economic growth process, the results from a materialism perspective. When reviewing the fundamentals of the actual process, the crux lies in the development of productivity. Those who think economic growth is making things bigger, increasing product value, and speeding processes up are wrong with biased and superficial views. They hold largely metaphysical philosophical views that require correction.

Firstly, the process of economic growth in a society must be based on productivity, and must rely on continuous development of productivity. As mentioned before, human need is both a starting point and a driving force of economic growth. Nevertheless, the foundation of this process is based on achieved productivity. In 1846, Marx wrote a letter to Pavel Vasilyevich Annenko, saying "people cannot choose their productivity – it is the basis of their history."[14] "Under the development of productivity, there must be a form of barter trade (commerce) and consuming. In order to implement this, there must be social systems, such as family, rank, and class systems."[15] These remind us that the foundation of economic growth is productivity acquired by a society.

Under a specific productivity development condition, one can gather a specific -scope and skill-level key elements in production. This in turn will help develop a system of productivity in a society. The economic growth of a society will depend on the quality of production, distribution, exchange, and consumption. Only through a proper management of systems, organizations, production units in a society can people further develop productivity and create more wealth for society. On the contrary, productivity will deteriorate, and be unable to create wealth. From the above analysis, the fundamental principle and the ultimate decisive force of wealth production, is not the social format of reproduction and economic growth, but the actual productivity.

We can measure the result of society productivity on the basis of wealth created, i.e. the growth of GDP. GDP can be used to estimate the scale and level of productivity a country, a region, or a society has achieved. However, wealth is not a sufficient indicator to measure a nation's power, its national income or the living standard of a country. Therefore, we must understand the principle of economic growth processes and the ultimate decisive power in realistic productivity. From this principle, if systems, regulations, and policies are reasonable and accurate, producers and proprietors will be fully mobilized, the existing productivity of a society can undoubtedly create more wealth for a society. To allow the economy to make a big leap in production varieties, there must be further development of social productivity in total sales and product quality, as we cannot solely rely on adjustments of systems and policies. The function of systems and policies belong to the function of a society's production regulations, while total benefits must be adjusted and wants must be satisfied for transferring to production processes. Full applications of existing productivity can then be accomplished. However, the ultimate decisive power of the continuous expansion of societal re-production is the certain social productivity which depends on a historical achievement and continuous development in the productive process within a society.

Secondly, the structure of social production and the development of material technique determine the structure of economic growth. As a result of economic growth, product is being used as a form of wealth expansion. The various structures of products reflect property, industry, technical division of labor in the growth processes of an economy. Through the perfect product structure with value-added quality and fulfillment of wants, industrial technical structure of an economic growth process is reflected. This structure of economic growth process is determined by the level of productivity. The so-called "horizontal structure" of productivity refers to the nature and condition of productivity in a certain space (country and region), over a specific time. It restricts the structure of society re-production process and economic growth process. Among all of these, essential factors of production form the basic structure, exercise and elaboration intention of productivity in a society. In fact, productivity that functions in social production and economic growth is a composite organism. In this organism, the essential factor is actually the technique structure, which is derived and evolved into a series of primal structures. For example, department structure of economy, property structure of society, product composition in societal re-production all are the derivations of the technique structure, and are also the results which different labors use divers work resources and act in different work objects.

Not only this, the phrase of economic growth process is also decided by the stage of productivity development. Technology is the result of human knowledge about controlling over natural forces, and it can be expressed in a form of humanization of natural forces, and is a power that human acts as a principle combined to his own power. To curve up from the equipment level of labor, productivity development process in a human society has already experienced three phases – hand-made tool phrase, heavy- duty machinery phrase and machinery automation phrase, and is now under intelligence automation phrase. According with this, the world economy has already experienced a primitive society economy as well as a slavery society economy, and the slow expansion of a feudalist society economy. In modern times, capitalist society made tremendous achievements exceeding the total productivity and economic expansion in earlier societies in less than 100 years. Also, the present society made the manufacturing industry the second most important industry leading towards speeding up the economy and moving into a high quality stage, and is gradually transmitting itself into a service economy with a high degree of development in economic growth. Based on the historical analysis of the world's industrialization process, many economists revealed the relationships and rules between the economic growth cycle and the improvement of the technological and productivity revolution after the middle period of the 18th century. They also state that basically because technological transformation leads to productivity revolution, there forms an economic cycle of growth-recession. Famous economist Nikolai Kondratieff from the USSR studied economic cycles of a capitalist society during the period of 1780-1920. He issued a series of research papers in the mid 1920s, creating the economic "long wave" theory. He not only concluded that there exists two half "long wave" cycles in a capitalist economy, but also forecast the long wave decline during in the 1920s. Due to his contribution to the study of long wave theory, he was praised as "the father of long wave theory". After that, other famous economists like Germany's Mons, Netherland's Doin, U.S.A.'s Rostow, Lewes, etc., focused their studies on the long wave theory, while each one of them discussed the range of possible cycles. To sum up, we can say that from mid 18th century onwards, complying with the technology revolution and productivity development period, economic growth of industrial countries in the world has experienced the following periods and stages as below.

-       the first stage was during 1790-1842, its direct decisive power is the first Industrial Revolution, invention and application of weaving machine and coal for iron-smelting techniques.

-       the second stage was during 1842-1897, it came as the railroad became the center of steam engine technology and steel technology was expanded.

-       the third stage was during 1897-1945, when the electronic industry was a symbol of the period, with a big leap in the chemical industry and the automobile industry.

-       the fourth stage was during 1945-1973, from the outcome of the second scientific & technological revolution and a further step ahead of property transform. The automobile, chemical, electric power and electronic appliance industries, as well as the traditional iron and copper industries were developed during the two world war periods; with the result of third scientific & technological and revolution as a foundation, the astronavigation industry, the computer industry, genetic engineering, and synthetic material industries were developed. People forecast that the productivity of a society will have a revolutionary development, while the global economic growth will enter the fifth rising-tide stage during the end of 20th century to the beginning of 21st century. The technological revolution gives rise to a phased leap of productivity development, the law that encourages the formation of economic growth phases tells us that economic growth has its own patterns and is restricted by the productivity development phases, especially restricted by scientific & technological revolution, and the gradation of technology improvement.

We cannot simply assume that promoting the speed and quickening the steps of economic growth are equal to "making things up", spreading out stalls in low-level items, and expanding fixed capital asset investment. This assumption violates the economic laws. Leaders, who understand economic rules and have experiences in leading economic work, must regard technology and productivity improvement as the basis of economic growth. By doing so, total production quality will be improved, while production level will rise. Wise leaders like this are the ones we need for the future.

Thirdly, social productivity development results from the formation of economic growth poles and the transit of regional economic growth. Economic growth pole is the economic developmental aggregation of a country, or a region with economic activation, speedy growth, and prosperous production value. This economic pole is formed by large scale technical equipment, together with other factors of production. Since an economic section or districts concentrates a big scale of production and a high level of productivity, they lead to the formation of economic aggregation and extension to the hinterlands. It also leads to social production growth with a radiation effect in economic growth, while becoming the center of economic development.

Besides, under the radiation effect of economic growth pole, the pattern of social productivity development restricts the shift of regional economic growth. Honestly, everyone in each country desires for economic growth and speedy economic development, but this is restricted by social productivity development regulations. These important elements include asset structure adjustment and transformation, export and import of foreign investment and technology. This kind of transformation is also restricted by the productivity and the combination of other factors in a country or a region. For example, social conditions, natural resources, geographic location, transportation communication, current economic asset, public security, human geography, economic policies, labor quality and income, and government services etc., all can restrict the economic development. These in turn are the basic constraints of social productivity in a country and a region. From the result, by forming the capability of consuming capital, technology, and human resources, economically developed countries or economic growth poles will transfer a portion of assets to those countries or regions with a kind of economic-level differences. (Based on this, the author raised the concept of "lowland effects" that attracted foreign investment, technology, human resources, and management experiences when he was the General Secretary of City Committee in Jiangmen, Guangdong Province. This concept had a great influence upon real production and the whole society). It leads to a chain reaction of social productivity among countries or regions, which helps to pilot economic growth and to create an economic growth chain. The same story happened in Guangdong: first came the formation of the high speed economic growth of Pearl River Delta, then the economic growth gradually spread into the inland areas The process consists of transit and transmittal of capital, technology and labor asset, and industries. It is also the same with the whole country of China: first, choosing areas around the coast for creating four special economic zones in Guangdong and Fujian provinces, opening 14 coastal cities, creating the economic open-door area of Pearl River Delta and Minnan's Xia-Zhang-Quan Delta, and economic growth poles in particular areas. Then, the openings and developments in the Yangtz River Delta and along the river, railways and interior provinces appear. As there exist a comprehensive opening situation in the country, investments from abroad and lateral ties at home are strengthened, attracting foreign capital and technology, accelerating social productivity, improving the economic growth of the coastal areas, which stable the economy of the whole country in a fast and healthy way.

The economy of the world has similar conditions: in the middle and late period of the 19th century, the Industrial Revolution laid the foundation for large machinery in England. First developing labor concentrated in textile industry, which helped to create a "world's factory" and a world's economic growth center. As adjustment and upgrade of asset structure occurred in England, the textile industry gradually rotated to America, Japan and the "Four Little Dragons" in Asia during the early 20th century, mid 20th century, and late 20th century. From the late 20th century onwards, this translocation of economic growth has led Asia to become a fast growing economic region. In other words, economic growth shows up after the occurrence of asset structure adjustment of social productivity development and capital transfer.

Last but not least, social products rely on social productivity development. Material and cultural products are what humans want, but two conditions must be fulfilled in order to satisfy their wants: one is the ability of monetary payment; the other one is the ability to get pleasure from the products. The formation and rise of the two abilities help to measure actual social productivity. On a basis of social productivity development, people can then earn their income through economic exchange and resource allocation, creating the ability of currency payment. Different productive technologies are created through science and technology and the development of education, raising the ability of acknowledging, grasping, and enjoying these products. As stated by Marx that through development of productivity, people create sufficient spare time, and correct allocation, "one can gain a suitable proportion of knowledge and satisfy his demands", fully enjoying the results of economic growth, achieving "pleasure of social life and comprehensiveness of activities".[16]

2.2 Effectiveness is the Base Line of Economic Growth Strategy

Economic growth is not only a basic theoretical topic, but also a practical subject based on contemporary development. After the WWII, each country treats economic growth as a matter of life or death. So they established different economic growth strategies in the western world - from "Growth in Fever" to "Growth in Maniac". G. L. Bach even claimed that: "the debate of economic growth based on socialism and capitalism is paramount in gaining hearts of the public."[17] Another famous American economist, Domar Evgey D. also pointed out that, "under the conflict of modern international societies, growth is the condition for survival."[18] In a highly competitive economic world, less advanced countries or regions usually choose the strategy of high speed of growth for quick economic development in order to catch up with advanced countries. Through this process, the economic growth of a society, a country, or a region is the result and behavior of its productivity development. Social productivity follows its own motion pattern and adjusts its speed while developing under different societies. This in turns restricts and decides the speed of economic growth.

From ancient to modern times, many economists and practitioners have done theoretical studies and practical discoveries on social economic development. For theoretical studies, western economists mostly believe that economic growth equals the growth of national wealth. This is why entrepreneurs think about economic growth as a result of increase on currency. People who place an emphasis upon agriculture would claim that economic growth is an increase of agricultural products. Classical economist Adam Smith explained it as an increase of national wealth that leads to an increase in gross national product or national income. Some modern western economists refer to it as the increase of national wealth, or the increase of GDP or GNP. Some of them mix up the term "growth" with "development". The publication of the "New English Encyclopedia" in 1980 did a fantastic job of separating "economic growth" from "economic development" with two unique explanations. Thus, for a long period of time, people have confused "growth" with "development". Putting these two terminologies into practice, there were discoveries in many countries with success and failure stories. Successful examples of growth and development are: post war Germany, Japan, the "Four Dragons" in Asia, and USSR in the middle 20th century. There were also unsuccessful cases, such as capitalism countries - Brazil and Mexico. Although their economies have grown, they have not yet completed modernization, but already have foreign loans that they cannot pay back. Some socialism countries, including China, also received many lessons from setbacks.

The USSR was famous for its high speed of economic growth during the 1950s and 1960s. In the 1950s, the annual economic growth rate was over 10%. Although there was a drop in the 1960s, the growth was still over 7%. From 1970 onwards, the annual economic growth rate was greatly slowed down. In the 1980s, the annual economic growth dropped to the lowest point in the post war period. The annual growth rate of national income dropped to 5.1% during the "Ninth Five-year" National Plan (1970-1975), 4.2% during the "Tenth Five" National Plan (1975-1980), 2.5% during the "Eleventh Five-year" National Plan (1981-1985). It dropped even lower than the American level from 1983 to 1984. Annual average growth rate of labor productivity dropped more then 50% (from 7.2% to 3.1%) during the periods of "Nine Five-year" National Plan to "Eleven Five-year" National Plan.[19] Until 1991, the passive situation of economic growth and development was unable to turn over, resulting in an extreme shortage of living necessities and difficulties in the life of people. These have mounted up to the disintegration of the country. In the end, the political power changed hands. In the middle 20th century, the USSR's prosperous economy depended on its speeding-up growth with sacrificing the living standard of its citizens. This unfortunately led to an undesirable outcome. The reason is that speedy growth is hard to maintain as labor productivity would continuously decrease along with the input of a large amount of capital and labor. Hence, they had fast growth yet slow development.

China also learned an impressive lesson about economic growth. From 1953 to1978, the accumulation (investment) rates were mostly above 30%, with the highest up to 43.8%, this had rarely been seen in the early industrialized countries. In the same period, China had a total production value average increment of over 10% each year while the total production value in industry and agriculture increased 8.6% each year. This was also rarely found in the history of world economic growth. However, the actual yearly national consumption only increased 1%. The slow economic development and poor livelihood was due to the fast increase in population, low labor productivity, wastage in fixed capital investments while a large proportion of investment was not able to grow. Statistics shows that there was a low efficiency in investment projects and a low usage in factories and equipment during these periods, which led to the 54% loss in total factories and equipment investment of over 3,500 billion RMB.[20] Although the condition in China has changed a lot after the 15 years of revolutionary opening-up policy, the problems of investment are still happening. The unbalanced situation in production structure is still unsolved, with existing problems in low-quality duplicated construction and unused facilities. During the period of 1984-1988, the national yearly fixed capital investment increased up to 25.7%, while national income merely increased by 12%. From the newspaper of Southern Daily in May 19th, 1992: "the productivity of nine important products of China including ethylene, automobiles, color TVs were seriously redundant. There were serious wastes of unused facilities, while 33% productive equipment for cotton and wool yarn were left idle, 50% for color TVs, 50% for refrigerators, 38% for washing machines, 75% for automobiles." Because of this, the problem of structural conflict and low economic efficiency were unable to resolve. Therefore, high tuitions were paid by China to learn from the lesson that an ill economic growth mode should be changed. This was not only for China but for other developing countries. It was a problem for the economy, society and political affairs. It was not only a theoretical problem, but also a problem of putting economic growth into practice.

From the above, pin-pointed implications have been those that the starting point of economic growth strategy must be put on an effective growth, and attention must be paid to the growth method, or it will cause serious economic consequences, evolving to crucial political problems, and might even endanger the existence of the nation and country.

According to Marxism economic growth theory, economic growth was actually productivity growth, and must be based on an objective rule of productivity and the condition of the international economy for driving a better model for economic growth. Adhering to this pattern and the various modes of actual economic growth, we must choose a kind of effective growth as a mode of fast development and a starting point of growth strategy. The strategy of effective growth must be firmly established in actual economy so as to have a fast economic development. To analyze the problem thoroughly, now we investigate several input and output conditions in the economic growth process. First, let us look at the productivity and reproduction flow chart:

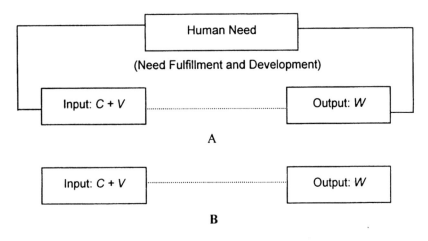

Figure 2.1

① $\triangle$ (C+V) > $\triangle$ W
② $\triangle$ (C+V) = $\triangle$ W
③ $\triangle$ (C+V) < $\triangle$ W

In order to analyze the above flow chart, indicators and measures for national levels of economic growth and development must be explained. For market economy based western countries, the national economy at macro level can be shown by Gross Domestic Product (GDP), Gross National Product, Net National Product and National Income which are claimed as System of National Accounts or the western system. For Eastern socialist countries, economic growth was long stated as an increase in Total Social Product (TSP), and is usually measured by $C+V+M$. China also uses this method for measuring its economic growth. Besides $C+V+M$, there are also the Final Social Product (FSP) and Net Social Product (NSP). They comprise of the so-called the Material Product System or the Eastern system. Up to now, we can see that China has made a lot of efforts in dealing with the problem of establishing a marketing economy system and linking up with the world economy. At the same time, there have been big improvements in economic statistics and measurement methods, by using the GDP for macroeconomic statistic calculation, and suggestions of the green economy and green GDP in the early 21st century. Although there were big leaps, the traditional GDP and others (TSP, FSP, and NSP) are still the important elements for China's statistical measurements of economic growth and development. It can be clearly shown as follows.

First, in social reproduction, there are two conditions for actualizing effective economic growth and development: 1) production quantity and quality must fit the aggregate demand of people for survival and development, while this is the objective of growth and development; 2) as for input and output, input must be fewer than output, while this is the ultimate result of reproduction. The first condition is easier to understand because people might not want the extra products that are over produced and cannot be actualized, which makes no sense for economic growth and development. So, let's concentrate on analyzing the second condition.

Second, in *The Introduction to Productivity Economy*, Professor Xiong Yingwu analyzed three different types of the second condition stated above.[21] He thinks that economic growth actually is due to growth in productivity, by that, a larger quantity and a better quality of products can be provided. High-speed economic growth does not necessarily equal wealth increase. There are two types of economic development and growth. One is "Speed Type", that is the increase from quickening economic development. This is a common type of increase, especially valued by countries that are looking to catch up with the rest of the world. Second is "Structure Type", which is caused by the improvements in property, technology and product structures.   Sometimes it is also called the "Efficiency Type" of increase. This type is always being ignored. In reality, these two types are neither totally different nor opposing.   In economic development, if there is no speed, there would be no efficiency. In contrast, if we only talk about speed without efficiency, effective growth cannot be attained.

Third, let's take a look at chart 2.1 B – input and output condition. Increase in material consumption of production shows that there is an increase in $C+\triangle C$ from the total output value. Increase in labor consumption reflects the increase in $V+\triangle V$ from total output value. Total output value (W) = C+V+M, increase of W can be the increase of M, or can be the increase of C+V. In ①, $\triangle(C+V) > \triangle W$, $\triangle(C+V)$ represents new input, $\triangle W$ represents new output.

From ①, we can see that if economic growth of this year increases 10% from last year, we cannot say that there is 10% increase in the wealth of the society, which brings more economic benefit to the nation. If $\triangle(C+V) = 20\%$, $\triangle W = 10\%$, the national wealth of last year would only turn out to be 50% of this year, while the other 50% disappears and gets wasted. In the long run, the economy has no realistic increase, and might even fall back and collapses. In ②, $\triangle(C+V) = \triangle W$, new input equals new output, where the wealth of the society does not increase. From ③, $\triangle(C+V) < \triangle W$, there is more new output than new input. In this condition, as economic growth speeds up, the wealth of the society also increases. The three mentioned situations point out that an economy can only be really developed under the third condition. Thereby the wealth of the society can be increased while development and growth can be balanced thus leading to effective growth and development.

The chief leader of China's revolutionary opening-up policy, Deng

Xiaoping, said that development is the biggest politics but it must be integrated with speed and efficiency. In the first and second condition, there seems to be both development and growth. But in the two conditions mentioned, new input is greater or equals to new output, and thus there is no actual increase in social wealth. This kind of development and growth cannot bring realistic economic benefits to the nation and might even do it harm. It compresses the actual national income, suppresses the national consumption level, and weakens the ability of economic activities.

During the previous "leaps" and "speeding-ups" of China's economic construction, especially the "Great Leap" and "High Speed" in 1958, its investment of basic economic construction increased 97% when compared with 1957, which meant that input was greater than output. Superficially, it looks as if there was fast growth in statistic value of industry and agriculture (32.2%), with a 54.5% increase in total output value from industry and 2.4% increase in agriculture, but there was negative increase for the next few years after 1958. This created huge waste in social wealth, while the superficial increase was no longer sustainable, leading to a three-year period of economic difficulties from 1960-1962, and the first economic big adjustment from 1963-1965 that brought about the fall back of productivity. There were four more economic adjustments, which happened in the years 1972-1973, 1977-1978, 1984-1985, and 1989-1990, respectively. This is a historical lesson for China to review and remember. Since the establishment of new China, it has been shown that the strategic pursuing of "speed-type" increases will harm economic development. The features of "speed-type" strategy can not realize an effective growth, but show on a route towards "high accumulation, high speed, slow development, and low consumption", which may cause disastrous consequences in national economy. The consequences may be described as follows.

(1) The economic structure was unbalanced and destroyed the stable growth of the national economy. The 3-year "Great Leap" followed by the negative growth of agriculture for 3 years, and industry for 2 years, in addition to the 5 years of the first adjustment, adds up to 8 wasted years. Together with the next four adjustments, a total of 18 out of 40 years were wasted. In between the 5 adjustments, the amplitude of industry increase was as follows: 94.0%, 35.5%, 10.3%, 9.7%, and 14%. This kind of amplitude rate is rarely seen in the world's economic growth. The larger the fluctuating margin, the more destructive power is brought to economic growth and development.

(2) The steepness of investment rate of fixed capital causes huge waste in limited investment capital. The fixed capital investments of the nation caused by 5 adjustments are as follows: 147.0%, 64.0%, 32.5%, 20.0%, and 31.3%. The drastic fluctuation of fixed capital investment leads to the extension of the investment period with junk constructions, overstocking of investments, and

lowering the result of investment. During 1950-1988, basic construction investment amounted to 1.5 trillion Yuan (RMB), with not more than 1.1 trillion Yuan being able to be formed into fixed capital. The completion rate in fixed capital investment was only 72%, 20 percentage points lower than that of the USSR. Nearly 1/4 of the investment was not formed into productivity causing the loss of 300 billion Yuan. Through calculating each hundred million RMB of investment that yielded GNP of 360 million Yuan (the yearly investment efficiency rate in 1981-1988 was 3.6), the loss of GNP was 1,008 trillion Yuan.

(3) The economic outcome was not good while the national livelihood suffered. From the famous writings of economist Xue Muqiao, between the 20 years of 1957-1977, the national livelihood basically remained at its original level. The income and provisions of ordinary workers and peasants did not increase, while 1/3 of the peasants' lives were very tough.[22] As an example in 1989, the fixed capital investment dropped by 11% compared with the previous year, excluding the price element, it actually dropped by 20%. The market was weakened with impact on lowering the national demands, lessening work hours of enterprises, lowering the increase rate of workers' income than that of living price, and leading to a fall in livelihoods.

(4) It incurred a series of social problems, and increased social instability.
Fourth, we should learn from experience and lessons that when promoting economic growth, solely pursuing a speedy growth strategy without relying on technology improvements and productivity enhancement, and only relying on investment of fixed capital and labor for increasing total output value, will finally result in the deterioration of the economic strength and the national livelihood. This strategy cannot accomplish the "catching up and surpass" goal, but in return compared with other economic advanced technological countries, an undesirable lag will be found.
Therefore, we cannot only pursue high speed without considering efficiency for the growth strategy. Only ③ in Figure 2.1 B, $\triangle$ (C+V) < $\triangle$W can achieve effective growth and development. To achieve this, investment, property, technology and product structure must be continuously optimized for increasing the productive quality. At the same time, it leads to economic growth according with human need for existence, relish and development. We should run towards the road of "structure-efficiency type" growth and development. Insisting on running towards this goal, the basic point of growth strategy must be put on effectiveness, while placing human need on top of the growth list, relying on technology improvement for driving economic development and growth, adjusting and optimizing investment and property structure, and increasing the quality of the national economy. In one sentence, enhancing economic returns (including macro and microeconomic level) should be the center, and satisfying material and cultural needs of people must be the highest principle. This should

be established as the basic strategy and policy of China's socialist economic growth and development.

2.3 Productivity is the Key Factor of Effective Economic Growth

Historical materialistic believers advocate that the development of a society is in essence the development of productivity and social production, that this is also a result of continuous improvement in productivity, and is the most important standard of human progress and development. Looking back to the history of the development of human society, the primitive living standard and slow development in the ancient times came from low productivity and the slow development of productivity levels. Modernization, social development and economic growth also came from productivity development. The high speed increase of productivity has led to wealth and a prosperous society. The fast development of modern economy, huge increase in the wealth of societies, and drastic changes in today's world also came from productivity development and its high-speed growth. Productivity is the leader of social economy, and is an economic theoretical topic which can be discussed endlessly. History and practice show us that improvement in productivity is a common trend and a key factor of social development. If China wants to increase the speed of economic development, achieve the increase of economy effective growth, and establish socialism with its own characteristics, it must adhere to this law.

What is productivity? Because of its importance as an everlasting theoretic topic in social economic growth and development, it has been explored by many thinkers and economists from the past to the present. Famous thinkers like Aristotle and Plato from the ancient Greece, and modern economists, like Adam Smith, Marx and Engels, both of whom criticized the classical economics of the capitalist class, all pursued and discussed the topic. They not only defined the category of productivity, but also used it as a starting point to create a system of productivity theories. Because of the limitation of its publication, we will only focus on analyzing Marxism and the main western economic theories regarding productivity.

In the development of western economic theories, the founding theorist and the main promoter of French "Agricultural School", Quesnay François, brought out his "productivity" concept for the first time in 1766. He indicated that: "the higher the labor return of artists and industrialists, the higher the productivity of these disciplines."[23] In 1883, Littre defined productivity as "capacity of production". In the early 20th century, Early defined productivity as "the relationship of the data used by output and produced output". After that, a lot of economists made their own definitions for productivity, like Davis in 1955, Fabricant in 1962, Sigel in 1976. Japanese economists also analyzed the issue of productivity, while dividing it into technical terms of productivity, and social and economic terms of productivity. The former one included object productivity (output/input), value productivity (NNP/input), and integrated productivity; the latter one pointed out the living quality of labors, the environmental coordination, and other societal-related productivity.

At the same time, some international organizations made their own definition of productivity. In 1950, the OEEC stipulated that productivity was "the quotient that is gained by output divided by the first production element", while extending to concepts such as investment productivity, raw material productivity. ILO pointes out that those products are the result from the input combination of land, capital, labor and organization. The ratio between the product and one of the above elements is the productivity of that element. The European Productivity Association (EPA) stipulates productivity as an effective use of the production elements. These elements include capital, facilities, raw materials, fuel materials, labor, exploited technology, and operational management. The output results of the above six elements are industrial products and output benefits.

The above shows that productivity issues were concerned by western economists from the beginning. The basic meanings of productivity are converging. In comparison, the productivity concept of Marxism economics is still the most clear-cut scientific concept. Marxism states that acting as a strict economic concept, productivity means labor productivity. It not only decides the usage value created by the work unit but also influences the amount of value created by the commodity unit. The founder of Marx once said: "on the whole, labor productivity is the same as using the smallest amount of labor to get the largest number of products, so that the cost of products can be lowered. In the capitalism type of production, individual capitalists do not have power to overturn the rule mentioned above."[24]

So, why is productivity said to be the key factor of effective growth, and how does it work out to be so important? The concept of productivity implies that there are three principles to improve productivity. Firstly, the more productive materials each labor puts into the production process, the more products come out, leading to fewer labors involved in a unit of product and more products are produced within a period of time. Secondly, the fewer materials needed for unit production, the more output will be yielded. Thirdly, the increase of productivity is the increase of the social technical capacity level. So, with the rise in productivity, more quantity of products will be produced, while the variety and quality of products will also be increased, being more conformed to aggregate demands. That proves that the increase of productivity is the increase in the production technology level and is the ultimate result and most important symbol of social production development. It also means to use fewer inputs for social production to give more outputs, achieving $\triangle(C+V) < \triangle W$. This is the only route towards effective economic growth and development.

The history of social economic growth and development actually is equivalent to the history of social production and capacity development which lead to the history of improvement in productivity. As we know, labor is the most dynamic and most important element of productivity and the priority of productivity is labor development or development of workers' physical strengths and intelligence. The history of productivity and labor capability show that labor capability develops along two different routes towards two different directions (i.e., physical strength and intelligence). Up to now, labor instruments have experienced three different stages of development: (1) handmade tool stage; (2) general machine system and automated machine stage; (3) intellectual automation stage. Accommodating with that, the development of productivity has also experienced three different stages: (1) handmade tool capacity stage; (2) modern machine capacity stage; (3) modern intelligence capacity or scientific capacity stage (information capacity). This is a vertical sequential development pattern of productivity. This pattern shows that, the change of a productivity stage calls for quantity change to quality change and from a part to the whole, from gradation to giant leap.

Moreover, the horizontal development of productivity has also become a basic law. According to this law, the development of productivity in a country or a region does not follow a gradual systematic routine but through introducing and absorbing other countries' advanced capacities, thereby improving its productivity even by a quantum jump. Ancient productivity development evolves from its former one, and modern productivity development has put more emphasis on following and relying on the use of horizontal quantum jump over the development pattern. Under this influence, a country or region can quickly shorten the gap between its productivity and that of advanced countries. Then it can also formulate a global development and productivity growth strategy, promoting the speed of development of capacity and growth of productivity.

As productivity becomes more socialized and modernized, labor capacity in social economic development and growth need to rely less on physical strength, but more on intelligence development. Due to constraints of productivity and labor capability, ancient productivity level was very low, labor capacity levels were also low, so economic growth and development was slow. In the whole development process, especially in the past few decades, the productivity development is speeding up. The level of labor productivity has risen with the speeding up of the development of labor productivity, leading to fast economic growth and development. According to a UN research report, "in the 1960s, 80%-90% of industrial output was contributed by the increase of labor productivity." Comparing developing countries with developed countries, the labor productivity contribution of the former to their economic growth is 1/2 of the latter. Labor productivity decided the trend of the world economy's speedy development after WWII, creating productivity and social wealth twice as much as in past times. It also decided the unevenness of developing countries: some caught up while some fell behind, and the gap between most developing countries and developed countries also widened.

History shows that restrained by the basic law of capacity development, the acceleration growth of productivity is a basic law of social production and economic development. When getting rid of backward positions, catching up with advanced countries in the world, China must follow the law, put economic efficiency as the center, and set speedy productivity growth as the basic strategy of economic development and growth. If betraying the law, backward countries cannot catch up with advanced countries, and will even become more and more backward; advanced countries will become back-warded, and might finally end up being a developing country. Some scholars claim that if advanced countries, like the U.S.A., do not pay attention to developing high technology and continue to promote the growth of productivity, they will fall back as a developing country in a short period of time.[25]

Let us take a look at the economic growth and development examples of using productivity law in typical countries:

The first example is in the U.S.A. The yearly economic actual growth rate was 3.3% between the years of 1950-1960, 4.1% between years of 1960-1973, 1.2% between the years of 1974-1975, 4.4% between the years of 1976-1980, and 2.5% between the years of 1980-1984. The labor productivity growth rate was 3.2% during 1948-1968, 2.2% in 1968-1973, and 0.6% in 1974-1980. During the years of 1978-1980, an negative growth firstly came out since 1909. As a result, the foreign trade of the U.S.A. was under trade deficits for many years in the 1970's. With the increase of labor productivity growth and slow down in social economic growth, USSR, Japan and Asia's "Four Little Dragons" gradually caught up to its development level. In the 1980s, however, the U.S.A. made a strategic adjustment for its national economy, at the same time information technology was largely used, which increased its labor productivity. In 1990, the U.S.A finally ended negative economic growth, achieving a GDP growth rate of 1.2%. In the following ten years, it maintained the momentum of economic growth. Until the year 2000 its GDP was still increasing at a high growth rate of 5%. At the end, it again lengthened its distance ahead of other countries. During this drastic change process, the new technology revolution created higher labor productivity.

Now, let's take a look at the annual economic actual growth of the USSR, Japan and Asia's "Four Little Dragons". The economic growth rate in USSR was: 10.2% between the years 1950-1960, 7.2% between the years 1960-1970, and 5.1% between the years 1970-1980. By the respective years, its yearly labor productivity growth rates were 8.4%, 5.9%, and 4.1%. Although in the 1960's, the economy of the USSR was stagnating, it became the world's second largest economic entity, with a composite national power second only to the U.S.A. Before the war, it only spent 20 years to accomplish the economic development journey which capitalism countries took longer to complete; after the war, it only used about 20 years to catch up with the advanced capitalism countries.

The actual economic yearly growth rates of Japan were: 8.2% between

1950-1960, 10.3% between 1960-1970, and 4.4% between 1970-1980. The labor productivity yearly growth rates were: 6.9% between 1950-1960, and 8.5% between 1960-1973. The high-speed growth of Japan's economy made it possible to recover from its losses in WWII in a period of only 20 years. In the 1960s, it has already caught up with the advanced economies in the world, becoming the third largest economic country, while at the same time the second largest capitalism economy country. The case of Asia's "Four Little Dragons" was similar to Japan's situation. Actual economic yearly growth rate and the yearly growth rate of labor productivity are listed in the table that follows:

The Table 2.1 shows us that Asia's "Four Little Dragons" were similar to Japan, not only relying on the high-speed growth of economy, but also relying on the high-speed growth of productivity. It only used 20 years to shorten its economic gap with advanced countries, becoming or getting closer to moderately developed countries.

Table 2.1

Country or Region \ Year Growth	1960-1970		1970-1980	
	Yearly economic growth (%)	Yearly labor productivity growth (%)	Yearly economic growth (%)	Yearly labor productivity growth (%)
Korea	8.9		9.5	5.7
Taiwan	9.3		9.8	7.6
Hong Kong	13.7		9.3	7.0
Singapore	9.4		8.5	6.8

Resource: *The Emergence of Asian "Four Little Dragons": Myth and Strategic Comparisons,* Financial and Economic Press of China (1990), p.28 and p.286. (In Chinese)

In contrast, years after the liberation of China, the economic growth speed was high: 30 years before the opening-up era (1978), the yearly growth rate of gross output value had already achieved 8.4%, while the yearly growth rate of industry was up to 11.3%. At this velocity, the growth rate was very high compared with the rest of the world. After the opening-up era, in the 15 years during 1979-1993, the GNP yearly growth rate was up to 9.3%. It did not only surpass western advanced countries but also was at the top of speedy developing countries and regions. However, China's economic development level was still very low; during the thirty years before the opening-up policy, the economic distance with the western advanced countries was lengthened. Until 10 years after the opening-up policy, this distance gradually had been shortened. One of the main reasons was that labor productivity growth of China was rather slow:

3.4% during 1953-1978, with a rise of 6.0% during 1979-1985, the yearly growth rate during years of 1953-1985 was 4.1%, lower than the yearly national income growth rate of 6.9%. The growth of productivity did not contribute much towards economic growth.

In sum, an economically backward country which is trying to catch up with the world's advanced economies should adapt a strategy of "catch-up type" economics; it can not only pursue economic development speed, but also needs to increase labor productivity through scientific innovation and technology improvements, making use of productivity while promoting its growth.

A lesson of China's economic development during the past years was that it should not only pursue high speed and should not ignore the increase of labor productivity. It did not achieve its goal to catch up with the advanced world. The secret of the USSR, Japan, Singapore and Hong Kong to achieve an economic strategy of catching up with the advanced world was that: they maintained their actual economic growth speed for a long time, while maintaining the speed of productivity growth, balancing both speed and effectiveness.

History, reality and economic growth theory tell us that: if China wants to achieve three steps of "catching-up" strategy, it must maintain the speed of economic growth and productivity growth, and continuously increase the contribution of productivity growth to economic growth. So, how can China's "catching-up" economic growth and development be designed?

Some scholars have professionally analyzed the topic, claiming that when comparing the year 1952 to the year 1981, the starting point of "catching-up" in China was still lagged behind. The year 1952 was the starting point of the founding of socialism in China. In that year, the social labor productivity level in China was US$155 per person each year (according to the basic exchange rate of 1: 2.27 to convert). In the same year, the social labor productivity level in U.S.A. was US$4433, USSR was US$1791, Japan was US$431, Germany was US$1961, Britain was US$1863, and France was US$4796 (amount during year 1954). They were 28.6 times, 11.6 times, 2.8 times, 12.7 times, 12.0 times, and 30.9 times bigger respectively when compared with China. China was under this situation when heading towards the socialist economic construction route. When measuring it with the process of productivity growth, the economic level of China during the year 1952 lagged 142 years behind Britain and 114 years behind Germany.[26]

How about the situation in 1981, after 40 years of economic construction? Up to year 1981, China's social labor productivity rate was US$545 per person a year (according to the basic exchange rate of USD: CNY= 1: 1.7768). In the same year, the social labor productivity level in U.S.A. was US$25934, USSR was US$6471, Japan was US$17634 (amount in the year 1980), Germany was US$6471, Britain was US$21804, and France was US$24092. They were 47.6 times, 11.9 times, 32.4 times, 43.9 times, 40.0 times, and 44.2 times bigger when compared with China.

When comparing with the year 1952, the labor productivity distance of China with advanced countries not only did not shorten but rather lengthened. Although the distance of average growth rate was lesser, China was still lagging far behind. During the years 1953-1981, the average growth rate of China, U.S.A., USSR, Japan, Germany, Britain, and France's labor productivity were 4.4%, 6.3%, 4.5%, 14.2% (During 1953-1980), 9.0%, 8.9% and 6.2%.[27]

We can see that, after years of economic development, although the social labor productivity of China made some progress, there is still an increasing distance when compared with advanced countries. The social labor productivity of Japan was the highest, up to 2.44 times of that in the U.S.A. Over the years, the economic growth speed of China has caught up or even surpassed that of advanced countries but productivity growth level has remained, thus somehow lengthened the distance to advanced countries. The economic growth speed of Japan was higher than that of advanced countries, like the U.S.A.; its productivity growth level was also high. Thus, Japan was able to achieve the strategy of catching up with the U.S.A.

Using this as a principle, if China is going to achieve the new-age strategy of socialist construction, how long does it have to go? Which way does it need to go? The key factors are still economic growth rate and productivity growth rate, and the latter one is especially important. Some scholars believe that, if the U.S.A is taken as a target to catch up with, assuming that the labor productivity in the U.S.A. does not change, while the growth speed in China is 6.7% annually, it can achieve the labor productivity level of 1981 in the U.S.A. in 60 years. Under this calculation, Zhang Delin listed a time table of productivity per capita required by China to catch up with other advanced countries in 1981.[28] It can be shown in Table 2.2 (assuming that the labor productivity level of these countries does not change).

Table 2.2

	Yearly growth rate for catching up in 60 years (%)	Yearly growth rate for catching up in 50 years (%)	Yearly growth rate for catching up in 40 years (%)
U.S.A.	6.7	8.0	70.1
Japan	6.0	7.2	9.1
Germany	6.5	7.9	9.9
Britain	6.3	7.7	9.6
France	6.5	7.9	10.0
Average	6.0	7.3	9.2

Resource: see the note number 17.

So, if the social labor productivity of China grows by 6.0% to 9.2% annually on average, it will need 40 to 60 years to achieve the productivity level of advanced countries in 1981. From this estimation, the productivity level of China will still be 40 to 60 years behind the advanced countries during the period of 2020 - 2040. Indeed, while China needs a composite national power or a gross economic scale for catching up with the advanced world, it must strive for a moderate level in 2050. The problem is that economic growth and development of China may lose its correct way if solely considering about gross economic value while the productivity level remains unchanged. Therefore, China needs to pay more attention to productivity growth. At the same time, China has to increase its productivity level. This is an important thing for solidifying and developing the Chinese socialist system, and is an important way for showing its socialist superiority.

By a horizontal comparison, China is going to face severe challenges. When assuming that there is no growth in the labor productivity of advanced countries, China needs 40 to 60 years in order to catch up with the labor productivity level of them in 1981. If their labor productivity growth rate is 2% annually, it will take China as long as year 2060 to catch up with advanced countries' 1981 levels. If the growth was even greater than 2% (which can happen, it will take China an even longer time to achieve their 1981 level.

In conclusion, labor productivity growth is the key factor for sticking to the center of economic construction and concentrating on developing productivity. Labor productivity is the leader of economic growth and is also a key factor for stabilizing and developing a socialist system and the future fate of socialism itself. High-speed labor productivity growth is not only a matter of economic development but also a matter of choosing appropriate developmental strategy and economic models. Under the condition of fast technological development in 1990s, traditional industrialization is heading towards modern industrialization. New patterns of industrialization and new types of modernization take information technology and newly-developed high technology as a foundation. Examples of these technologies include bioengineering technology, new energy resources, and new material technology. This is an important transition of productivity revolution. In order to have higher productivity, we must seize this transition and run towards a route of new industrialization, at the end, achieving continuous, effective high growth.

Anyhow, if ignoring the high-speed growth of labor productivity, and ignoring the economic growth model, the basic policy of setting economic construction as the center will not be realized, the superiority of the socialist economic system will not come true, and socialism with Chinese characteristics will not be fully established. But, we believe: under the leadership of the Chinese Communist Party, the labor productivity growth can be obtained at a 6% annually average. With this criterion, Chinese people have the ability to speed up labor productivity growth. At the same time, socialism with Chinese characteristics can be achieved, leading China towards a bright future. The future belongs to the Chinese nation, and great Chinese socialism.

Chapter Three

Resource Environment: A Basic Constraint

Condition of Economic Growth

The process of social production and economic growth is a process of interaction between human beings as the subject and nature as the object. In this process, four main relationships exist: first, the recognition relationship of human beings as the subject to nature; second, the practical relationship of human beings as the subject to nature; third, the material technology relationship (materials and energy exchange relations) of human beings as the subject to nature; fourth, the mutual relationship among human beings as the subject, in other words, the production relations. These four kinds of relationship demonstrate that the process of social production and economic growth with human beings as the subject can not be separated from nature, society, or the resource environment formed by nature and society otherwise social production and economic growth will be hindered. In a nutshell, social production and economic growth is always subjected to resource and environment constraints. Therefore, when we try to study the social production process, to make decisions about social economic growth and development, or to organize social production, economic growth and development, we have to base them on practical situations to study the resource environmental system and its restrictive impacts.

3.1 The Basic Structure and Characteristics of Resource Environment

Resource environment is a comprehensive system consisting of natural and social factors that are involved in the social production process and can be used to achieve an exchange of materials, energy and information. The basic structure of resource environment includes four parts: natural resources, geographical location and transportation resources, actual economic and industrial resources, and social environment resources. These four elements are interconnected, interacted, and act as a basic structure of resource environment. Resource environment is the environmental support for social production and economic growth process. It is also an important condition for a nation in carrying out economic production. Following is a specific analysis on the basic structure of resource environment.

First, let us look at the condition of natural resources. Natural resources hereby mean the natural materials and natural forces that are well-known and have economic value. The abundant natural resources involved include creature resources and plant resources. Natural resources consist of land and water resources with geographic and climate characteristics, earth surface resources like the forest and animals, underground resources like minerals. Natural resources can be both living resources (known as living materials by Marx), and production materials (known as labor materials by Marx).[29] According to the natural characteristics of natural resources, the above can be categorized into four different types. The first one is bio-ecological resources, like sunshine, air, moisture, etc. The second one is organism resources, like plants, animals, and micro-organisms. The third one is land resources, like area of land, and fertility of soil. The fourth one is mineral resources. If we use the reproduction characteristics of natural resources to make classifications, there will be two different categories: The first one contains renewable resources, like bio resources, organism resources, and fertility of soil. The second one is nonrenewable resources, like mineral resources, and area of land. Obviously, although the content of natural resources is very rich, but when it is basically classified into four main categories, the most fundamental natural resources are nonrenewable resources, like land and mineral resources. Humans, after evolved out as the dominator of the natural world, have become relatively independent on natural resources, and have been able to increase their capability of transforming the natural world. However, the existence and development of humans as well as their social productivity and economic activities still rely on natural resources, and can not be separated from the nature environment. Human beings still rely on the natural world and its resources for living and production. Wealth comes from the natural world and labor productivity, and these two elements need to be combined together to perform wealth. Humans must integrate natural power into their own power, so that to roll out a larger amount of wealth. Without natural resources and natural power, human beings will lose their own power and productivity, and thus social development and economic growth will not happen.

So, how is the condition of natural resources throughout the world and China? This is the foundation of economic development for achieving the strategy of economic growth. The condition can be simply shown in Table 3.1 below.

From the information above, scarcity of cultivated land is a very important element in economic development. Although the cultivated land area of the world is 5.5 acreages per capita on average, this cultivated land is spread unevenly in different parts of the world. In some countries, cultivated land per capita is far greater than the rest of the world, while cultivated land per capita in some countries does not reach the world average. For example, USA and USSR respectively have about 13 acreages and 16 acreages of cultivated land, while Thailand has 6.3 acreages and China has only 1.2 acreages. The cultivated land per capita in Guangdong Province is even less than 0.6 acreages (dropped to

0.4125 acreages per capita during 2004, one time lower than the warning line of the United Nation). Although people always say that China is big and full of resources, its cultivated land per capita does not even reach average world levels. Cultivated land is particularly scarce in Guangdong Province. Of course, land resources do not only mean cultivated land but at the same time it is the most important element. The unfavorable condition of land resources in China has influenced its economic development. In order to speed up economic growth, China must treasure its land resources, especially its cultivated land. Any misuse of the land is a sin of not being responsible to the next generation. The abuse of land will also worsen the resource environment and is harmful to long term economic growth and development.

Table 3.1

Natural Resources	Possession amount of the world	Amount per capita in the world	Possession amount of China	Amount per capita in China	Amount per capita of China in amount per capita of the world (%)
Land	22.05 trillion acres	49 acres	1.44 trillion acres	14.4 acres	29.39
Forest	6.975 trillion acres	15.5 acres	1.83 trillion acres	1.8 acres	11.61
Cultivated Arable land	Hundred million acres	5.5 acres		1.2 acres	21.81
Grassland	5.13 trillion acres	11.4 acres	430 million acres	4.3 acres	37.72
Fresh water	Hundred million cubic meters	10,800 cubic meters	25.63 trillion cubic meters	2563 cubic meters	23.73
Coal (geology reserves)	1415.70 trillion tons	3146 tons	146.5 trillion tons	1465 tons	46.57
Oil (geology reserves)	42.3 trillion tons	94 tons	3 – 6 trillion tons	30 – 60 tons	31.60 – 63.83
Water power (total reserves)	0.495 trillion kilowatt	110 million kilowatt	676 million kilowatt	0.676 kilowatt	61.45
Iron mine (Proved reserves)	39.15 trillion tons	87 tones	4.68 trillion tons	46.8 tons	53.79

Resource: edited from *Encyclopedic Almanac of China*

Taking a step forward to look at the economic value of natural resources, land resources are always the most important resources of all. For developing countries, as their economic development level is relatively low, agriculture becomes an important industry for their economy, with a large percentage of peasants. Agriculture leads to industrial development and at the same time stabilizes industrial processes and social revolutions. As we know, agriculture production needs to use land as a foundation. Agricultural work can only be done on land. Not only that, the development of economic construction of transportation networks, factories and commercial buildings, and social facilities also needs land. Therefore, for countries with prosperous wealth and dense population, the role of land is even more important for a higher level of development, while its value is "an inch of land as high as an ounce of gold."

At the same time, mineral resources are also very scarce. From the above chart, we can see that China is a place with a large population and little resources, which restricts industrial and agricultural development. As in China, there are 46.8 billion tons of reserved iron mine, 5 trillion tons of reserved coal (guaranteed reserve of 901.5 billion tons), and the oil reserve is 30 to 60 billion tons, which ranks at the top of the world. China is also rich in other types of mineral resources and ranks highly in the world. Nevertheless, the resources per capita in China are far below the world average. Most of the resources level can not reach half the world's level. In Guangdong, there is a lack of coal and iron mines. There are only 300 million tons of reserved iron in the Yun Fu, Da Bao Shan and Da Ding mines. This shows that, as non-reproducible resources, mineral products are scarce in China. In order to modernize industries and to speed up economic growth, China must carefully make use of mineral resources.

Other natural resources are generally reproducible and will not be described in details. From the point of being a part of nature and having natural power, the characteristics of reproducible and non-reproducible natural resources under the economic growth condition are stated below.

(1) The limitation of a static state. This kind of limitation in one dimension comes from the limited capacity in a certain period of development when people exploit and process natural resources and materials. In a second dimension, it comes from the limited amount of natural resources the earth can provide. Although the universe is boundless, the weight and area of the earth is bounded. The weight of the earth is nearly 6.6×10^{33} tons, with a surface area of 1.1 billion square kilometers. Therefore, the earth is limited when facing the economic growth of the world. If the world population is to expand without limit, economic growth will not be sustainable under the earth's restrictions. In the end there will be a population that the world cannot bear. In a third dimension, it comes from the limited amount of the earth's resources that people can utilize by human ability. In a fourth dimension, it comes from the limited renewal time of

natural resources. Up till now, humans can neither fully utilize all the natural resources nor fully renew the reproducible resources already consumed. According to studies of the United Nations, if the world's natural resources are reused at their maximized potential by all nations, (under a stable and unchanged economic growth condition before 2000), it could only reach 75% of the potential resources.[30] If the economy continues to grow, the rate of resources utilization will fall under 55%. This implies that under a certain condition, natural resources are scarce. Therefore, we must save our resources through making good use of them. By doing so, an economical society will then be formed and an recycling economy can be developed.

(2) Infinity in dynamics. From epistemology, knowledge of human beings is both limited and unlimited. Through widening the horizon of humans, their knowledge about nature begins to expand. This strengthens their understanding of the economic value of natural resources and the renewing value of reproducible resources. Humans might also be able to create things that do not exist in the natural world. Hence, natural resources are infinite in this respect. From the existing resources on earth, minerals that people can discover and exploit are buried a few thousand meters deep the ground. There is still a long way to go before reaching the radius of the earth. Deep inside the earth, there are a lot of elements like iron, nickel, and platinum. Rich minerals are hidden under the sea. An example would be the Pacific Ocean that has 1.7×10^{12} tons of manganese nodule, 400 billion tones of manganese, 9.8 billion tones of cobalt, 8.8 billion tones of copper, 16.4 billion tons of nickel. Manganese nodule is still growing at a speed of 10 million tones annually. It is estimated that there are 2.6 trillion tones of marine creatures, 1.4 trillion tones of which live under the sea. Each year, there are 20-30 billion tons of green plants under the oceans, making use of photosynthesis to transform carbon into glucose and protein. If its ecosystem is not destroyed, the ocean will produce 3 billion tons of products annually. As we know, the earth is only a member of the Solar System, which is a member of the Milky Way System, and the Milky Way System is only a member of another outer space galaxy. Various galaxies together form the universe. No boundary can be found within a universe and its resources are infinite. Therefore, the natural resources which humans rely on are unlimited.

(3) Uneven distribution in geographic location. As mentioned above, natural resources of the world are dispersed unequally across different geographical regions, for example the natural resources in each province of China are extremely unbalanced. This unbalance was due to the formation pattern of natural resources. The resources quality found in regions are not the same, not to mention their quantity, characteristics and evolving directions. In China, 80% of the coal reserve is spread in northern China, while 56% of it is concentrated in north central, 10% in the southwestern regions, and only 9% in

11 provinces in south central China. The best quality of coal is found in the northern part of China. The reserves of iron and mineral resources in Ji Dong and Chuan Xi are 50%. 80% of oil reserves are spread in the Northeast and Northwest of China. 90% of phosphorous reserves are concentrated in three provinces of the southwest, Hunan, and Hubei. 90% of Bauxite is spread in Shanxi, Henan, Guizhou and Guangxi. Wolfram mineral is mainly spread within the four provinces of Hunan, Jiangxi, Guizhou, and Yunnan. 90% of Sylvite is concentrated in Qinghai. 80% of asbestos is concentrated in Sichuan, Shaanxi, and Qinghai. Provinces, like Guangdong, Fujian, are relatively poor in mineral resource supplies. Under a certain productivity level, the unbalanced pattern of natural resources has made noticeable differences in the economic growth and development of regions.

(4) Diverse functions of natural resources. Natural resources are usually considered as a whole; however, they are only one part of the whole unit under the production process and the creation of wealth. Due to the various features of natural resources, some of the natural resources can be used as an integral part of the whole to fully function well, such as geographical location, the sea, the lake, mountains, the plain, and the climate. Some other natural resources can function as separate parts, or even can be moved to different places, like mineral, water, and organism resources. From the perspective of stable unity and mobility of natural resources, some regions that have geographical advantages will also have obvious economic benefits. Some regions, such as Japan and Singapore lack natural resources advantage and are actually very short of them. In fact, it will not be a problem for these countries as they can make use of the mobility of resource to promote their economic growth and development for having greater success. With various kinds of characteristics in natural resources, economic growth and development will continue unceasingly. Under a certain condition, regions without a rich hinterland of mineral resources can still achieve a high level of economic growth and development. Oppositely, regions which are rich in mineral resources may not be guaranteed to have a high level of economic growth and development.

To sum up, natural resources are the foundation of the natural environment. Different natural resources have their own characteristics which impose different degrees of restrictions on economic growth. So, natural resources are the first key component of the structure system of the natural environment.

Now, let's consider the importance of geographical location and transportation. These are the things that humans rely on for production activities and development. They are the conditions humans in which undergo the production process and also the social economic bases for controlling productivity and the variety of wealth in a society.

Geographical location is the space structure of one country or region on the surface of the earth. It is also a result of natural and human evolution. Therefore, geographical location is the endowment of nature and history. Geographical location is a unity of humans and nature under the natural and historical process (Organism–Economic Loop). To give an example of this unity, the lands and the oceans occupy 30% and 70% of the earth respectively. Lands are separated by the oceans into Eurasia, Africa, North America, South America, Australia, and the South Pole. The oceans are separated into the Pacific Ocean, Indian Ocean, Atlantic Ocean, and Arctic Ocean. From the structure of lands and oceans, each region is separated into rivers, lakes, mountains, plains, and basins. All these are formed by the earth itself and its motion process. That is why we say that geographical location is the endowment of the nature. The geographical advantages of different parts of the world are closely related to the long history of humans. For example, China is situated in the East Asia, and China's land is huge with wide plains and high mountain areas. There are also large bodies of water such as the East Sea, the Huanghai, and the Bohai with Yangtze River and Yellow River. In fact, there is no definite geographical benefit for a region. It all depends on the kinds of and the results of human activities. It is a condition which every generation has to inherit to carry out its own activities. For locations with geographical advantages, a favorable climate and sunshine can provide other countries easy access to them, thus stimulating speedy economic growth and development. If a region does not possess geographic advantages, the pace of its productivity development will be restricted to a certain degree. Hence, other local resources need to be exploited. When these resources are put into the production process, their force will be realized. Up till now, a better economic growth always needs a relatively better condition of natural resources. Provinces, like Guangdong, have good geographical locations. It is close to Hong Kong and Macau along the coast. After the reform and opening policy, its economic development has sped up. Geographic location has become a kind of economic resources, which is due to the advantage of economic and technological communications among regions and countries.

When we talk about transportation conditions, we are talking about nature-based transportation. For example, transportation by water or rivers and by coastal lines with natural ports can be seen as a kind of transportation condition. All these make it easier for ships to get through. For land without mountains, it is easier to construct broad roads, highways, railways, stations and airports. If a country has better natural transportation advantages with a balanced level of productivity development and economic growth condition, it will favor the economic development of constructing transportation facilities. In the end, this advantage will help achieve economic prosperity which leads to faster economic growth and development.

The geographic and transportation conditions mentioned above belong to a category of natural resources which is not movable like the mineral resources that can be transported among countries. The characteristics of geographic location and transportation are holistic and stable. Therefore, there is a high degree of restraints in economic growth and development. Because of this characteristic, there is a big difference between countries having geographic and transportation advantages and those short of these advantages. There will be obvious differences in terms of speed and level of economic development. The differences in economic growth and development cannot be changed within a short period of time. However, if productivity development is developed in the right direction, like developing highly manufactured products with great value, the disadvantage of geographic and transportation conditions can actually be modified. The economy of inland and mountain regions can also be developed quickly under this circumstance. Electric products are the prime output of Japan, while central business is placed in large cities and component production is placed in remote mountainous regions. This helps to speed up the economic development of the mountain regions. Transportation has stronger restrictions in the early stages of productivity development. The higher the speed of productivity of today, the more important transportation is in an economy. Even the huge distances of an ocean can be shorten with advanced transportation. This breaks away space limitation and lets communication activities flow easily. From this point of view, a demerit can actually be turned into a merit, making great changes in transportation. It is important to weaken the geographic and transportation disadvantages of economic development and to make full use of other aspects of advantages for offering help in transforming disadvantages into advantages.

Now, we are back to the actual economic and industrial resources. This is the result of historical human production, from each generation or each government to the next. These kinds of resources are the material technology foundation of the economic growth and development strategy, from production to reproduction. If natural resources, geographic locations and transportation conditions are caused by nature without from the influence of people, then actual economic productivity resources are a target for development of natural forces. These resources are also a kind of transformation using natural forces as an intermediary. This is something that people can choose and make decision when conducting their own activities. Because of the above reason, the historical differences of countries' economic development are demonstrated clearly. It is also the result of the previous generation, and a reminder for the next generation. It can be treated as a historical starting point when economic growth and development are being considered.

What elements should actual economic and industrial resources include? One of them is gross economic production. It is mainly the net value of fixed capital and the gross national economy. Second is the stage of economic production development, like an agricultural stage or an industrial stage. An agriculture stage can be sub-divided into general machinery or bio-agriculture. An industrial stage can also be divided into a general machine system stage and a general automated stage or an intelligent automated stage. Third is the developmental degree of economic productivity. For example, whether a series of complete production departments, industry departments, and the facilities of the whole society can be formed in primary, secondary or tertiary industries is a big question we have to consider. Agricultural water conservancy projects, seeds, fertilizers, machinery, pesticides, agricultural systems, formation of production units, deep-processing agricultural products, and quality of peasants and technical workers should be all considered under the production of primary industry. Completeness of light and heavy industrial departments, such as industrial settings on raw material, machine-manufacturing, foods, clothes, and electrical appliances, should be considered under secondary industry. Fourth is the optimization of the industrial structure. That is the idealistic conditions of the relations between mainstream industries and supporting industries, and the co-ordinations of the whole production structure. Fifth is the advancing degree of the industrial structure. History in the past has indicated a certain path of economic development in developed countries. The path of advancing industrial structure went through this order: relying on primary industry or first industry (mainly agricultural and mineral production) → relying on second industry (mainly construction and manufacturing production) → relying on third industry or tertiary industry (mainly service industries, such as science, education, finance, trade business, and high-tech production). All of the above have created an organic synthesis of production. This is a critical consideration for countries starting their economic growth and development.

China is in lack of resources for production. When new China was established in 1949, the fixed assets of the state-owned manufacturing corporations were only $10.7 billion (1952). Modern industrial production value was only 17% of the total value of industrial and agricultural settings. Steel production was 158 thousand tons (the highest yearly production in history was 900 thousand tons). Coal production was 32 million tons (the highest yearly production in history was 62 million tons). The industrial gross output value was $34.9 billion (measured by year 1952), while tertiary production still had not started. Up to 1980, when China started to build a new age socialist society, China was still closely attached to an agricultural industry at a primitive stage. The nation's industrial fixed resources were $34.56 trillion with 37.12 million tons of steel, and 620 million tons of coal. The industrial gross output value was $48.97 trillion. The ratio among primary, second and tertiary production was 31.2: 48.3: 20.5. Besides, these industrial resources were unevenly distributed throughout the country. The above was not only the foundation for China to build up its socialism economic society but also acted as a basic consideration for the Chinese Communist Party and the central government.

Lastly, let us take a look at social resources. Some people say that social relation (guanxi) is a kind of productivity in the developing market-orientated economy. From the perspective of social relations as one of resources for economic development, this saying is correct. Social resources are also the result of accumulated human activities, including human quality, culture, education, operation management experience, capital raising and capability of market development, and capability of technology. Other activities included are socio-economic geography, socio-political and public security conditions, quality of civil workers, government public services, democracy and legal systems, economic legislations, tax laws and the international environment. All of these are critical in initiating a country's economic growth and development, forming production types and structures, and raising social economic benefits. These human activities are the socio-economic foundation for advancing an economic region. Starting from the implementation of the opening-up policy, due to better social resources and preferential policies, coastal provinces and cities, opening-up economic areas, and especially the special administrative zones have had much better economic performance. The characteristic of the social resources is what can be created by the people. The quality of people and the capability of social citizens affect the formation, development and application of social resources. If the quality of the social citizen (particularly the leaders in government) is high and makes good use of economic policies and other social relationships of economic activity (e.g., businessman living abroad), this kind of social resources will be developed in a more desirable way. The functional value of social resources in economic growth and development will be relatively high. Otherwise, the functional value of social resources will be restricted and will not promote local economy to a certain extent. For example, some coastal cities, even economic special administrative zones with good developmental conditions, are not more desirable in economic development than their counterparts in China or in Guangdong because they are deficient in using their social resources.

In this chapter, we have mentioned four kinds of resources – natural resources, geographic location and transportation resources, actual economic and industrial resources, and social resources. All of these resources help form the basic structure of a resource environment system for a country's economic growth and development. These resources have their own characteristics which are well-connected with functional values to each other. The first two kinds of resources form the natural foundation of the resource environment. Economic and industrial resources form the actual economic foundation of resource environment. Social resources form the adjusting lever of the resource environment. Each and every country that is developing its economy must face this reality. It cannot escape from the reality when setting up its economic growth and development strategies and objectives, nor can it form the social production strategy without putting the reality into consideration. An economic strategy escaping from this kind of reality will be unpractical and disastrous failure will occur.

3.2   The Function of Resource environment in Economic Growth Process

Acting as a structural system on the whole, resource environment constraints economic growth and development; meanwhile, it also constitutes the basic production components such as aforementioned natural resources, geographical location and transportation resources, industrial resources, and social resources etc., which respectively have an individual function of economic growth and development in accordance to their own features. Then, what is the function of resource environment in economic growth? How is it used? How can we accurately use the function of resource environment to promote economic growth and development? In fact, all these have patterns to follow.

(1) The function of integral promotion of investment. This function means an inseparable promotional effect on economic growth and development imposed by the resource environment. The integral promotion of investment forms a kind of cohesion and attraction, while promoting the grouping of production elements, like capital, labor, technology, and management experience. This helps speed up productivity and the growth of corporations. At the same time, through material or physical conditions, societal wealth can be created by making use of different productive elements in the production process. If a country or a region is rich in land resources and mineral resources, situated in coastal areas, has good geographical and transportation conditions, with established economical productivity and opening-up policies, it can easily attract huge investments and advanced technologies to support the development of heavy industries, such as iron and steel projects, oil refinery projects, automobile projects. In return, the scope of productivity will be expanded, while the productivity level will be raised. Thus, this country's economic growth and development can then be promoted. After the opening-up policy, compared with other inland and mountainous areas of China, the open coastal open areas, such as the Pearl River Delta of Guangdong Province, have more favorable resources like geographic location and transportation, productivity and social resources. Only the natural mineral resources are not as favorable as those in other inland and mountainous areas. This enables the Pearl River Delta area to form a competitive advantage in economic development and speed up its economic growth. Hence, the introduction of investment from abroad and the establishment of lateral ties at home can be expanded. It can then participate in international economic technology cooperation and exchange projects while attracting huge investments.

Through the promotional function of resource environment, advanced technology and management experience can be imported into Guangdong Province, forming a new advanced productivity capacity. Guangdong's development cannot be separated from its resource environment as it helps promote investment for production. Up to as late as 1993, Guangdong Province actually used US$29.5 billion in foreign capital from 44,705 foreign-invested corporations, while importing 1.4 million sets of equipment and over 5,000 production lines. Foreign investments also helped 50% of Guangdong's industrial corporations in transforming technology (up to 2004 Guangdong actually used US$15.04 billion foreign capital, from 110,000 foreign-invested corporations). On the whole, different parts of Guangdong have different resources, especially when compared mountainous areas with the Pearl River Delta area. This led 70% of all the actually used foreign capital in Guangdong concentrated in the Pearl River Delta area. Throughout the whole nation, as Guangdong Province was a major testing region for the opening-up policy, this enabled Guangdong to have the advantage of special policies and time preference in economic environment. The social resources of Guangdong are much better than other provinces therefore allowing its resource environment to be better developed. Therefore, Guangdong's foreign capital accounted for about a third of the whole country's actual used foreign capital (as of 2004, while the whole country was running under the strengthened opening-up policy, Guangdong actually used 26.8% of the whole country foreign capital). This is the result of the "Lowland Effect".

(2) Enhancement or blockage in improvement of productivity. Marx said, "productivity is decided by many factors, including the level of labor proficiency, the level of science development, and the level of workmanship application. Other elements include social structure, the scale and efficiency of productive materials, and the natural conditions that relate to the production process."[31] The above elements belong to the concept of resource environment. Therefore, if a country or a region has a resource environment advantage, its increase in productivity will be faster. If a country does not have resource environment advantage, its increase in productivity will be comparatively slower. If countries have the same conditions in production, capital, and technology, while the basic components and the structure of resource environment are different, the productivity in these countries will be different even though they may use the same amount of labor. In this situation, advantages of resource environment go hand in hand with high rates of productivity. Hence, we can then say that, resource environment has a big influence on economic growth and development.

We must understand that the function of resource environment on economic growth and development is not spontaneous, but man-made, that is, the hard work of the people and the society. History has seen many examples of achieving economic growth and development through the effort of people and the excellence in resource environment, such as the natural resource environment, geographical location and transportation conditions. In the late 19th century to early 20th century, America's economy developed at a high speed. This high speed development is due to several factors, like economic relationships and population. But, the main reason for the high speed development was the richness in natural resources. The opening of western areas of America could not be separated from the broad land resources owned by them. The mass forests and rich mineral resources helped develop the economy of America. After 1960's, the economy of the Middle East countries sped up. This fast development was also the result of the advantage of oil resources. No wonder Marx regarded the productivity which was generated by natural resources as the natural labor productivity rate and suggested that this kind of natural labor productivity play a very important role in economic development.

(3) Providing an actual material foundation and social assurance for forming an entity of products. Material product is the basic formation of social wealth and economic growth and development are the increase of social wealth in forms of products. But material product is the result of natural resources processed by labor and it is also the result of transforming the shapes and functions of natural materials. Therefore, natural resource, as an element of productive realization, helps decide the quality, variety and quantity of products. At the same time, production is processed under the foundation of economic productivity and a series of social conditions which include different policies, legal systems, and laws. So, for increasing social wealth, social resource has an important protective function which acts as an economic foundation and social adjustment lever.

(4) Controlling industrial structure and productivity distribution. The industrial structure is a system of industries and departments based upon social division of labor and cooperation. There are many factors controlling industrial structure, but resource environment, especially natural resource environment, is the most important factor.

As we know, a country's natural resource environment has a certain kind of structure, which influences labor structure, leading to specific labor types in different countries or regions. The differences among specific labor types will form a country's unique characteristics of social division of labor and productive departments. To build relatively complete and coordinated development in productive departments, a country must have a rather complete and rich storage of natural resources. Otherwise, the country will not be able to form productivity departments which are in a relatively complete production structure system. Globally, in a country like Japan, there are lacks of natural resources (especially in mineral resources). So, natural resources have always been a big existing problem for Japan's economic development. Under this condition, over 90% of Japan's mineral resources rely on imports. This also determines that Japan's economy must be built up upon producing manufactured products. After 1973, under the influence of the oil crisis, the Japanese government was forced to adjust their productivity structure, changing their industrial structure from capital-intensive heavy industries to knowledge-intensive light industries, while developing high-tech products and energy saving products. Guangdong province is also relatively poor in natural resources, especially mineral resources. So, this province adopted light industrial structure as a major production structure. People might think that light industrial structure would easier for Guangdong. Consequently, Guangdong once did not fully recognize the importance of heavy industries for further economic advancement. These aforementioned examples show that natural resources constrain the formation and developmental variations of productive structure.

Besides, natural resources also determine the space layout of productivity. Since natural resources are distributed unevenly around the world, it makes the space layout of productivity also uneven. If policy makers decide the layout of productivity subjectively without considering the geographic spread of natural resources, it would not only be contrary to the rule of economic benefit, but also lead to irreversible difficulties in economic development. This already shows the law of "productivity layout versus resource restriction". Currently, with improvements in science and technology, the law of resource restriction has been weakened but its existence and continuous occurrence will not change.

To sum up, the role of resource environment is multi-facet and objective, with a series of patterns and functions for economic growth and development.

3.3 The Functional Patterns of Resource Environment upon Economic Growth (Tendency)

We must acknowledge that the multifunction of resource environment on economic growth and development embed a certain kind of pattern, the function of which is shown by reversing the trend of development. On one hand, it works towards a weakening direction of development; on the other hand, it works towards a strengthening direction of development. A weakening direction of development means that with improvement in science, technology and productivity, the constraint of natural resources upon social economic growth and development gradually decreases. Such rule is called gradual decreasing law of natural resources. This pattern shows the restricting effect of natural resources upon economic development is in inverse proportion to the level of productivity development.

Up till now, categorizing by the shape of labor materials, the development of social productivity has experienced five stages, namely, hand tools, machinery, electrical forces, electronic forces, and information. Productivity structure also has experienced five styles -- resource-intensive, labor-intensive, capital-intensive, technology-intensive, and knowledge-technology intensive. Through these styles, the critical role that natural resource played in economic development has been replaced by other kinds of productive elements, such as labor, capital, technology and knowledge. That is why economic growth occurs in recent times, while the consumption of natural resources decreases. Some statistics show that, ever since 1900, the need of raw materials has been decreased by 1.25% annually in the world. In the 1980's, the industrial raw material needed by a unit of industrial product was at most 40% of that in 1900. Currently, the industries of the whole world have been shifted from raw material-intensive style to knowledge-technology intensive and value-added process intensive styles. As new products continue to mushroom, and new crafts and new technology continue to be promoted, the proportion of raw materials in the production costs of many products have gradually decreased. Semiconductors are a good example: now it is only 1% to 3% of the original production cost. The energy needed to produce 100 tons of glass fiber is only 5% of producing 1 ton of copper conductors. This proves that with the diminishing pattern of the function of natural resources, the function of natural resources towards a country's economic growth and development restriction reduces. Especially under today's advanced technology and the prosperity of marketing economy, natural resources, like richness of minerals, no longer plays a decisive role in the condition of economic development as in the past. Japan and Singapore are also poor in natural resources, especially the latter, which has to import water from Malaysia. But their economic development has not been restricted by the deficiency in natural resources. Japan is now becoming a strong industrialized country and a huge economic entity, while Singapore has become a modernized and industrialized country. On the contrary, some developing countries with rich mineral resources are slow in economic development. This is due to the lag behind in productivity development.

Similarly, countries that are well off in social, economic and industrial resources cannot automatically make the country's economic development. China, India, Babylon, and Egypt -- the four ancient civilized countries lagged behind after the Middle Age. These countries were not restricted by the historical foundation of actual social economic productivity resources.

America is a young country with about 200 years' history, but its weak historical foundation has not restricted its economic development. Actually, the historical foundation may not have a great impact on realistic social economic and industrial resources. Its influence towards a country's future economic development has already been weakened. For instance, countries of the Asian "Four Little Dragons" (including Singapore, Korea, Taiwan and Hong Kong) have been growing tremendously within a short period of time in the last few decades. Although they used to lag behind in terms of their economy and their technological foundation, they are fast in catching up with other countries with a long historical foundation.

Nevertheless, in another aspect, social resources, like laws and regulations, items of economic and non-economic policies are affecting today's global market economy. There is a trend of strengthening the position of the above social resources on a country. In some aspects, market economy can also be called legal economy. Therefore, as market economy develops, the function of marketing as a foundation in resources configuration is greater. Hence, a country needs to have various sound laws, regulations and macro adjustment policies. This will help maintain a good order in the market, while strengthening the macro adjustments towards its citizens. It also leads to a configurative cooperation among various kinds of resources to achieve the fine cycle of social economy, while promoting economic persistence with speedy and healthy development. After the world wars, the economic development of Japan and Asian's "Four Little Dragons" have made full use of their social resources. As a developing country, to achieve a speedy economic growth and development, China must create a modernized socialist country. It cannot overlook the right conception and also should grasp and use the functional patterns of social resources to create a good resource environment in this aspect. Under these patterns, when we set up strategies of economic growth and development, we need to consider mobilization and organization of people for achieving economic growth strategy. We must comprehend the restricted function of resource environment and while realizing the increasing function of social productivity development and the level of science and technology advancement. Based on the above, we must have the faith and the determination while trying to catch up with the world's leading level. At the same time, we must have the belief of surpassing the advanced level of world and make this kind of leap on the actual foundation with a consistent strategy and a revolutionary and scientific attitude.

Chapter Four

Strategic Target: Driving Power of Economic Growth

It is not easy for a developing country like China to speed up its economic development to the level of modernized countries. It is a long-term historical process of continuously expanding production. During the process, many things are involved and lots of problems need to be overcome while integrating a variety of economic production resources to strengthen production for achieving healthy economy growth. When determining strategy for social economic growth, the whole process of economic growth, the pattern of each economic stage, and the elements involved in economic growth, all of these need to be understood. The scope of economic growth strategy includes strategic targets, strategic key issues, strategic implementation plans, strategic steps and strategic thoughts, etc. Among them, strategic target of economic growth is the most important one, while the others are under its constraint. In this chapter, we mainly study the issues of economic growth target and its guiding function.

4.1 Fundamentals of Strategic Target on Economic Growth

From our point of view, we will limit the strategic target of economic growth to the economically less developed countries. We know, this is not the case in reality, but developed countries are under different circumstances. It is partial to say that economic growth theories can only be applied to those highly-developed countries, while development theories are the main concern of developing or underdeveloped countries. Actually, development comes along with growth. It would be better to say that economic growth remains an issue in both developing and developed countries. In order to reach a world-recognized advanced level, qualitative and quantitative measures are required to actualize economic growth. Economic target is the first thing needed to be determined for economic strategy.

So, under market economic conditions, how should we define the economic growth target of a country or a region?

First, from the theoretical viewpoint of economic growth, the strategic target of social economic growth is a summation of growth targets in all levels and is linked to society with the ultimate goal of fulfilling the needs and development of people. The vertical and horizontal summations of targets are scientific decisions that need to be well considered for economic growth and development strategy. Vertical targets include primary, secondary and tertiary industry, as well as education, science, technology and culture. Horizontal targets can be divided into four levels. The first target level concerns total social production value, total production value of industry and agriculture, gross national production, national revenue, and national revenue per capita. The second target level concerns total production value, net production value and total revenue generated from major business settings or industries, such as agriculture, manufacturing industry, construction, transportation, commerce and trade, medical care, science, and educational. The third target level concerns total production value, net production value and total revenue generated from farming, forestry, fishery rearing animals activities under agriculture, light and heavy industry in manufacture. The fourth target level concerns growth in products and services yielded from all departments – a fundamental of strategic target in social economic growth. Multilevel human needs are actually reflected through multilevel targets of economic growth and their accompanying multilevel structure of industry; they are also reflected through interactions among satisfying human needs, level of human development, and consumption structure; as well as interactions among production target, multilevel distribution structure and multi-facet circulation. All in all, economic growth is to satisfy the needs and the multi-level development growth of people.

Second, from the operational point of view, if a nation or a region want to set a strategic plan, generic and specific stage-based indicators are required for measuring its strategic economic performance. For example, under the leadership of Deng Xiaoping, the economic growth and development strategic target was: during the twenty years from 1981 to the 20th century, China's GDP should be doubled, and the average GDP per person should reach US$800 – 1000, reaching a relatively well-off stage. On this basis, fifty years later, the average GDP per person should come to US$4,000.00 – a stage of actualizing modernization. Deng Xiaoping said: "what does this mean? It means that China can become a medium developed country by the middle of the next century. If we can achieve this, it means that: 1) people in China have accomplished a very demanding task; 2) the country has made great contributions to human beings; 3) people can experience the excellence of a communist society. The amount of GDP per capita – USD $4, 000.00 means something different to people in China than to and in the States as the population size in China is huge. If China's population reaches 1.5 billion at that time, with an average GDP per capita of USD $4, 000, its GDP would amount to 6 trillion US dollars, ranking among the top in the world. Then, this would prove to be the right path for the Chinese people and to be an example for three quarters of the population in the Third World. Also, it would show that socialism is the best path for the Chinese people to follow, and socialism is superior to capitalism."[32] Hence, strategic target includes both economic indicators and the system itself – demonstrating the integration of comprehensive national power and the average development level of people. The excellence of socialism can be strengthened through economic growth and creating a profound economic, social and system-wide environment for human development. This is basically different from the economic growth strategic target of capitalism. The dynamic economic target is to narrow down the economic gap with developed countries – continuously catching-up with the developed countries, instead of just only catching up at an initial stage but lagging behind again in a later stage.

Third, from the perspective of realizing strategic target of economic growth, generally, no matter which country or region wants to achieve a long term goal, it has to face the problem of setting several stages. Based on the opening-up policy made by Deng Xiaoping, there are three steps for the target. First step, during 1980 – 1990, the average GDP per capita reaches US \$400-\$500 and people's basic survival needs are fulfilled. Second step, by the year 2000, the average GDP per capita shall be doubled to US \$800-\$1,000 and people's living standards should be maintained at a satisfactory level. Third step, from 2000 to the middle of 21st century and beyond, the GDP per capita shall be about US\$4,000 after 50 years' of hard work. At this point the life of people will reach the level of the developed countries and the stage of modernization will be basically reached. At that time, the country's GDP would reach 6 trillion with a calculated population of 1.5 billion. This is an aggressive strategic target of China. On the 16th CCP National Representative Congress held in 2005, the third step of the strategic target was further divided into three phases: first, by 2010, the GDP will double the amount in 2000; second, by 2020, the GDP will double the amount in 2010; third, by 2050, socialist modernization will basically be achieved, reaching the level of a medium developed country.

Fourth, from the perspective of geographical distribution of strategic target, a nation with different regions shall have different strategic targets of economic growth. China is big country, with different provinces and regions. The economic foundation of each region is so unique that differences in strategic target of economic growth will exist. The central government of China is eager to have speedy economy growth in all regions, especially coastal areas, like developing Shanghai into an international economic, financial and trading centre in order to stimulate economic performance in other areas in Yangtze River Delta, or along the Yangtze River. Guangdong, Fujian, Hainan and Circum-Bohai Sea areas should also accelerate their economic development. With twenty years' efforts, Guangdong and other regions should become the first areas that achieve modernization. Hence, individual regions shall determine their own unique strategic targets of economic growth.

The above has described China's strategic target of economic growth up to the year 2050. As the focus of the book is about catching up economic growth theory in general, sub-classification of strategic targets in China economic growth will not be covered in details.

4.2 Key Principles for Determining Economic Growth Strategic Target

Most of the developing or under-developed countries intend to catch up to modernized countries' levels of economic performance. This is actually an important issue to the people of developing and under-developed countries. Hence, a 'catching-up' economic development stage and a number of newly-industrialized countries and regions have emerged since 1945. Some of these countries' economic performance has already outweighed that of those developed countries (this is based on an average income standard of the richest countries in the 1950s). To quote an example, even as a defeated country in the World War II, Japan has developed into an industrialized country after 20 years' effort, and its economy has caught up with and is trying to surpass that of the United States.

Looking back at the history of the countries that developed fast, almost each of them has determined its own long-term strategy and target of economic growth and development. Then, generally speaking, what are the guiding principles for them? This is especially important for China – a developing socialism country. Based on the situation in China, there are five principles that need to be followed.

(1) The principle of human need. Human need is the highest principle of any economic growth. It is also an everlasting motivator and logically the starting and ending point of economic growth. To set up a growth strategy for the economic development of a nation we have to consider whether human motivation, such as newly-added materialistic and cultural wealth, can meet the development and need of people and whether they are favorable to achieve the developmental level of the nation. This is especially important for all newly-developed countries, especially socialist countries. A lot of economists have a general thinking that socialist countries are eager to maintain high economic growth because this is a basic condition for socialist countries, including China, to survive in this competitive world. They think that their responsibility and mission is to build such an economy. But, the thing that we need to consider is the level of economic growth to be achieved. From a subjective point of view, three things need to be taken care of when determining the level of economic growth: responsibility of a nation in its history, willingness of its people to sacrifice short-term benefits and the ability to endure pressure from investment. If the level of economic growth reaches a level that is beyond the level the nation's people can carry or tolerate, it will not be an appropriate one and the people will not support it. If the strategic target is not supported by the nation's people, it will only meet the political need but not the people's need. Hence, the target of economic growth to be achieved falls on the hands of the people; otherwise, it will not get any power from people. This case actually

happened in China in 1958 during the revolutionary plan of the "Great Leap Forward" (a strategic 15-year plan to catch up with the United States and the UK). This plan was totally unsuccessful because it was unrealistic, and the high input and the high accumulation exceeded the psychological endurance of Chinese people and the country's economic foundation. As a result, China only achieved short-lived growth. It could not achieve what it planned to achieve, instead it suffered a three-year famine and following that several years' of negative economic growth. The former Soviet Union also learnt an impressive lesson in this respect. It concentrated on developing its heavy industries and overlooked its light industries. The result was that the living standard of its people did not improve while the gap with other western developed countries widen. In the end the nation collapsed. This was a tragedy as the economic growth targets set by the central government were not well supported by its people.

Oppositely, production surplus will appear if strategic target of economic growth is set beyond the human needs of a nation. Problems that may occur include: a weakened market; goods are being stocked without turnover; social wealth is not being accumulated at a desirable level. In fact, this should be followed when determining or executing strategic target of economic growth – aligning the economic target with the human needs of a nation without making the economy overheated and go off track. A nation needs to keep its eyes wide open and take the global market into consideration. Otherwise, our exposure to the outside world will be limited. The balance between demand and supply is dynamic. The reason is that the currency demanded by a nation to make payment for its liability is a kind of market demand. On the other hand, supply will also limit the actualization or creation of demand. Take the region of Taiwan in China for example, in 1953, the textile industry had 167,000 spindles and 6,700 spinners. The supply had exceeded the demand of the island and its growth rate and aim had been limited. If the productivity was solely determined by demand on the island, its textile industry would not grow and develop. However, it continued to grow: in 1980, the number of spindles had increased to 3.36 million and the number of spinners had reached 5.66 million. Then, textiles became one of its pillar industries and provided many employment opportunities. The key point is that exploring international markets expanded the needs and stimulated the fast growth of the textile industry in Taiwan. It is the same case with other industries or even the entire economy. The strategic target of a nation or a region cannot go beyond the needs of the nation or the region; meanwhile, it cannot only consider the needs of the nation or the region. Newly-developed countries shall take this into account when determining their strategic target for economic growth otherwise economic development will be very limited.

(2) The Principle of Capability. Economic establishment relies on the capability of a nation. Strategic target of economic growth cannot be set beyond

its capability or the target would be like building on sand, with no foundation. This is a fundamental and objective principle that a nation is required to follow. The capability of a nation is based on its use of internal and external resources including the profound spiritual cultural resources of a nation, to support its economic growth and to develop its materialistic and spiritual power. Materialistic power has a dominating power in this aspect as it exerts power in economic growth. Hereby, the capability of a nation also means the material and spiritual constraint of economic growth. This is a common issue for most developing countries. The limit of material constraint of developing countries and socialist countries is much higher when compared with developed countries and capitalist countries. China is a developing socialist country; the quantity and quality of material resources supplied for economic growth is limited. The main problem that these developing countries need to face is that they need to overcome poverty by means of economic growth, that is, to shorten the economic distance with developed countries. Most developing countries, including China, intend to increase the input of material resources for generating maximum economic growth. However, the input to increase productivity, especially capital input, is limited. When compared with developed countries, this problem is even more common in developing countries. Though developing countries can import natural resources for production, this poses another problem of balance of international revenue and payment. The debt-paying ratio[33] will also skyrocket due to importing capital, technology, entrepreneur...etc. All in all, there is a limitation for developing countries in the sense of availability of resources for production. Hence, consideration of availability of resources and the capability of a nation are required when determining the strategic target of economic growth.

Market resource is another kind of constraint. The domestic market represents the needs of the society. It has a decisive power in the actualization of total supply under economic growth. In an open economy, the domestic market can not be sealed up, instead, it can be affected by the international market through imports and exports. Part of the market is suppressed by the amount of imports. Though entering into international trade is good, competition is keen too. Market resource is a reflection of a nation's capability. Hence, the scale and speed of economic growth will be affected.

From the above, we see that a nation's material resource can affects the quantity of economic growth in the nation, but it can actually limit the quality of economic growth. This covers two areas: the quality of material supplies – the provision of production facilities and the level of labor tools; the quality of labor – the level of competence of labor, technology, and management of labor. This implies the capability of a nation to attract capital, new projects, expansion of production scale, capital for productivity enhancement, and the potential for economic expansion. China seems to overlook the lessons learnt and ignores the continuity of productivity history. For example, in 1958, steel production was

6.2 million tons, increasing 15.88% from 1957, which was relatively realistic. However, in the second half of, the "Great Leap Forward" required that steel production double, reaching 10.7 million tons, which was in contrary to the law of capacity. As a result, people all started to make steel: they went to do mining, cut down trees and broke ironware, causing millions of dollars in losses. The steel industry input in 1958 was much more than the total during the first Five-Year plan, and its proportion in GDP jumped from 6.4% to 14.4%. During the three years of the "Great Leap Forward," thousands of blast furnaces were built, some of which were even smaller than one cubic meter, much smaller than the first furnace (10 cubic meters) found in Belgium 500 years ago.[34] It is known that severe consequences will occur if the capability of a nation, when establishing its economic infrastructure without realizing its blind spot when moving toward its economic target, is ignored. Not until the opening-up policy in the late 1978s did China started to realize the importance of conforming to a nation's capability. If fluctuation in economic growth is smaller, economic development will be faster and at a steady pace.

Though spiritual elements have been included into the capability of a nation, they are not that rigid when compared to the material resources in economic growth. However, spirit can turn into a materialistic element. Eagerness to escape from poverty and the spirit of hard-working by the people in developing countries can motivate people to work enthusiastically and creatively. This spirit will push people to make intensive use of available material resources for economic growth. This kind of motivation is strongly felt by the people in a socialist country like China. This is a competitive advantage for China over the developed countries. The desire to live on one's own feet with one's given effort has had a positive impact on the economic growth of China.

(3) The principle of late-starting advantage. This idea was first put forward by T. B. Veblen (1857-1929). Late-starting advantage is hereby referred to as the advantage enjoyed by underdeveloped countries with technology and capital of developed countries and the cheap labor of its own. The underdeveloped countries may make use of this kind of competitive advantage to develop their economies at a faster pace. That is why sometimes they can catch up with or even go beyond the economic performance of the developed countries. This can be treated as a base for economic growth strategic target. This kind of competitive advantage is derived from the economic cycle of products and the horizontal regularity of productivity improvement. According to a U.S. economist named Raymond Vernon, there are usually four stages of producing new products in developed countries like the States. They are: first, input of products and exploitation of exports; second, growth of products and emergence of new products in developing countries; third, maturity of products and competition found in international markets between products produced by developing and developed countries; and fourth, developed countries shift

exports from themselves to imports from developing countries. Oppositely, a similar theory called the "flying-goose" has been brought up by a Japanese scholar named Kaname Akamatsu. Using the development of the textile industry in Japan as an example, he suggests that there are three waves. The first wave of introducing advanced technology in product development; the second wave of fulfilling market needs; and the third wave of exporting products (similar to the fourth stage of product life cycle by Raymond Vernon). From the above scholarly concepts in the United States and Japan, we realize that developing countries can avoid lots of risks and costs of technological development through transnational economic exchange and cooperation, and through the utilization of advanced technology and spare capital from and developed countries and low-wage labor from themselves. This undoubtedly can nurture the growth of modern economy in a better and more mature way.

At the same time, economic development of advanced countries are affected by the economic cycle of technology of production and its re-production cycle with a slow-down intermittent period during the time of development. For example, there are five long waves of technological development from the 18th century to the 19th century. Each long wave of development started and ended in developed countries, and the pace was usually slow. The time for high tide and low tide lasts between 10 to 30 years with an average of 20 years (see the Table 4.1). This brings good chances for developing countries to catch up with the developed ones.

Table 4.1 Long-wave Division Summary Table

Author	The first wave		The second wave		The third wave		The fourth wave		The fifth wave	
	Up	Down	Up	Down	Up	Down	Up	Down	Up	Down
J.A. Schumpeter		1780	1810~1817	1844~1851	1870~1875	1890~1896	1914~1920			
		1801~1810	1844~1852	1870~1875	1890~1896	1914~1920				
Mandel	1789	1826	1842	1873	1898	1914	1940~1948	1968		
	1815~1825	1848	1873	1897		1940	1967			
Rostow	1790	1815	1848	1873	1893	1920	1933	1951	1972	
	1815	1848	1873	1893	1913	1933	1951	1972		
Duyn		1845	1848	1873	1896	1948				
		1815	1873	1896	1920	1973				
			1873	1893	1929					
		1872	1892	1929	1948					
D. Brize	1759~1792	1808~1814	1846~1851	1872~1873	1895~1896	1930	1936~1946	1974		
	1808~1814	1846~1851	1872~1873	1895~1896	1930	1936~1946	1974			

Source: [Neth.] Duyn: *Long Wave in Economic Life*, George Allen and Unwin Press, 1980, English edition, P162; [Amer.] J.A. Schumpeter: *Business Cycle*, the 1st volume. McGraw-Hill, Inc., 1939, English edition; [Rus.] Kondratieff: *Long Wave in Economic Life*, *Modern foreign Economics Papers*, the 10th series, Commercial Press, 1986, P11; [Belg.] Mandel: *Long Waves of Capitalist Development*, Cambridge University Press, 1980, English edition, P105~106; [Amer.] Rostow: *World Economy: History and Prospect*, McMillan Company, 1978, English edition, p.110.

During the intermittent period among the long waves, production horizontal shift and regularity of expansion are found. It is common for developed countries to disperse their capital and technology into the developing countries to gain a better margin of profits. This is to make use of the expansion of productivity to enhance economic return of technology. This undoubtedly helps boost economic growth of the developing countries or regions.

With the late-starting advantage of developing countries as mentioned above, it is possible for developing countries to spend a shorter period of time to go through the longer period that the developed countries have spent. This has been proved by the history of economies in the past. For example, making the ratio of primary industry down from 50% to 20% when moving from industrialization into modernization, Britain spent almost 300 years and the States spent about 100 years, while German spent 70 years and Japan spent only about 50 years. Hence, late-starting advantage plays a definitely important role in the economic growth of developing countries. China should have confidence to achieve the same amount of success as experienced by developed western countries, especially with the idea of socialism.

(4) The principle of competiveness. Competiveness means not only the comprehensive power scale of developing countries, but more importantly, the integrated quality of national economy, the social productivity development, industrial development, diversified products, the excellence demonstrated through international economic competition and diversification...etc. Keeping this excellence, the strategic goal of economic growth can be achieved. Otherwise, it is hard to make sustainable economic achievement in the long run.

(5) The principle of stability. Stability means balanced growth in economy, in social politics and the society as a whole. This kind of desirable environment relies on the healthiness of economic growth. If the growth is not balanced but instead unsteady, shaky social situations may appear which might possibly damage the realization of economic goals.

The aforesaid five principles can be grouped together under one main principle – achieving a developmental, stable economy with benefits to people in a nation. This should be followed by not only developing countries, but also those under-developed regions within a country. Though sovereignty differences may be found in economic policies or non-economic policies in various regions of a country, alignment among regions shall be maintained for reaching strategic goals.

4.3 The Guiding Function of Strategic Target of Economic Growth

As mentioned previously, strategic target of economic growth is the sum of qualitative and quantitative indictors from a dynamic process of social and economic evolution – from traditional economy into modern economy; from developing into developed; and more importantly, it is centered on meeting human need and promoting human development. The strategic target of economic growth is also based on materialistic and spiritual conditions, and accumulates the persistence and eagerness of the leaders and ordinary people in a country. Hence, strategic target of economic growth is a live organic system to give direction for production and economic development of a nation or of a region. This guiding function has to direct the behaviors and thoughts of people, the diversified elements and formats of production, the decisions and adjustments of all different departments in relation to economic development. The strategic goals serve a motivational purpose if the goals are reasonable, realistic and appropriate to a nation. Besides, they shall reflect the patterns of economic development in a nation; otherwise, they will hinder the nation's economic growth and development.

Through describing the different, interactive elements and factors in the following Figure 4.1, the guiding effect of strategic target clearly demonstrated. What kinds of guiding effects in economic growth can be illustrated from the above chart?

(1) Mobilizing and Organizing Effect

Strategic target of economic growth does not only actualize the real needs of the
people but also reflects their idealistic needs. It is also a kind of requirement for social organizations to gain benefits for themselves and for the whole society. Once a reasonable and scientific target is set, it will act as a lighthouse, with a coherent function to pull all levels of people in a society to work toward the goal for the benefit of the society. The long-term goal can, in fact, integrate manpower, materials and capital altogether for achieving required performance. Through different goals at individual levels and different goals from individual departments, and through the power of the market and its distribution mechanism, productive elements will flow to high-efficient, strategically-directed industries, departments and regions. Hence, economic productivity will be enhanced and social benefits will be maximized.

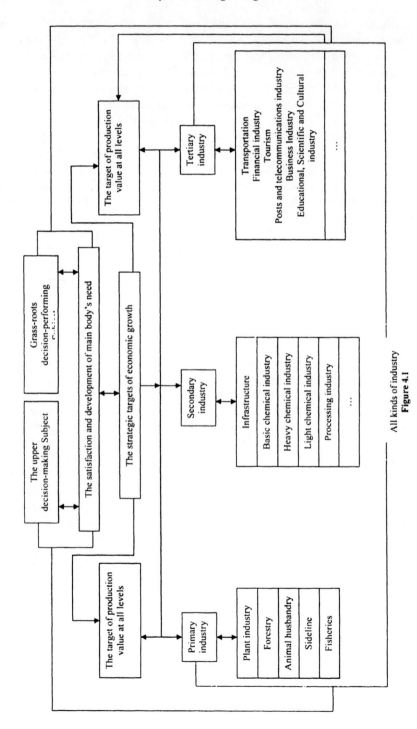

All kinds of industry
Figure 4.1

China's strategic goal through three stages and realizing modernization by 2050 has been described as a "full of legendary economic potential" by the U.S. magazine *Fortune*.[35] The reason is that the China's strategic goal follows Deng Xiaoping's socialism theory with consideration of social context and the benefit of people in the nation.

(2)   Strategic Guiding Effect

During the economic growth process, a few issues need to be considered to actualize the growth target. These are: choice of strategic direction, focus of strategy, stage of strategy, and implementation of strategy. A Growth target has a guiding effect on all these named issues. The strategic direction should be based on the growth scale and speed required by the target; and strategic focuses, strategic stages, and strategic measures should be decided by the integration of the scale and speed required by the target, the national power, and overall external economic conditions. Hence, strategic target acts as the directive goal of the economic operation on one hand; on the other hand, it needs to make sure that strategic direction, strategic focuses, strategic stages, and strategic measures are all aligned with the set target. If they are off the target, no single country or region can successfully achieve economic growth.

(3)   Tactic Guiding Effect

Economic policy is a reflection of the interaction of all economic activities and economic relations; on the other hand, it redounds upon economic growth. To make a nation become a modernized economy, setting an appropriate strategic target and applying appropriate tactical policies in economic growth both are crucial. The relationship between economic policies and economic strategy is like the relations between the means to the end. Economic policies are means to reach the economic target, as economic policies are supposed to be aligned with the growth development target. Economic targets, in both quantitative and qualitative aspects, are decisive in the choice and in the implementation of economic policies. If the requirements of the target are sufficiently clear, the impact of tactical economic policies will be much greater and hence there is a guarantee of target actualization.

(4) System Guiding Effect

No matter if it is a country or a region, during its economic growth process of modernization, there is a system linking up all adjustments between productivity and productive relations. Hence, from a holistic point of view, inter-dependency is found among the organizational structure of an enterprise, organizational internal management system, and societal guidance on economic activities in the market. The guiding rationale, direction, and routing in the process of economic adjustments should all depend on the strategic target of economic growth. Moreover, the strategic targets should be consistent with the nature of productivity development and its requirements. We have learnt our lessons of economic development from the past. Tracing back to the time of the barter system to that of manual labor, to that of machinery production, to the latest productions with advanced scientific technology, our society has evolved from a state of natural economy, a state of commodity-oriented economy to a state of product-oriented economy whilst our economic operation system has been changed from a self-reliance stage to a market economic stage and then to a planned economy system. China's socialism was established from a semi-feudalism, semi-colonial state with backward economic technology while production remained at a stage of manual labor. This actually determined the China's economic growth in the revolutionary progress, and also helped boost China's economic development at an abnormal pace. Finally, strategic target of economic growth should be matched with the capability of a nation, the nature, the level and the requirements of its productivity development so as to build a new economic system.

(5) Self-development Guiding Effect for Human

Fulfilling the needs of human self-development is one of the uses of setting a strategic target of economic growth for a nation. Moreover, it also serves a dynamic guideline in the sense that economic growth should be based on the reasonable ratios of accumulated wealth and consumption wealth of a society, such as the ratio investment and consumption in social production and reproduction process, and the ratio among survival material, luxurious materials, developmental materials in social distribution and consumption. Under the basis of ensuring people's living standard at a level of gradual improvement, the strategic target can motivate people to accumulate more capital for social production and re-production, and put more effort on self-development and productivity development. The strategic target of economic growth can lead human development on a proper track; besides, it can guide human development in a variety of dimensions and push people to strive to increase the quality of their lives.

All the above elaborations of the guiding effect are based on the assumption that strategic targets of economic growth are reasonable and scientific. If the targets are set without considering the human need, and the targets are unrealistic and out of the capability of a nation, then its negative impact will appear – mislead social production and people's live, and put the national economy in a chaotic and instable situation. To conclude, economic development and enhancement should be taken on with great ambition but should not be aimed at an unrealistic "high speed" or "high indicator".

Chapter Five

Industrial Movement: Historical Opportunity

for Latecomers' Catching-up

Modernized economic growth started from the 18th century, when a few capitalism countries, such as England, achieved industrialization through the Industrial Revolution and gained economic prosperity. The historical opportunity for developing countries to jump out of poverty is to realize the ways and the patterns of industrial evolution and to take advantage of the industrial adjustments found in developed countries during the process of economic globalization. Developing countries take the benefits of the manufacturing industry as their mainstream industry in order to make them develop even faster than developed countries. Hence, developing countries need to realize the historical opportunity to speed up their economic development and to enter into a new era of modernization.

5.1 Trend of Industry Upgrading and Expanding

The process of social re-production and economic growth actually is a reflection of the expansion of the production system in a society. This includes the integrated quality of reformation and the overall upgrading and interaction of all economic activities. It is an actualization of production expansion in a society. Understanding past economic development can help developing country realize the existence of opportunity for speeding up their economic growth.

First, let's have a look at the trend in upgrading of industries and the possible historical opportunity. The development of industries has been moved from a lower level of production into a higher level of production. In 1935, Professor A.G.D. Fisher in New Zealand put forward a concept of "Three Industries" in his book of "Conflicts in Safety and Progress". In the 1940s, a British scholar named Colin Clark made use of the "Three Industries" to illustrate the relationship among the interactions and upgrades of industries in his book called "The Elements for Economic Growth". The idea of Clark has been further elaborated in details by an American economist Simon Smith Kuznets to explain the upgrading of industries, the factors and the outcomes of economic growth and development. Hence, when people talk about the concept of the "three-industry category", they often link Fisher, Colin, and Kuznets together. As the scale of production was small and the standard of production was low in an agricultural-based and animal-rearing society, agriculture was the primary industry, even the only industry. For industry at that time, it still remained in a manual labor stage. Commercial activities were centralized in the hands of individual merchants. Both manufacturing and commercial activities were not mature enough to be an industry. This was the time of self-reliance of people in history with agriculture as their main resource for survival. This is the first stage of industrialization. The second stage was from the middle 18th to the middle 19th century with the secondary industry as a landmark of economic growth. Secondary industry then featured with a large scale of manufacturing expansion, and began to impact the first or primary industry. During this stage, there was a wide range of products available for purchase and wealth was fast accumulated by industrial production in a society. The third stage is the stage where primary and secondary industry is fully developed and when people start to have money to spend for their enjoyment and the entertainment business starts to boost. All this improves the living standards of nationals. Nowadays, the ratio of tertiary industry in the overall GDP of some developed countries is up to 60%, and is the prime economic activity for these countries. Hence, some people say that biological-based industry (a focus in agriculture) is the starting point of economic development whilst physics-based industry (a focus in machinery) makes the shift into secondary industry, and scientific management of social live and production is the key for the shift towards a tertiary industry. This is the historical path of upgrading economic activities based on time sequence and a reliance of people on natural resources, as well as the importance of industry in social development. As the following Figures (5.1 & 5.2) show, the clearer the arrangement of the three kinds of industries, the upgrade of the industrial structure looks more obvious.

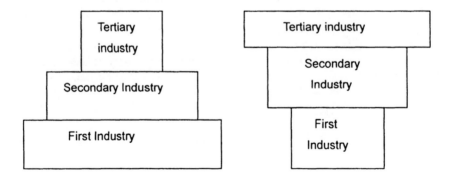

Figure 5.1 Based on the order of life   Figure 5.2 Based on importance and ratio

Based on the development of the above three kinds of industries, some scholars predict that a fourth and fifth kinds of industries may actually exist. This indicates that the industrial development follows a path from low-end to high-end.

The upgrading rule of the three kinds of industries is especially clear in the secondary industry – continuously expanding while upgrading. In the past 200 years of the first and second industrialization, there were three stages of structural changes in the economic development of developed countries. The first stage lasted from the midst of 18th century to the end of 19th century during the first industrial revolution. With the invention of evaporator and textile machinery, industries like metal, heavy machinery, coal mining, ship-building, railway and textile were developed gradually. This established a foundation for the secondary industry and countries like Britain, France, Germany, and America have all undergone the process of industrialization. The second stage happened at the end of 19th century with the invention and application of electricity. With the rapid development of second industries, industries were then diversified into industries of electricity, automobile, aerospace, gold mining, chemistry, and oil refinery. This is a tremendous progress moving from the primary industry into the secondary industry. The third stage occurred in the 1940s during the third industrial revolution. Productivity had been greatly advanced with the wide use of nuclear energy, electronic calculators, and spatial technology. It entered into an era of automation with value-added industries – a stage of enhancing the structure of industries. Starting from the 1960s, the landmark for actualization of modernization is the application of electronics, aerospace technology, nuclear energy, and other high-end industries. The fourth stage is the forth industrial revolution found in developed countries, in which the economy has emerged from the base of electronic technology into the base of information technology, and mass standardized hard structure has been upgraded into specific, diversified soft structure. Some people have named this stage as "emptying the industrial heart" as there are not any standardized rules for production.

During the expansion and upgrading of the secondary industry, re-structure was found in all levels of industries in the economy. For example, agriculture industry has been changed from manual work into mechanic work with a parallel move of ecological farming, where products evolved from small production with low quality into mass production with high quality. Different kinds of value-added in-progress technology have been implemented for product development. In the tertiary industry, the speed of economic development has been straightened up with technological advancement as a foundation. Besides, services offered are continuously diversified with a higher level of standard. Up till now, the distance among people in the world has been shortened, and the globe has become a "global village", with progress in transportation, and telecommunication, the allocation of computers and mobile intellectual technology. Undoubtedly, there is a spiral improvement in the overall structure of industries in a national economy.

From the above, it is obvious that there is a pattern of industrial development, a small to large scale expansion; from low-end to high-end. The trend is as follow: farming activities – light industries – fundamental industries – heavy and chemical industries – highly value-added processing industries – modernized service industries. The movement from light into heavy industry and then into light again at a higher level has shown that there is no absolute pattern in economic evolution. First, the overall implication that we can grasp is that: there is a trend of movement from resource-intensive industry into a labor-intensive one, further into capital-intensive, and then technology and knowledge-intensive production; and from industries for living materials into industries for productive materials. Examples were that bulky machinery replaced manual labor work and labor–intensive textile industry replaced resource-intensive farming; the emergence and development of mechanic industry and electronic industry had made capital-intensive industry replace those labor-intensive industries. Later on, electronic and information technology has become a mainstream industry and has replaced capital-intensive ones. Second, we should realize that the advancement of industries is motivated by the leading industries. Most developed countries, while undergoing the four-stage industrial development, chose machinery industry, electricity industry, electronic industry and information industry as the leading industry respectively. Third, there must be a mechanism of adjustment in industries – a group of mainstream industries and a group of peripheral industries shall be put in place to support the leading industries to establish a production network and industry systems so that the potential of each kind of industry can be developed. For instance, historically, when machinery was the leading industry, there would also be related supporting accompanying industries such as metallurgy, mining, textile, printing, etc. When the electricity industry was the leading industry, there was also the machinery, electronic appliance, petroleum, chemical engineering, automobile, steel industries, etc. Fourth, science, technology and education must be taken into consideration, when we try to determine leading industries and peripheral industries.

Next, we are going to have a look at the motivation power of industrial upgrade and expansion in the economic growth of a society. During the 100 years from 18th century to 19th century, the secondary industry was born and grew up in the industrial revolution. It is both a signpost and an outcome of productivity development in a society. It turned a group of less developed European countries successfully into industrialized ones at a 10 times increment in the total global industrial output. This made human society transit from feudalism into capitalism. Concerning this change, Marx and Engels wrote in the *Communist Manifesto*: "the conquest of the nature, adaptation of the machines, application of chemistry in industry and agriculture, sail of ships, run of railways, usage of telegraph, cultivation of the continent, passage of rivers, emergence of explosive population—who could ever perceive such productivity embedded in societies?"[36] In the almost 100 years between the late 19th century to the middle of the 20th century, upgrading and expansion of industries pushed the development of productivity and made a 20 times increase in the total global industrial output. Some developing countries even escaped from poverty and lined themselves up with advanced countries. About 30-40 years after World War II was the third time of revolution in technology and there was another time of industry upgrade and expansion. This was when productivity of society took another big step forward as there was about two times the amount of new wealth created. Simultaneously, Japan, Russia, and the "Four Little Dragons" in Asia and other developing countries and regions speeded up their economic development to match the advanced standard of the world. From this, we can conclude: first, there is a upward movement of industrial upgrade and expansion over the last few decades and some developing countries have benefited through and caught up with the developed countries; second, industrial upgrade and expansion is a worldwide dynamic motivator for all countries to gain economic growth, which is the demonstration of its "driving force" and "shaking force". Only the people and the leaders in less developed countries who have the great desire to improve their countries' economic performance will have the feeling of the impact generated from industry upgrade and expansion, and will warmly embrace them and actively grasp opportunities from them.

The last thing is to summarize the reasons for the accelerating industrial upgrade and expansion. The history of science, economics, and philosophy can prove that the developmental history of human societies essentially is the history of knowledge and the history of productivity and social production. A dual relationship has been illustrated from this historical process: the first is the practice relationship of human beings as the subject to the nature, which results in the development of materials and production; the second is the perception relationship of human beings as the subject to the nature and society, which results in the development of knowledge and sciences. The dual relationship can increase the knowledge-acquisition ability of people, can motivate a continuous development of sciences, can integrate the nature and the power of human beings, and can stimulate an overall productivity development of a society and make structural changes within industries.

For categorizing the stages of industrial revolution, apart from the long-wave theory by the Russia scholar, Kondratiev, some other scholars used the features of human organs to analyze industrial revolutions. Someone said that the first industrial revolution was marked by enlarged physical strength of human beings; a steam engine replaces a great part of human physical power. The second industrial revolution was marked by extended human limbs; making use of machinery, rail, and automobile greatly expanded the length of human hands and feet. The third industrial revolution was marked by extended the five senses of human beings through the invention of telecommunication, allowing people to see and listen across thousands of miles. Now the fourth industrial revolution is to widen our intellectual ability. The application of electronic computers has greatly eased our minds. Hence, we can learn something from the historical process: each improvement of science, each advancement of technology, and each upgrade and expansion of industry can extend the uses and performances of our organs; enhancing the quality of human beings is the ultimate source for making the revolution happens. We can understand that we need to allow people to use their minds for production rather than for labor. We need to grasp the intermittent period in the industrial reform and movement to actualize the economic strategic goals. In order to increase people's quality for catching-up in industrial reform and movement, education and science are absolutely necessary. Otherwise, the opportunity for industrial upgrade will be lost, and particularly, we will not adapt ourselves in industrial evolution or in newly created industries. Hence, increasing people's quality is a must for speeding up modernized economic growth.

5.2   Common Trend in Adjustment of Industrial Structure and Transfer of Industries

After World War II, there was a tremendous economic growth which lasted for a quarter of a century in the global economy. Such a long period of growth at such a fast pace was very rare in history. A famous economist named W.S. Rostow mentioned in his book *World Economy: History and Prospect* that during 1948 to 1971, there was an average worldwide industrial growth of 5.6%. This is equivalent to twice of the 2.8% growth of 200 years from the 18th century to the 20th century. However, after the 1970s, the growth turned into a low state. It was predicted that during the 1900s – 2000s, people would still find it hard to run out of the low growth tide. The global economy is still at the intermittent period before the high growth period comes in the 21st century. During this period, the global economy growth is about 3.5% while that of western countries is about 3%, 5% for those developing countries and the same growth rate for Russia and other Eastern European countries. Asia becomes the most active region with economic growth rate above the world average, hitting up to above 5%. China experienced wonderful economic achievement during its first-stage reform. With the establishment of market mechanism under the reform, its economic growth percentage is around 10%. It not only occupied a leading position in the global economy but also among Asian countries.

In the global economy, the adjustment of industrial structure and transfer of industries among countries or regions are the necessary outcomes of industrial revolutions and productivity development. It is an objective pattern of social economic development. In this process, as developed and moderately developed countries or regions have to maintain their competitive advantage in productivity development, they need to explore new industries with new technology to transform the old traditional industries into advanced and updated ones. They need to transfer "sun-setting industries" to developing countries or regions. On the other hand, as developing countries lack capital, technology and management experience, they need to absorb the re-located industries from developed or medium-developed countries or regions in order to create economic growth which can act as a foundation for future growth. Those industries are "sun-setting" industries in developed countries: low productivity compared with newly developed industries; high labor cost; and low economy of scale. However, for developing countries or regions, as their economic scale is small, labor cost is low, and industrial structure is either unsatisfactory or mismatched, those "sun-setting" industries still can be developed well, and welcoming these industries may also help them to attract foreign capital, technology and management experience. In addition, some of the problems in capital, technology and other key elements in production then can be solved. To developing countries, the industrial relocation also lays a good foundation for industrial expansion, for adjustment of industrial structure, for enhancing labor productivity, for absorbing surplus labor, for speeding up economy growth, for improving the livelihood of people, and for building a base of productivity development and economy up-rise.

What will be the trend of adjustment and re-location of worldwide industrial structure in the 20th century?

First, technological development in developed countries or regions is going fast. Competition in technology can be reflected in the economic performance of a nation and its overall strengths. As developed countries intend to escape from the slow-down development stage, they put forward strategies of economic modernization, such as increasing investment in new technology, developing new products, and nurturing new industries, etc. These are the motivating factors for pushing economic growth. For example, in the 25 years from 1965 to 1989, R&D expenses of Japan have increased 7.1 times, the index of which kept at a higher level than 2.45%; at the same time, GNP jumped 7.4 times. For French, the above numbers were 4.6 times, 1.8%~2.3%, and 12.6 times. During the process, those that can best reflect economic modernization direction were "re-industrialization" of the U.S., "vitalization of industries" of France, and "invigorating the country through technology" of Japan; the core of which is to promote economic growth via technology. The proportion of high-tech investment to total R&D investment has risen from 22.1% in 1970 to almost 60% in the 1990s', or even 70% in some countries. Nowadays, in developed countries, from grassroots to congress, from rural areas to urban areas, high technology is treated as the core and decisive force to accelerate economic growth. Just as the book *Global Gambling: the Future of U.S. High-tech* by Potter King mentioned: during the reform of the global industry, high-tech has become the pillar of economic growth. In the U.S., on one hand, traditional industry is shrinking; on the other hand, information industry is developing. In the past five years, small and light computers in the U.S. have increased 6 times, with production value increasing from USD 945 million in 1980 to USD 6.5 billion in 1985; the sales of software have increased four times, from USD 1.7 billion to 7.5 billion; the electric product market has expanded form USD 100 billion in 1980 to 200 billion in 1985, which equals the sale of 30 million cars. According to estimation, the work load done by computers in the U.S. annually equals to that of 400 billion people working for one year, and to that of 200 million U.S. people working for 2000 years. At present, people that work in service and information sectors take up 70% of the total labor force and this number is going to reach 86% by the end of the 20th century or by the beginning of the 21st century. The electric industry is second to the energy industry and will become the secondary industry setting. At the same time, the optical fiber communication industry, biology industry, new material industry, laser industry and space and aircraft industry have gradually become new emerging industries. As they become more commercialized, they become strong driving forces in modern economic development. West Europe and Japan are all undergoing industrial structure adjustment, aiming at developing high-tech industry. Newly-emerging industrialized countries and regions such as Asia's "four little dragons" are on the way to catch up with the new trend.

Second, advanced technology has been used to transform traditional industries. This is a key direction in the adjustment of industry structure for developed countries or regions. Automation is the fundamental goal of transforming traditional industries, like integrating electronic and mechanical technology, using industrial robots in production, transiting the mechanic stage into intellectual automation stage. In Japan, it will only take 9 hours for a factory with robots to produce a car; however, in the U.S., it will take 31 hours for an ordinary factory to produce a car. The cost of a car in Japan is USD 2,000 which is less than it in the U.S. In 1963, the automobile industry in Japan lagged 50 years behind the U.S., but in 1980s' the former has far exceeded the latter, ranking top in the world. The success of Japan depended on the high technology used in the automobile industry by adopting robots. At present, the application of robots has been popularized from the automobile industry to many other traditional industries, such as heavy engineering, metal, electric engineering industries. Under such a competition, the U.S. has also made great reform to its large steel industry. As a result, more than two thirds of steel industries have been equipped with computer and other engineering systems so that they are closely connected with electronic, information and energy industries. Besides, it has invested USD 160 billion to reform the automobile industry from the 1970s to the 1990s, making it become the industrial sector with the most microprocessors. The U.S. has spent USD 900 billion to reform the traditional service industry via information technology. Roughly 45% of the fixed assets investment goes to information technology and equipment, to quicken the strategic adjustment of the industrial structure so as to maintain its leading position. The textile industry is the most traditional industry, as people cannot live without clothes. So it too has been reformed, becoming an automated industry. The trend is pretty evident in other countries, which are just like Japan and the U.S., using high technology to reform equipment and techniques of traditional industries. For example, the textile industry, just as the steel, construction and railway industries, has started using new high-speed technology. All these are the result of using high technology to reform traditional industries.

Third, adjustments in industry structures needs to be sped up and part of the industries need to be transferred. Industrial structure is a diversified, milt-level system, which is more than the combination of primary, secondary and tertiary industries. It may also include the national output of leading industries, major industries, and peripheral industries. Adjustment and re-location of industries mean to adjust the ratios among industries and to transfer some of the down-turning industries into other countries or regions. Through the transfer of industries, profits may be gained, and a nation or a region can establish its new leading or major industries so that the industrial structure may then be upgraded into a higher and more advanced level. Agriculture is the fundamental base for a country's economy and no country or region can survive without it. However, under a modernized global economy, adjustment and re-location of industrial structure mainly happen in the secondary industry, the leading industries, and the major industries. For the developed countries, the goal of adjustment and re-location is to move the "sun-setting" industries into developing countries or regions where they still can have enough resources to be utilized. As we know, every industry has its own life cycle – growth, maturity, improvement, and recession. These periods are tied up to the technology levels and economic conditions of a nation. Simultaneously, the second industry is trying to move from high energy-consuming into low energy-consuming and from high material-consuming into low material-consuming industry. Materials used for production have also experienced a shift to the more delicate pottery-like or fiber-like materials, instead of the natural ones. This can make "bulky, thick, long and big" products evolve into "light, slim, short and small" products; can replace mass production with small scale and specified production; can make manufacture-based secondary industry ultimately turn into information-based tertiary industry. The industrial adjustment and re-location of developed and medium-developed countries or regions undergo the following three-level path.

(1) Transferring those machinery-based traditional, labor-intensive and capital-intensive industries emerged from the previous industrial revolutions into developing countries or regions. For example, as newly-developed industries such as Asian "four little dragons" are facing the pressure of soaring currency rates and rising labor cost, they have to turn into developing capital-intensive and value-added in-process manufacturing industry, and then propose some kinds of reform plan (like the "second industrial revolution" of Singapore, "industrial diversification" of Hong Kong, "industrial upgrade" of Taiwan and

"industrial top-up" of Korea). The aim of making these plans is to squeeze themselves into one of the developed countries or regions through moving the capital-intensive and labor-intensive traditional industries to the under-developed countries or regions in order to upgrade their industrial structure.

(2) Re-locating the so-called "sun-setting" industries into developing countries or regions that have relatively better economic conditions. These "sun-setting" industries emerged from the middle 18th to the middle 20th century were all modernized, technology-based, capital-intensive, and mainly heavy industries. For instance, during these years most of the iron industry, oil industry and chemical industry have been transferred out of developed countries or regions.

(3) The most developed countries such as the USA and Japan have moved out some lower level modernized, high-tech industries that emerged from the third and forth industrial revolution, for example the installation of electronic products to developing countries and regions. This matches the needs of developing countries or regions as they want to seek business partnership from the developed countries, meanwhile the developed countries have an intention to kick out of their downstream industries. In fact, this is a business opportunity for developing countries to jack up their economic growth and to establish a high-level industry structure.

Fourth, the life cycle of leading industries and the period of industrial transform have been shortened. From the 1760s to the 1860s, as the result of the first industrial revolution, the textile-based industrial group was formed with the textile industry, metal-smelting industry, coal-mining industry, and primary manufacturing industry and transportation industry followed. From the mid to the end of the 19th century, as the invention and application of electricity and as the result of the second industrial revolution, the iron-based industrial group was formed and replaced the textile-based industrial group; This helped the core industries change into the electrical industry, railroad transportation industry, heavy machinery industry, automobile industry and telecommunication industry. From the end of the 19th century to the early 20th century, at the extended outcome and the intensification of the second industrial revolution, the automobile-based industrial group was formed with several leading industries such as the automobile, petroleum, chemical, electrical, and steel-iron industries. This was maintained up till the third industrial revolution occurred in the 1960s. As the result of this revolution, information-based industries, like the aerospace industry, electronic-calculating industry, bio-engineering industry, new material industry, new energy industry, became the core industries. Experts predicted there would be a new industrial revolution in the early 21st century which would generate a great impact upon the whole world economy and the industrial division with the bioengineering industry becoming the leading industry. In sum, the cycle of industrial evolution, formation and transformation among industries from textile, iron, automobile, information, and then bioengineering, has been shortened, with each from around 150 years to around 20-30 years. This is the result of the fast-pace development of productivity. It is also a symbol of accelerated global economic development which also brings imbalanced economic stimulation effects among different countries. This helps developed countries sustain their business excellence and also gives an opportunity for developing countries to catch up. If a country can make good use of the opportunity, it will become a leader in the worldwide economy. If not, it will lag behind and lose its competitive advantage gradually. Britain was a good example of grasping the opportunity that appeared in the 18th and the 19th century and the period between the late 19th to the early 20th century. By doing so, Britain made itself the "global factory" and the absolute leader of the world economy at that particular point of time. However, Britain did not maintain hold of this opportunity after the world wars, but instead the U.S.A. and Japan did. This let USA and Japan take over Britain's economic leader position.

Fifth, the condition of industrial adjustment and economic competition becomes more severe. As the worldwide economy keeps on expanding and the quality of industrial structure keeps on increasing, there is a need of re-structure and re-location of industries in both developed and developing countries. Competition has become keener in the 1990s as these changes are found in the worldwide economy, adjustment of policies and transformation of technology in developed countries; increasing competition of traditional industries; and minimizing the impact of labor cost in total production cost. This made labor-intensive developing countries lose their attraction in the international market. Their low labor cost will no longer attract input of foreign capital. According to a survey about Japanese manufacturing industries' foreign investment intention conducted by the Japan's Planning Board in January 1987, market share was the most important factor while increasing product competitiveness ranked second and low labor cost ranked third. This means that the once high attraction of manufacturing low labor-cost products or inputting capital for value-added manufacturing in the developing countries or regions since the 1960s-1970s now has been weakening. However, developing countries or regions still have advantages of making use of foreign capital, introducing outside technology, and developing 'out-going' economy in the 21st century. The main reason for this situation is that developed countries or regions become more internationalized, while their industrial structure needs to be re-adjusted, like the output of capital, and the establishment of own or joint-venture factories and in overseas countries other than their homeland. Examples of moving factories overseas are capital-based industries such as iron, chemical, paper-manufacturing, metal, etc., and technology-based industries such as transportation and installation of electrical appliances. A Japanese economist has named this kind of phenomenon as the "hollowing-out of economy". On the other hand, industrial competition has become more severe in developing countries including China. The developed and newly-industrialized countries need to sustain their economic development and gain more market share among labor-intensive exporting business. In the 1950s-1960s, only Japan tried to do so. Afterward, the "four little tigers" in the 1970s, then Southeast Asian countries and Latin American countries in the 1980s, joined in the competition. Thus, the one who can first seize the opportunity and hold on to it tightly, will be the winner in the worldwide economy.

5.3   Seizing the Historical Catching-up Opportunity

Looking back at recent times, it has been found that the occurrence of the catching-up opportunity was due to the use of the global industrial re-structure and re-location opportunities by late-coming countries and regions. These countries did take advantage of the opportunities made by exploration of technology and the industrial cycle during the up-and-down economic waves to expand their economic growth. Examples can be found in America, Germany, Japan, Russia, and the Asian "Four Little Dragons". During the period of the 18th century and the middle 19th century with first industrial revolution, the textile industry was a leading industry. This motivated other related industries and modernized the economy of Britain at a high-flying pace. Later on, the textile industry and other related industries moved to the States at the end of the 19th century and to Japan around the middle 20th century. These opportunities reached to the "Four Little Dragons" in Asia during the 1960s and 1970s and to other developing countries or regions including China and other Asian countries in 1980s. It had a significant historical impact on the economic modernization of developing countries. These countries made good use of the opportunities brought by the re-location of the textile industry and other industries like heavy industry. However, the restructuring and re-location of the textile industry played the most important role in this aspect. The history indicates a simple rationale: to developing countries or regions, the re-structuring and re-location of growing industries in global economy can provide fair opportunities; the most important thing is to treasure the opportunities to advance to levels of developed countries or regions.

Then, why could the industrial re-structuring and relocation of the developed countries or regions bring such kind of historical opportunity to developing countries or regions?

First, re-structuring and re-location of industries takes time that may cause an intermittent period. Generally speaking, the stage of growth, maturity, development and recession in an industry, and the formation of a reasonable industrial structure, would be actually affected by the needs of the society, the speedy economic growth, and the constraints of scientific technology development and industry revolution. Hence, due to the re-structuring and re-location of industries in developed countries or regions, saturation in some declining industries even in some major industries may appear. At the same time, the replacement of new technology in these developed countries or regions has not been fully realized. Consequently, it slowed down the economic growth of the developed countries or regions. Even worse, a period of negative growth may then emerge, which, over the last few centuries, created the long economic waves altogether five times: the first long wave was found from 1780s to 1840s; the second long wave appeared between the late 1840s to the 1890s; the third wave was between the mid 1890s to the middle 20th century and to the end of World War II; the fourth wave was after World War II while the fifth one began from the early 21st century. The recessionary period was formed between economic up-downs of two long waves. The peak of the fourth long wave was in 1973; afterward a recessionary time occurred until present. By the early 2010s, the total years of the intermittent period will be about 40 years. This actually offers a historical opportunity for developing countries or regions to catch up with the developed countries or regions. What they need to do is to seize the opportunity through speeding up economic reform, widening their exposure, creating a good social and economic environment with a good system and introducing and implementing new technology.

Second, another outcome of the re-structuring and re-location of industries in developed countries or regions is the transfer of industries from labor-intensive, traditional technology into knowledge-based, modernized technology with multiple levels. This outcome can help developing countries or regions to have a much greater space for industrial upgrade and diversification, through integrating their traditional skills with modernized technology, their foundational industries with assembling industries, and integrating various productive resources. This trend implies that, under new information technology, developed countries or regions intend to split their industrial locations. They keep their "minds - gimmicks" at home, such as in research and development and brand creation, but leave exploration of marketing channels and those less value-added, such as in-process manufacturing, for developing countries or regions. This is to create zoning areas for industrial re-structuring. This kind of arrangement results from the developed countries or regions' sound economic foundation established in the past 200 years. However, for the developing countries, taking the "sun-setting" industries and some high-tech-based but labor-intensive industries transferred out from developed countries could let them only spend about 20-40 years to go through the journey of 200 years that the developed countries went through, and to catch up the economic performance of the latter. For example, Japan only took around 40 years to catch up with USA after World War II, and the "Four Little Dragons" only used about 30 years to realize their industrialization and economic modernization. So, there is an objective pattern that we can observe, that is, developing countries or regions can spend less time to catch up with developed countries or regions.

Third, the inflow of international capital can help developing countries or regions solve the problem of insufficient funding. Seeing the problems of high-rising monetary cost, high labor cost, and low profit margin, most big enterprises have to seek for better investment channels and aim at developing countries. The mobility of cross-country investment from developed countries or regions has soared since World War II. Examples are securities investment, direct investment, short and long term capital loans and other kinds of funding. In 1945, the total amount of direct investment from developed countries was $20 billion; but, the amount reached $625 billion by 1983, and $2,660 billion by 1995. In 1980, there totaled $5,000 billion in the global capital market; but, the number rose to $35,000 billion by 1995 and to $83,000 billion by 2000. The international transactions in the global stock market amounted to $250 billion in 1995; afterward the annual amount was increased to $1,000 billion or above. Japan was a fast-growing Asian country after the war and has become a developed country. Starting from the end of the 1960s to the beginning of the 1970s, its industries had undergone re-structuring and a lot of these industries were transferred into Southeast Asian developing countries. Examples included labor-intensive industries, fiber manufacturing, installation of home appliance, sundry-goods industry; capital-intensive industries, iron, ship-building, oil, chemical industry; and technology-intensive industries such as automobile parts manufacturing, and the electronic composition industry. Among these transferred industries, the first tier occupied 58.9% of foreign direct investment in 1972; the second tier was 43.9% in 1984; the third tier was only 21% in 1972, soaring to 23.7% in 1982 and up to 26% in 1984. Since the 1970s, traditional industries have been either moved out or faded in Japan and there was a tremendous increase in overseas investment. The total of foreign direct investment during 1972 – 1980 was 32.062 billion dollars, which was 7.23 times more than the amount of 4.435 billion US dollars recorded within the 20 years from 1951 to 1972. Some 54.7% of Japan's investment money flowed into developing countries or regions along with the transfer of the first tier industry. There was a big jump in the total investment amount during the period of 1981 – 1989: average annual investment amount climbed to 10.155 billion US dollars in 1984, comparing to 220 million US dollars in 1951 – 1971, 3.56 billion US dollars in 1972 – 1980, and 6.98 billion dollars in 1981. The Japanese currency had appreciated a lot in September, 1985; thus Japan made a historical increase in foreign investment with 12.2 billion US dollars in 1985, 47.02 billion US dollars in 1988, and 67.54 billion US dollars in 1989.[37] Though there was bubble that emerged in the Japanese economy in 1990s, Japan still achieved economic growth through foreign investment initiated from the adjustment of industrial re-structuring. Continually, Japan's foreign investment reached 305.5 billion US dollars in 1995. At the same time, a large number of foreign currency reserves were found in the "Four Little Dragons" countries or regions, of which they need to find outlets through restructuring their industries. This trend still continues, and is a good opportunity for developing countries as it brings an inflow of capital and an exposure of advanced technology, management, and methods of production.

Fourth, developing countries can offer low labor cost, policy privileges and huge markets that can create an enormous of room for the industrial adjustment and relocation of developed countries. This is a win-win situation for both developed and developing countries and regions as both benefit from the historical opportunity. Though the attractiveness of the low labor cost and the preferred tax rate received from developing countries were weakened in the 1990s, the advantages were still valuable to developed countries. However, market power is a fascination for developing countries or regions as it can help them have an inflow of capital and new technology. China is a great socialist developing country as its open and reform policy has made it become a very active player in the global economy. The percentage of its economic growth in the period of 1983-1987 was 11.1%, 12.3% in 1992, 13.4% in 1993, and maintained at 9.1% in 2003 which were much higher than that of any other Asian country. In 2003, the total production value of China was 1.32 trillion US dollars which was equivalent to the level of Japan in the 1980s, and China's production value per capita was roughly 1,100 US dollars. Though this amount lies within an average of low income level in developing countries, China is a potential major market for the world economy. China has formed a three-tier market composed of "inland, coastal open cities, and special economic zones." This will generate a complimentary economic effect between China and other developed countries and regions attracted by China's huge market.

In sum, if developing countries, especially such a big country like China, can make good use of its historical opportunity, they certainly can advance their economic development to match those of the developed countries. This kind of historical opportunity may only show up once from the late 20th century to the early 21st century. If the opportunity has not been grasped effectively, the economic distance between developed and developing countries will be further widened. If it was said that, in terms of GDP per capita, the distance between developed countries and developing countries was 24.3 times in 1950, and was 61.5 times in 1991; then the distance will be over 100 times by the first half of 21st century. Hence, this is a critical, historical topic for developing countries or regions. If they want to realize "catching-up" strategic objective of economic growth and shorten the economic distance with developed countries, they shall tightly seize the historical opportunity and spend about 30-40 years time to undergo the almost 300-year journey of economic development that developed countries have undergone, and to go through the process of industrial nurture, industrial upgrade and industrial re-structuring. Otherwise, they will lose their foothold in the globe. Comrade Deng Xiaoping has a deep understanding about this trend of global economic development and the urgency of developing countries' catching-up in economy. He stated that "from the present to the middle 21st century will be the most critical period, we must work very hard,"[38] "the fundamental truth is to have persistent development."[39] "Our political pathway should focus on realizing four aspects of modernization and strive for developing our productivity. We must closely grasp this central niche unless there is an outbreak of wars. Even so, we must be back on economic building after a war."[40] He also mentioned that there would be a three-step developmental strategy in the first half of the 21st century. This statement shows a historical insight, an aggressive goal for Chinese people, and the hope for China's catching-up. A famous Japanese economist working as a banking consultant once spoke highly about China's future development that "China would become the first economic giant in the coming future."[41] RAND company, a US strategic research agency predicted that the national production value of the US will surge up to 7,859 billion US dollars in 2010 while that of China will be 3,791 billion US dollars – the second highest in the world, and, Japan will rank the third while the Commonwealth of Independent States (former Soviet Union countries) will be the fourth with 3,714 billion US dollars and 2,873 billion US dollars respectively.[42] We strongly believe that our goal can be actualized in the 21st century, a century with China's economic take-off!

Chapter Six

Capital and Investment: the First Motivator

for Economic Take-off

The first problems for less developed or developing countries to solve are accumulating a large amount of capital and expanding the scope of investment in order to develop modern industry, to enter onto the right track of economic development, to accelerate economic growth, and to realize economic take-off and modernization. When analyzing the ways of enlarging re-production and economic growth in a capitalist society, Marx pointed out that "capital was the first motivation in the whole process."[43] A well-known US economist Lewis stated that this was "the focal point of economic growth theory."[44] Hence, to achieve the strategic goal of economic growth, the issues and roles of capital formation and investments in economic take-off should be covered so that we can make full use of capital and generate the greatest economic benefits.

6.1 Capital Formation and Capital Function

The source of capital is the fundamental issue for formation and accumulation of capital. This has been brought up by lots of economists in the past and proved by economic practices. Formation of capital is a dynamic process, which involves the formation of people's saving and the transformation from saving to investment. In this process savings go beyond the value preparation stage and can take the realistic form of capital.

Capital has imposed a fundamental constraint for developing countries or regions for economic growth under the condition of a modern market economy. However, the constraint of capital is in essence the constraint of the mechanism of capital formation. This is a core issue in the theory of economic growth and development. Contemporary history in economics has showed that availability of natural resources is crucial to economic growth and a level of development. Actually, besides natural resources, the other consideration is the deprivation of capital. This is the greatest barrier that needs to be overcome by most developing countries. Capital shortage is a relative concept which bears both static and dynamic characteristics of. It is static, as capital constraint is derived from the level of capital stock. It is dynamic, as the constraint of capital formation comes from capital growth constraint. As the concepts of growth and development are dynamic, the scale and speed of capital acceleration places constraints on economic growth and development. Normally, if the scale of capital growth is larger, its speed will be higher and capital supply will be more sufficient and economic growth and development will speed up and the level will be much higher; and vice versa. The mechanism of capital formation is a critical point. Different capital mechanisms will make the sale and the speed of capital growth different. Capital supply, effect of capital accumulation, and their impact on economic growth and development will be totally different too. Capital plays a decisive role in economic growth and the development of developing countries. Instead of an absolute concept, capital constraint is actually a relative concept. Capital constraint can be changed and improved, economic growth can be fulfilled, and development goals can be achieved through establishing a healthy mechanism and enriching the source of capital supply.

Capital formation mechanism is influenced by economic systems. In a planned economy, a national fiscal mechanism is the basic way for capital formation; capital accumulation, use and even its transformation into investment all display as fiscal activities, such as fiscal revenue, construction plan, and so on. As the capital comes from a single source and is formed in a single channel, its expanding scale and rate will be small and very limited. Constraint of administration other than of the economy itself may appear when transforming capital into investment. With limited uses, the capital cannot meet the requirement of economic growth and development. Hence, under such kind of mechanisms, the constraint of capital in economic growth and development is harder while the constraint on expansion of investment is softer. Conflicts occur under the hard and soft constraints, which lead to adjust once a few years. As a result, capital waste and low quality of investment will be often the solution for the conflicts. And, the cost of adjustment will be paid and a vicious cycle of capital formation will occur. This is a weak point of the Soviet-style planned economy. It needs to be changed in order to obtain better economic growth and development.

Under the system of a market economy, monetary mechanism is a common way for capital formation. The opening-up policy of China motivated the transition of a planned economy to socialist market economy in which the market played a fundamental role in the allocation of different production resources. Since 1979, there was a big change in the distribution of national income among residents and enterprises along with a deepening effect of economic system reform. The disposable income of enterprises and residents has been increased and this makes the source of income turn from a single-outlet (government) into multi-outlet (government, enterprises, residents). The savings of residents have been replaced by the saving of the people in a nation. This turns the fiscal-based capital formation into a finance-mediated one as there is enlargement in capital sources, like personal saving, corporate profit accumulation, credit finance of security market and overseas capital, etc. In 1978, the debt of China's financial institutes (the national financial assets amounted to 115.5 billion Yuan) composed of: fiscal savings at 39.5%; corporate savings at 42.3%, while individual savings were only at 18.2%. In the year 1991, the debt of national financial institutes amounted to 1.2 trillion Yuan: fiscal savings decreased to 7% of the total; industrial savings made up 41.9%, while individual savings increased to 51.1%. During 1978 - 1990, the annual growth rate of the national individual actual saving ratio (the ratio of incremental saving to incremental income) reached 18.6% on average. At the same time, the whole individual saving rate also increased greatly: 13.0% in 1985; 15.8% in 1988; and 16.6% in 1993. During the 13 years after the opening-up, in the increment of savings deposited in banking institutes, fiscal savings made up 4.7%, industrial savings 42%, while individual savings amounted to 53%. Up till 1993, the total asset of monetary reserve and the currency in the nation reached 2.2 trillion Yuan, of which 1.2 trillion Yuan were owned by residents (more than 50% of the total). Till the end of 2003, the total local and foreign currency held by monetary organizations climbed up to 16,977.1 billion Yuan, with 135.8 billion Yuan from security markets. Besides, up till 1993, China had absorbed and utilized foreign investment of about 137.8 billion Yuan, which took up 10% of the fixed asset investment of China. In 2004, China utilized 60.63 billion Yuan in foreign investment was which was about 7.16% of the total fixed-asset investment. The reform of the economic mechanism has brought a high savings interest rate, a high growth rate in savings, and multi sources of capital. It has also provided a historical opportunity for China to develop its economy by solving the problem of insufficient capital, demonstrating that China can make use of the monetary mechanism to increase capital resources, and to accelerate the growth of the national economy by maintaining a steady growth in savings and attracting more foreign investment. This indicates that a new market economy mechanism can benefit capital formation, can solve the problem of insufficient capital, and can promote economic growth and development. Hence, reform can bring new capital formation, more capital investment and quicker economic development.

Under the market economy system, what is the impact of capital formation on economic growth and development?

First, capital serves as the function of carrier. Modernized market economy is a highly developed commercial economy. The social production and circulation process under a market economy can be divided into four points: production, exchange, distribution and consumption. All of the points need to be market based and capital driven. From the viewpoint of commercial economy, use-value is the physical carrier of value, so capital as a form of value can only be carried by various substances, but itself cannot carry any substances. However, from a dynamic perspective, differentiating from the value of a single commodity, capital serves as the form of pre-paid value during the circulation of commodities, and it actually represents all the production elements. Centralization, movement and change of capital are the outcome of integration, operation and change of production elements in the process of economic growth and development which unified social production and circulation. The join and withdrawal of production elements are reflected by the circulation of capital. The enrichment of capital can trigger the operation of the whole commercial economy. It is the cycle of currency capital, production capital, and commodity capital, instead of the cycle of materials that makes the economy develop and grow. Hence, expansion of social reproduction relies on the input of new and expanded capital. Otherwise, the enlarged scale of economy cannot be achieved. The increase of total production and then national income, and the development of social economy all demonstrate as capital growth in their value forms and they are the result of increased capital. Therefore, capital serves as the carrier for the circulation of commodities in social production, the operation of the whole market economy, and the growth and development of social economy.

Second, capital serves as the function of cohesion. This refers to the ability of capital to pull all the production elements and economic resources together under the market based economic system. There are four coherent functions of capital. (1) Capital could promote the formation of means of production. Before entering into the production process, production materials scatter individually. With the existence of capital they are all pulled up together into production according to certain technical (quality) and value proportional (quantity) requirements and serve as a means of production. (2) Capital could integrate laborers and other means of production. Laborer is the one to transform means of production into actual products and the transformation relies on the use of capital. This is because on one hand laborers can work only when means of production and labor objects are transformed from capital; on the other hand, capital can settle the difference between the period of salary payment and the period of value realization. Salary is a kind of pre-paid value and this value has to be transferred onto products through production and economic growth and then join the circulation of capital. Capital can integrate laborers into the production process and let them mix with means of production. (3) Capital could contribute to technology development and industrialization. Scientific technology is part of productivity and needs to be applied into the production process, or it is only a kind of potential productivity. Its development, application and industrialization can be realized only through improvement of existing productive processes and facilities, and technical reform, which need the input of capital. (4) Capital can transform natural resources into economic resources. All the production activities are generated from human beings' consciousness and ability of using and transforming natural resources. With the advancement of people's knowledge and the development of technology, availability of natural resources for production becomes an important constraint for the economic development of a country or a region. Under a market economy, natural resources cannot directly join in production. This leads to slow economic development of some countries with rich natural resources, and quick economic development of other countries with limited natural resources but abundant capital. Only with the help of capital, can the joining and transforming of natural resources be made possible, and speed up economic growth and development. The role of capital in this aspect can be shown clearly.

Third, capital serves as the function of linking and controlling. Capital performs a linking function in pulling all kinds of economic relations, industries and products together. It reflects the main interaction between the economy and technology required in a nation and has a decisive impact on the operation of a market economy. So, the control of capital is an important tool in the macro control of a national economy. Under a market economy, the nature of economic relation is the exchange of equal units of labor. As for each laborer and each product, labor is specific and not identical. The relationship of exchange of equal units of labor can only be realized through the exchange of capital. This relation exists among laborers to laborers, laborers to enterprises, enterprises to nations, laborers to nations, regions to nations, and even nations to nations in foreign trade. If the capital relationship gets destroyed, the economic benefit of all these parties will lose balance and therefore will negatively affect the economic growth. During the exchange, capital is closely linked up to production and products. If the use of capital goes smooth, product exchange among enterprises or industries will be made easily. Otherwise, it will be hindered. For example, in recent years, there was a trend of delaying payments in China. This phenomenon was called "triangle debt" which turned into a risk of debt with a stocking up of products and the breaking down of the currency chain. In sum, under present market economy circumstances, the linkage among different industries gets strengthened as a result of increased horizontal transactions across industries and regions. Capital becomes complex and inseparable to the economic network.

Fourth, capital serves as the function of direction. One of the differences between a market economy and a planned economy is that the former is capital driven using a capital structural change to adjust the economy while the latter one is administration driven using a subjective plan to adjust the economy. Moreover, the products under a modern advanced market economy are different from these under a simple market economy: the former uses value flow to direct products flow, while the latter uses products flow to direct value flow. As an advanced modern market economy, China's socialist market economy is capital-direct. Such directory function is reflected as follows. (1) The re-production and circulation are unified as capital movement. Production elements are distributed in the form of capital. It brings a great impact to the economic operation in a society through capital management and its format of operation. (2) Besides, the structure of capital determines the industrial structure from a macro perspective. It decides the allocation of production elements from a micro point of view. (3) Capital can also act as a tool for the macroeconomic control of the government. The government can make use of the regularity of the value derived from capital to make economic policy, to fine-tune the uses of capital, and to adjust the structure of industries.

6.2 Capital Accumulation and Its Efficient Use

As the income level in developing countries and regions is rather low, the possibility to save capital resources is limited. So, accumulation of capital and acceleration of capital formation are major necessary conditions for industrialization and economic take-off. However, owing to the insufficiency of capital, it is quite necessary to establish a mechanism for capital utilization to greatly improve its efficiency.

Some advanced countries and regions, which realized industrialization at an earlier time, adopted a "Blood and Fire" method to accumulate and centralize capital. Britain adopted "the enclosure movement", using aggressive and cruel methods of exploiting overseas immigrants and farmers to accumulate capital from local people or people from the colony. They thought this could solve the problem of insufficient capital. However, this method is now outdated. Neither modernized developing socialist countries nor capitalist countries will use these methods to accumulate capital any more.

Nowadays, for developing countries or regions, no matter socialist or capitalist, market economy or non-market economy, the following are the common methods for "primitive capital accumulation".

(1) Super-economic way to centralize capital from farming

This is a so called the "scissors difference" method adopted for farming and industrial products. It pulls all the surplus value of agricultural products together to encourage and subsidize the manufacturing industry's development. To an agricultural country, especially a large one, this is the only way to obtain capital as foreign capital is absent and the country is restricted from exporting primary products to obtain import of capital. In order to centralize the remaining value of the farming products, the government has to impose agriculture tax and land tax to get food stuff directly. They might also make use of their coercive administrative power to suppress the prices of agricultural products or to raise the prices of industrial products. This can widen the price difference between farming and industrial products so as to obtain the surplus value of farming products and keep the low labor cost, low material cost but high profit of the industrial products. Through these measures industry expansion would then be achieved. Moreover, the government always squeezes the remaining farmers' energy to help activities, such as irrigation, repairing work, digging the land, constructing or repairing railroads, highways, airports, and other transportation or buildings, as a form of direct physical capital.

There are mainly two ways to use this method to mobilize capital across countries and regions.

One way is "the forced mobilization under mandatory plan", which was adopted by socialist countries. This method was used by the Former Soviet

Union in the 20th century around the 1920s–1930s and by China in the 1950s–1970s during their industrialization period, and was called "socialism primitive capital accumulation".[45] Its characteristics were to use the authoritative power of the government, through unequal exchanges with farmers (i.e., the "scissors difference" method as mentioned previously), to accumulate and centralize the value of all the remaining farming products by coercive power and to use them as a kind of capital for industrialization. Some statistics showed that China accumulated 600 billion Yuan from 1950 to the end of the 1970s through adopting the method of "mandatory planned capital accumulation". Aligning with this capital accumulation method, a highly centralized organizational management system was also set up to control farming activities by the government. A trend of "uniform purchase vs. uniform sell" was found among farming products and the regular law of value of production was not appreciated. Oppositely, heavy industries were a main focus of strategy in industrial expansion. On one hand, this mandatory method accumulated a large amount of capital to establish a comprehensive industrial system and strengthen national defense within a very short term. It also helped enhance the sovereignty of new-born socialism and create a more desirable material technology foundation to catch-up with advanced countries. However, on the other hand, it costs a lot, discouraging farming activities and encouraging industrial activities which led to an imbalanced national economy. Under this situation, farming production was ignored; light industries were upset; heave industries were highly focused; resources were wasted severely; economy of scale could not be achieved; the living standard of people were improved very slowly; and the whole economy lacked motivation to move forward. Consequently, all these in return would hinder the development of industries and the realization of economic goals. Examples of experiencing this cycle of unhealthy economic structure were socialist countries as the Former Soviet Union, Eastern European countries and China in the 1960s - 1970s.

Another way was "market-driven capital accumulation" which has been adopted in rising countries or regions with a market economy system, such as Japan, Korea and Taiwan since the end of World War II, and mainland China since the implementation of the opening-up policy in 1979. This method is to reform the land ownership and land use systems in order to increase the productivity of farming laborers and their farming surplus. As a result, low labor and material costs for industrial expansion can be maintained. This paves the way for industrial products to enlarge the farming market. In order to utilize the function of law of value and to go with the capital accumulation method, the organizational system for farming was family run or farm run with a circulation system of farming products determined by the free market. As for industrial development, on the other hand, the priority of expansion was given from labor intensive textile industries to capital intensive heavy industries and technology intensive advanced deep processing industries. This capital accumulation method brought a positive effect as both farming and industrial activities were developed equally and were complementary to each other through the use of machinery and the sharing of technology. Productivity was then enhanced and a chain of positive results appeared. Countries or regions, like Japan, Korea, Taiwan (a province of China), and Chinese Mainland (after the execution of the opening-up policy), had better economic performances by using this method.

(2) Fiscal way to capital accumulation

As a commodity economy is usually laggard in developing countries and regions, currency and monetary markets are not fully developed. Capital for heavy industry construction projects is usually gained by some financial means. Government would require enterprises to pay taxes, and the state-owned enterprises to turn in most of their profits earned, or issue bonds, in order to centralize the reserves. Hence, government plays the role of capital distributor in investment activities. This guaranteed that important departments could obtain their share of capital for development and expansion, especially the costly fundamental constructions, which were the initial activities in the early stage of industrialization and could not be paid by any single enterprise. However, as the scale of economy becomes larger, some weaknesses of this capital accumulation method start to appear, like depriving the right of capital accumulation and investment from state-owned enterprises. Enterprises don't have much say in their fund management and investment, as all these fall into the hands of the government. Enterprises are not concerned about their own performance but the investment role of the government, which is wrong as the government is not the major investor. This leads to the following predicament: on one hand, the economy would increase investment demand from enterprises; on the other hand, the economy would suffer from the problems of investment inefficiency and the increase of compensation, which becomes a big financial burden to the government. Moreover, the government only makes efforts to support large or medium enterprises and ignores small ones and farming organizations. As a result, a dual economy emerges. Because of inefficient use and unequal distribution of capital, waste of resources and imbalanced economic structure appear. This kind of capital accumulation method does no good for personal savings and enterprises investment activities, no good for moving capital to high marginal productivity departments, no good for increasing economic scale, and it even lowers economic productivity and weakens the foundation of future economic development. This method may be necessary during the early stage of industrialization, but the government should shift the saving and investment responsibilities to its citizens, enterprises, and especially the banking system comprised by banks and other money corporations. The responsibilities of the government should lie in the fundamental infrastructure of a society and other non-profit public affairs and national defense projects. In sum, capital accumulation and distribution shall be adjusted by the monetary market, and the investment system shall be reformed.

(3) Monetary way to capital accumulation

This is a common method used in modernized market economy countries. Starting from the execution of the opening-up policy in China till the end of the 1980s and the beginning of 1990s, capital was basically accumulated by using the first two methods as mentioned before. After intensifying the reform, the planned economy evolved into a socialist market economy which separated the political monetary system from the commercial monetary system. State owned commercial banks were the primary monetary organizations. People became more aware of the operations of capital market. Monetary organizations and policies were more open than before with disciplined competition and a stringent monetary management system. During the first 20 to 30 years after World War II, influenced by the Keynesian economics and Soviet-style industrialization and in order to accumulate capital, enlarge investment and accomplish economic strategic goals, developing countries and regions adopted the first two methods to gain capital. They accelerate capital accumulation and industrialization by planning, nationalizing and importing, but ignored the function of market adjustment in allocating resources. They did not take monetary policy as a way for economic growth and development. In these countries, including China, monetary system only served administrative purpose for distributing products or assigning labor. Instead of an independent organization, banks only received and paid out money for the government. There was not any development in the monetary systems at that time in those countries including China, which had not undergone the reform yet. Until the end of 1970s, some developing countries like China started to realize the importance of a monetary system in economic development. From then on, the monetary system has been a key method for capital accumulation in accordance with the market economy. Hence, banks and the monetary market make use of the interest rate to attract savings and centralize capital from depositors and investors. This could eventually increase the level of savings and investment and distribute savings for investment activities in a more efficient way to solve the problem of insufficient capital and to improve allocation of resources.

Based on the aforesaid information, three types of capital accumulation have experienced two different developmental stages in developing countries and regions. The first and second methods associate to the first stage while the third method fits the second stage. In order to boost economic growth and development, a monetary system for capital accumulation has been used widely in developing countries and regions to catch up with the advanced countries since the 1980s. This is to make their economies more internationalized and globalized and to let developing countries increased their economic growth rates in a much faster way. However, it does not mean that other methods of capital accumulation cannot be utilized. In fact, a monetary system can be incorporated with other methods as long as they can generate healthy economic growth for developing countries. The things that these countries should consider are their real needs, the extent of investment utilization and the degree of alignment with other peripheral facilities.

Ways to make use of the capital being raised is a more critical issue that needs to be tackled. Past experience shows that it is the misuse of capital rather than capital accumulation that hinders economic development in developing countries. They cannot minimize input and maximize output to benefit from a greater scale economy. After World War II, the accumulation percentages of Japan and China were both about 30% with similar amounts of resource usage. However, their generated national incomes were quite different. Hence, improving capital use efficiency is more important than increasing investment in the long run. Capital utilization mechanism means an integrated system that includes capital centralization, allocation, leverage and organization. According to the analysis of the above, administrative tactics for capital allocation should be changed. Efficient capital utilization mechanism can guarantee a higher rate of utilization, and this relies on monetary mechanisms and an adjustment of law of value. In order to make capital be utilized in a more efficient way, the following is needed.

First, it is important to handle the problems of capital utilization, choice of industry and labor employment. An initial pressure that developing countries suffer from is insufficient capital and labor surplus. Based on the key production elements in industrialization and economic development, a stable social environment is required. At the early stage of industrialization, the focus of development shall be placed on a labor-intensive industry rather than a capital-intensive one. This can lessen the pressure of labor employment as well as improve the income level and the living standard of people. Statistics shows that fixed capital of every 1 million Yuan can absorb only 94 labors in capital-intensive heavy industries, but can absorb 257 labors in labor-intensive textile industries, and even more in retailing and service industries. Therefore, a great employment pressure leads to a labor-intensive economy in a developing country and region. The historical sequence of industrial development is usually from labor-intensive, to capital-intensive and then to technology-intensive. However, this does not necessarily happen and the sequence may be different under different employment conditions. Labor-intensive industries would be preferred for a longer time with great employment pressures. The post-war Asian "Four Little Dragons" and China's coastal regions with economic take-off in the 1980s have enjoyed economic success as they decided to fully utilize a cheap labor force and chose labor-intensive processing manufacturing industries, often textile industries, as their primary industries.

Second, it is important to handle the relation between capital formation and technology innovation. To achieve real productivity, capital needs to be bound together with labor and natural resources. Here, technology combines all kinds of production elements and is crucial for enhancing productivity. Therefore, capital should be effectively used to promote technology innovation, to increase capital output ratio, and to raise investment profit. In the early stages after World War II, many developing counties, including China, knew little about "science and technology as the first productive force." They have learnt a great lesson that only increasing quantity of production does not suffice to sustain social re-production. They have also learned that investments in education, science and technology, and increasing quality of production are all very important.

Third, it is important to handle the relationship between the allocation of capital and the sizes and structures of enterprises. Such structures are actually the structures of a national economy which combines main parts and minor parts and embodies the overall strength of a nation and the lives of its people. As developing countries and regions aggressively intend to boost their national economy, they concentrate capital in large & medium enterprise and in capital-intensive industries and projects while ignoring a large number of labor-intensive small-size enterprises and those non-publically-owned enterprises. They did not realize that the latter enterprises can, in fact, offer employment opportunities and improve the living standards of their people. Hence, availability of capital shall be made to both large and small enterprises; well adjusting sizes and structures of enterprises need to be considered as a focal point in capital allocation.

Fourth, it is important to handle the relationship between investment decision and investment management. In order to speed up economic take-off, governments of the developing countries and regions often put emphasis on approving and organizing new projects, but overlook the expenditure of projects in their construction and completion, formation of productivity, and performance. This lengthens the production cycle and decreases the profit. In order to have better investment result, attentions should be paid to the management of the whole process: making investment decisions, implementing investment plans, completing projects on-time, forming a productive capacity, meeting production goals and standards, and achieving good profits. Ultimately, capital can be allocated appropriately, while usage and output rate of capital can be enhanced and economy growth can be accelerated.

Fifth, it is important to follow economic rules and efficiently utilize capital and resources. The fundamental economic laws in a society include law of value, profit-maximization and balanced development among regions. In order to appropriately allocate capital and to avoid waste in resources and repetitive low level construction, barriers among administrative regions need to be overcome together with a reasonable flow of resources in accordance with economic laws. Minimizing input and maximizing output can always help us increase efficiency in capital and resources. Simultaneously, reform on enterprises' internal structure and external management system needs to be intensified in order to improve the quality of enterprises, which is the micro-base for better use and output of capital and resources.

6.3   Ways and Principles of Changing Capital into Investment

For developing countries and regions, besides the problem of insufficient capital, there is another problem that needs to be solved, how to change capital into investment for capital growth and expansion. As mentioned in previous chapters, resources and the environment constrain the economic development in developing countries and regions. These countries cannot follow the process of investment actualization as carried out in developed countries and regions, integrating technology, projects, labor, and markets together. Developing countries and regions always face difficulties even after transforming capital into investment in social production. There are many other barriers that interrupt the transformation circle of monetary capital – production capital – commodity capital – monetary capital. This makes the process of re-cycling their capital difficult. This process can be simplified in the following formula:

$$G_0 \longrightarrow W_0 \longrightarrow G_1 \longrightarrow W_1 \longrightarrow G_2 \longrightarrow W_2 \longrightarrow G_3 \ldots\ldots$$

If which,

G_0 = monetary capital

W_0 = commodity capital as the output of production process

G_1 = monetary capital evolved from product capital

This tells us that the evolvement of capital into investment is in essence a value added process. During the evolving process, capital enters production, and changes from currency form to physical form. This change is hard in developing countries and regions. The author has worked in the mountainous areas in Guangdong, China for many years and experienced difficulties in organizing and leading economic development in undeveloped regions. It is difficult for them to raise capital, not to mention converting capital into investment and then productivity. The latter is about whether they can and how to make use of capital and about the ability to use capital or the ability to make investment or attract investment. Without such ability, capital cannot enter production through project implementation and only stays in the currency form without transforming into production capital, or commodity capital, or even investment activities for productivity in a society.

Here, a new concept, called capability of Investment, emerges in development economics. It refers to the capability to accept and absorb investment, which was determined by the availability of capital, technology, entrepreneurship, labor and mentality, and the resource environment. If the amount of investment is beyond the capability, the investment recovery period will be lengthened and investment return will be lowered, as people do not have the ability to absorb it. On one hand, this slows down economic growth; on the other hand, it becomes a burden to a country. Developing countries and regions have to face not only insufficiencies in capital, technology, human resources, especially entrepreneurs as well as economic and administrative experts, and in qualified workers, but also bad social mental environments. Capital is only one of the elements in production, and it needs to be combined with technology and qualified people for a better result in investment. Most of the time, even though developing countries can have new sources of capital or new investment projects, they still lack qualified people in enterprise management and are short of a certain number of qualified laborers. As a result, they can neither reach their targeted performance nor find a market for their products, and they even have to shut down their business. Hence, there is only the existence of ordinary investment, instead of value added capital circulation in the production process. Developing countries need to exert effort not only in accumulating capital, but also in developing technology and qualified managerial people and laborers with innovative ideas of economic reform in order to make the society a positive, aggressive and advanced one. Thus, capability of investment will be enhanced and capital can be transformed to investment smoothly.

So, is it true that we can randomly transform capital into investment without making any choice once capability of investment is improved? No, it isn't. Actually, there are five guiding principles in the selection choosing process.

Principle One: making use of competitive advantage. Though developing countries and regions have lots of disadvantages, such as weak economic foundations, low level of economic development, insufficient experts in technology and low quality but a large quantity labor force, they have competitive advantages, like unexplored natural resources, low labor costs and a large potential consumption market. Hence, the competitive advantages need to be incorporated into the limited capital in order to achieve a high output of investment with low input. Priority should be given to labor-intensive industries based on conventional technologies. As the production cost of these industries is low, production and sales volume can be enlarged, capital can be accumulated to a greater extent, and economic growth can be sped up. If those big technology-based and capital-driven projects are initiated at first, the transformation of capital into investment will be negatively impacted, as these countries' competitive advantages are not being used.

Principle Two: prioritizing leading industries. Leading industries are the most privileged ones which can be aligned with other supporting industries to widen the scale of the economy and improve national economic performance in all related sectors in developing countries and regions. Because of the forward and backward correlation, the development of leading industries can promote the formation and growth of a number of other industries. Therefore, developing countries or regions can transform limited capital into investment with less effort if they give priority to the development of leading industries.

Principle Three: prioritizing "bottle-neck" industries. In the process of economic growth, the developing countries' industrial structure is not mature. The industrial structure is imbalanced with those "bottle neck" industries bulging out, with transportation and telecommunications lagging behind. This situation cannot match with the needs of economic expansion. Therefore, the originally low social productivity cannot effectively promote economic growth. If the "bottleneck" can be removed, productivity generated from investment can be increased 10 times or more. Hence, exploring the "bottle-neck" industries can help improve the utilization of capital and efficiency of investment.

Principle Four: prioritizing projects that have a high capital output ratio. In the model of the Harold-Doma Theory, the two variables determining economic growth are capital and output. They are also used as important economic indicators by numerous economists. Hence, developing countries and regions need to choose projects with maximum output for every investment unit. That means they need to pick investment projects with the lowest capital/output ratio, and put all existing resources, including labors and materials, into these projects. This is an important principle to improve the efficiency of capital use.

Principle Five: prioritizing projects with products in growth stage. Developing countries and regions usually pick those industries with good product sales. However, the market for the industries may be saturated once they enter the industry market, which may lead to investment waste and facilities waste. The above situation is caused by the ignorance of the rule of the product life cycle and the violation of the principle of giving priority to projects with products in growth stage. According to the theory of product life cycle, there are usually four stages in the cycle: ① introduction stage (product technology has not been mature yet); ② growth stage (though the technology has matured, consumers do not know enough about the products and the market needs to be exploited); ③ mature stage (product market has been opened up with a good sales record, and enterprises can make great profit with a promising future); ④ decline stage (new products emerge and replace the old ones, and the old products are gradually made with increased production costs, shrinking sales and decreasing profit). Developing countries and regions lack experience in managing modern commodity production but are anxious to develop their economies. So, they usually invest in projects with high sales, which is not a correct way. Only by investing capital into the products that are in the growth stage will be a right way to cut costs in product development, to enhance market exploration, to increase product competitiveness, to obtain a better profit and investment return for enterprises, and finally to boost economic growth.

6.4 Expanding Investment – the First Motivator for Economic Take-off

The economic term "take-off" was first put forward by a U.S. economist named W.W. Rostow in his book "*Stages of Economic Growth: Non-communism Declaration*" published in 1960. He claimed that there were five social development stages for human societies: traditional society, pre-condition for take off, drive to maturity, and high massive consumption. Later on, he added one more stage "the pursuit of quality of life" after the "stage of high massive consumption" in his book *"Politics and Stage of Growth"* in 1971. We are not going to discuss the scientific logic of the sixth stage. However, there are some elements of truth in Rostow's interpretation of economic "take off". In his opinion, the "take off" of developing countries and regions means breaking away from their traditional under-developed economic condition and obtaining sustainable economic growth in a short period (about 20-30 years) through industrialization and reform in production. His idea is reasonable in that continuous economic growth and actualization of modernization rely on the actualization of industry and reform of the farming-based economic structure for enlarging the scale of the economy and for establishing a good foundation for modernization. So, how to actualize "take off"? Most economists believe that capital formation is a barrier for "take off". Economist Rostow takes the capital accumulation rate above 10% in a nation as the first condition for economic growth. Harold and Doma consider the capital formation rate (saving rate) as the only condition for economic growth. Lewis took the issue of raising the savings rate from 5% to 12% as the core question of developing countries and regions.

The author agrees with Rostow on the first condition for economic growth, but disagrees with Harold and Doma as they regard enlarging investment as the only sufficient and necessary condition. The correct interpretation is that enlarging investment could be the first motivator for economic "take off", which is only a necessary condition, not the only condition or a sufficient condition. There is a definite ratio among all sorts of production elements. During the process of social economic growth and development, these elements need to be put into the production process to get an interactive and complementary reaction. From the perspective of input-output, the causes for a slow economic growth in developing countries and regions are that the number of production elements into the production process is small, the quality is low, and the interaction result will not be good enough to have a high productivity level. "Key Production Elements" means capital, labor, qualified management, and all kinds of natural resources. Though labor quality in developing countries is not high, the volume is tremendous; there are not enough managerial and technological talents, but they can be trained, which needs a long period and a huge investment in education and technology. As for natural resources, they can be imported from other countries to solve the problem of insufficiency. Comparatively, capital resource is the scarcest one and its role is important as it can bring "economic life" to other factors of production through interaction. This has been brought up in the first chapter when the functions of capital are mentioned, such as when the coherent function and integrated function link up, allocate, exchange and consume in the re-production process in a society. Hence, developing countries and regions need to increase input into education and fundamental development, to develop key industries, leading industries and other industries, and to establish reasonable industrial structures to increase the overall economic scale. The input of capital and its expansion determine the scale of all other production elements.

Without capital, nothing can be done successfully, not to mention economic "take off". Therefore, capital is the first motivator for economic growth.

Economic theory comes from and has to be supported by real economic practices and experiences. From a global economy perspective, what is the reality? According to western economists' analysis of the economic statistics of developing countries, capital plays different roles at different stages of economic development. Based on the research done by economists such as Denison on all kinds of production elements, during 1952-1967, input of capital only contributed to 25% of the economic growth in America, already a developed country at that time; Britain 22%, Federal Germany 16%; on the other hand, Japan, a developing country in 1952-1967, the rate was50%; during 1950-1962, Mexico reached 47.2%, Argentina 44.8% and Brazil 30%.[46] This indicates that capital has a significant impact upon the economic "take off" for countries such as Japan, Mexico and Brazil. Please take a look at the following two tables.

Table 6.1 Average Growth Rates of Investment Scale and GDP of Eight Countries During 1954-1980 (%)

	U.S.	U.K.	France	The Former Federal Republic of Germany	Japan	Poland	The Former Yugoslavia	The Former Soviet Union
Fixed Asset Investment	8.3	11.3	12.8	9.5	16.2	9.6	20.6	5.2
GDP	7.8	10.3	11.6	9	14.2	8.7	20.2	4.7

Source: *Poland Statistical Yearbook* (1981), *National Account Statistical Yearbook* (1966, 1975, 1980)

From the two tables (Table 6.1 and 6.2), we can see that by comparing their relationships there is a trend that investment grows more quickly than national income. This trend is more obvious in countries with a lower level of economic growth, especially those in the stage of 'take off', than those countries with a higher level. Therefore, it is a rule of growth, the growth in scale of investment happens prior to economic growth, which is clearly shown in developing countries. Therefore, expanding investment is the first motivator for economic "take off". In China, during the period of 1953-1989, the average growth rate of the national income was 6.7%, while that of investment growth was 11.2%, the latter is 0.67 times higher than the former. This can clearly demonstrate the trend mentioned. The trend remains the same in different countries. To conclude, after the world wars, investment grew much more quickly than national income in the countries with a weak industrial structure but a larger rate of economic growth, examples of this are both Japan and China. But, this was not the case in America, which did not experience much destruction during the Second World War, and had a more developed economy. This showed that the annual investment growth rate became comparatively lower when approaching the maturity stage. Simultaneously, judging from a longitudinal point of view, in China the rate of growth during the initial period is the highest. However, this drops down along with economic growth, the advancement of technology, and the enhancement of productive standard. Because of the above rule, the growth rate in Japan during 1956-1970 accumulated to 40.3% while the growth rate in China was 26.8% during 1952-1976. The average rate for Japan was 36.8% while that of China during the same period of time was 27.2%.[47] During 1985-1988, China experienced a much faster economic expansion, its investment rates were 32.4%, 36.2%, 38.3% and 38.4% respectively. From this view, we can predict that the investment rate in China will be maintained at a steady and slower rate in the coming future before entering into a period of structural change.

Table 6.2 Average Growth Rates of Investment Scale and GDP of China (%)

Year	A	B	Year	A	B
1953~1962	24.1	7.5	1967~1976	8	5
1954~1963	13.4	5.5	1968~1977	12.9	7.4
1955~1964	11.1	5.1	1969~1978	15.6	9.9
1956~1965	11.7	4.7	1970~1979	12.6	8
1957~1966	3.3	3.3	1971~1980	7.7	5.3
1958~1967	7.2	3	1972~1981	6.5	5.1
1959~1968	-3.8	-0.4	1973~1982	7.4	5.7
1960~1969	-4.3	-1.5	1974~1983	7.2	5.4
1961~1970	-9.3	-0.3	1975~1984	7.3	5.5
1962~1971	9.6	7.6	1976~1985	6.9	6.6
1963~1972	20.1	10.3	1977~1986	9.4	8.7
1964~1973	12.5	10	1978~1987	10.6	9.6
1965~1974	12.6	8.5	1979~1988	10.3	8.5
1966~1975	9.7	7	1980~1989	10.7	8.9

Notes: A refers to average growth rates of investment calculated by accumulative approach;

B refers to average growth rates of GDP calculated by accumulative approach.

The economic "take-off" experience of the "Four Little Dragons" of Asia also demonstrates that the mentioned rule of growth is objective and has a definite function.

Table 6.3 Investment and Economic Growth in Asian "Four Little Dragons"

Type / Region	Investment Rate		Economic Growth Rate	Capital Contribution Rate
	1971-1980	1981-1985	1970-1980	1970-1980
Korea	25.2	32.1	8.5	29
Taiwan	26.2	26.3	9.5	33
Hong Kong	19.6	28.9	9.8	54
Singapore	34.5	45.5	9.1	62

Note: This table was sourced from *Japan's Investment and Asian Rise* (in Chinese) by Fan Yongming, p. 65 and p. 68.

Based on the above described information, people might wonder about the reasons for such a trend of faster annual investment growth, wide investment expansion and high investment rate in developing countries and regions. It is because of the following three reasons.

First, it is necessary to establish a more comprehensive industry structure mechanism to make the national economy transform from a traditional farming-based structure into an industrial-based structure, which is a revolutionary change of the national economic structure. In order to complete such transformation, a lot of fundamental elements need to be added into the production process, especially large scale farming and material-based industries in which there is extensive re-production and requires a large number of investments. That is why the rate of investment needs to be maintained at a high level.

Second, investment expansion and economic growth can be achieved through stimulating needs in a society. 40% of capital can be transformed into labor's salary and a consumption fund, while the other 60% can be changed into materials for production. This can expand the needs of a society, such as personal consumption needs and investment product needs, to create a better market environment for re-production and economic expansion.

Third, expansion in investment actually means expanding inputs into production in order to motivate economic growth, which can be done by increasing supply. The physical transformation in social production and then the formation of products cannot be realized without the increase of productive input, which really relies on the increase of capital.

However, there is a boundary in investment expansion. Developing countries and regions need to choose an appropriate investment percentage as a base for motivating economic "take off". So, what is the appropriate level? This has to link up with the choice of growth targets and the constraints in relation to the targets within a country or a particular region. The common criteria for choosing the target are: 1) the society is able to put up with the investment rate psychologically and materialistically, and the society can be motivated for a higher rate of economic growth in a stable way without much fluctuation; 2) the planned investment rate can be balanced with rate of investment demanded and rate of investment supplied, that is, $i_p = i_d = i_s$; 3) this variation in planned investment can be psychologically bear by people. The first condition is the summation of the remaining two conditions. If there is problem in the remaining two conditions, the first one may not be realized and hence economic growth will be hindered.

A few decades after the World War II, apart from the above mentioned countries, many developing countries and regions have put in a lot of effort, even with administrative means, to motivate a savings rate to 10% or even above 20-30%, so as to widen the scale of fixed asset investment. However, there is not any encouraging economic performance or "take off", as "appropriate investment rate" has not be chosen and set correctly. Moreover, the rule of investment has not been applied appropriately in these countries and regions at different points of time. The investment rate is not the only factor that makes economic "take off". Other subsidiary conditions are required, especially the input of other production elements such as well-trained labors, technologies, and talents in economics and management, as well as reasonable industrial structure, appropriate investment policies, and other social, economic or cultural conditions. Otherwise, economic "take-off" cannot be realized.

All in all, expansion of investment is only the first motivator and an essential factor in developing countries and regions for economic "take off". All factors, like capital accumulation and appropriateness in investment, need to be well coordinated and balanced for economic growth and development.

Chapter Seven

Corporate Quality: the Source of Power for

Economic Growth

As aforementioned, investment expansion is the first motivator for economic "take off". However, it requires enterprises to handle investment. Otherwise, the power of "first motivator" will be lost. In a modernized society, enterprises not only create wealth but also act as economic organizers for survival of a society. They are cells for production in a society to promote productivity, production development, and economic growth. Moreover, they are also entities for investment expansion, which widen the scale of productivity development and enhance productivity levels. Hence, the quality and vitality of enterprises will directly affect economic growth rates and economic benefits. Corporate quality is the profound source of power for economic growth. Either from the practical perspective or from the theoretical perspective, the implementation of an economic growth strategy is the fundamental issue that people need to pay attention to.

7.1   The Meaning and Basic Elements of Corporate Quality
Corporate quality refers to the vitality and dynamics of enterprises produced by the driving force due to internal and external elements of enterprises, as well as by the pressure under the market mechanism. Generally speaking, if the vitality of enterprises is strong, the quality of the enterprise will be higher, and the power for creating social wealth will be greater too; and vice versa. During the process of creating social wealth, corporate quality determines the quality and quantity of wealth that enterprises create and the overall picture of economic growth.

Then, what are the basic components of corporate quality? This point needs to be clarified; otherwise, corporate quality as the source of power for economic growth cannot be well developed, and economic growth of a society cannot be sped up.

The first element is the business management system. It refers to a synthesis system combined of all kinds of relations within an enterprise, as with other enterprises, with production elements, with the market, and with the nation. From a macro perspective, the business management system means the regulation and organization for guidance, adjustment, and management over enterprises from the government. From a micro perspective, it means the regulation and organization for the management of an enterprise's internal elements such as labors, capital and materials, the relationships between enterprises as independent legal entities, and the operation of an enterprises' autonomy of entering or leaving the market. This can be demonstrated in Figure 7.1.

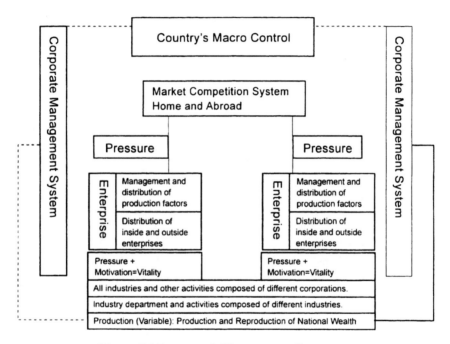

Figure 7.1 Integrated Management Systems

Figure 7.1 shows that under the market economy condition, based on the rules of economy and a macro-level adjustment of the market, the government exerts some control on enterprises in the form of systems and regulations to increase the competitiveness of enterprises and their chances of survival and development. Adaptation of the external environment will be determined by the extent of enterprises to put up with the requirements and pressures imposed by the government. Besides, an enterprise's capability, its internal mechanism of benefits, its autonomy of production and operation of business, all depend upon on the management and the allocation of the internal elements such as the employees' salary and payment, the level of tax and the amount of profit.

All these factors together form a motivation mechanism for enterprises, a motivation of self-development for enterprises. The pressure and motivation for an enterprise comprise its vitality. The stronger the vitality is, the higher the quality will be. Hence, the vitality comes from the management system of an enterprise. If an enterprise's management system aligns with its production capacity, the socialization level, the production level and its development requirements, then both quality and vitality of an enterprise will be higher.

The second element concerns the corporate management and decision-making. This element forms the main activities for top management and management staff of all levels and the center for production and operation of enterprises. It also determines the direction, width and depth of all corporate activities. Techniques of management and comprehensiveness of peripherals will help enterprises achieve correct decisions and efficient management. The production and operation, the initiation and innovation of the whole staff, as well as the utilization of existing production capacity in an enterprise, all rely on the quality of decisions, the determination and confidence of the management staff, and the implementation of decisions. If the quality of the management staff is high and decisions executed by the staff are correct, the management level of an enterprise will be higher. Enterprises will make use of their high-quality management system to enhance their production, energy and innovation. Hence, having a strong leading team for decision management and qualified staff for implementing correct decisions are extremely important. Under a highly centralized planned economic system, enterprises are like factories only focusing on production while ignoring management, production decision making, plan developing and target setting, the purchasing of materials, the utilization of laborers, the handling of products, salary and other compensation packages, etc. Enterprises do not need to make any decisions; instead they just need to follow instructions imposed by the government. Hence, their decision making power is exploited, their management power is limited, and the initiation and innovation of their staff cannot be fully utilized. As a result, corporate quality will be affected. Oppositely, if each enterprise is competitive enough to enjoy its autonomy in production and operational decisions under a market economy, its productivity will be increased and wealth will then be created to a greater extent. Therefore, an enterprise's management and its decision making power are an important part of corporate quality.

The third element concerns the scale of the production facility and the level of technology. This is crucial as it is the material and technology base for enterprise quality and a basic element for production. In addition, it determines the type and amount of production. Generally, the smaller the scale of production with a low level of technology will bring a poorer quality of enterprise. There is a positive correlation between the condition of an enterprise's production facility and the quality of an enterprise's material and technology. However, this may be applicable to a fast growing economy. The quality of an enterprise's material and technology usually is demonstrated through a large scale production facility, and the continuality, advancement and efficiency of the production process. If the economy is going to transform from the stage of "extensive" growth into the stage of "efficient" growth, the enterprise production facility needs to be more complex, more multi-functional with preciseness and automation. Information technology will then be applied to product research and development, design and manufacturing, and all aspects of enterprise management, including product sales and after sales services. No matter what level the economy achieves, an enterprise's production facility, its quality and quantity, and its level of technology shall form major parts of an enterprise's quality.

The fourth element concerns the quality of an enterprise's technicians and workers. This is the most active part of an enterprise's quality. Technicians and workers are required in all aspects of production, from operation of management, implementation of decisions, relocation of production facilities, actualization of production, etc. Their labor is a dynamic and very flexible process. If they are skilled, dedicated, and hard working, the enterprise's technology productivity will be stronger and the production facilities will achieve full utilization. The transformation of its internal elements will reach the effect of $1 + 1 > 2$ more quickly. Oppositely, the quality of an enterprise will not be that high. The performance of an enterprise reflects its labor productivity. Therefore, the average labor productivity of an enterprise is an indicator for an integrated quality of an enterprise.

The fifth element concerns sales and the information network systems of an enterprise. Under a market economy, enterprises need to have circulation systems of commodities and information to enter the markets, to balance their production, supply and marketing, and to make correct decisions about reproduction. It seems that this is an external part of an enterprise. However, it is closely related to production. The four basic elements of enterprises (i.e., production, exchange, allocation and consumption), are connected to the production and consumption processes of the whole society under a modernized market economy with highly developed products. Interaction can be found between production and circulation. As production becomes more complex, more multi-level and dynamic, enterprises need to exchange information at both local and international levels. This can help enterprises adapt to the dynamic market, get enough information about demand and supply, target the right products for production, increase sales and build a positive image in the overall market. Development of a sales networking and information exchange is needed to enhance the quality of enterprises. Some small to medium enterprises may not have the ability to do so and that's why their quality is lower. This is due to some constraints that they may have to face. It is the responsibility of the central government to provide services to them and allocate resources in a better way.

The sixth element concerns an enterprise's innovation ability. It is the last but the most important element for enterprises. It can make enterprises full of energy to explore and face challenges in the future, therefore it's the most up-to-date, most challenging and most creative part of an enterprise's quality. The innovation ability of an enterprise is actually derived from its talents in technology and management, from its management system, and from its interaction with the market economy. An enterprise with a qualified staff, good system, a desirable working environment and some pressures from internal and external sources, will have good innovation ability. Innovation can be found in the areas of systems, management, technology, products, production techniques, and people. Only if these areas are enhanced, can output be more diverse with good quality, good pricing and high labor productivity. This ultimately helps to speed up economic development for the whole society.

Based on the aforesaid, corporate quality is a dynamic and integrated system comprised of relevant factors such as management systems, operational and decision making activities, quality and quantity of production facilities, qualified talents and workers, sales and information networks, innovation ability, and the interactions of all these factors. It displays as the vitality formed by the pressures that enterprises face and the motivations that enterprises hold.

7.2 Function of Corporate Quality in Economic Growth

Assuming corporate production and sales are balanced in a market economy, corporate quality and economic growth shall have a positive correlation, which means that in social production, if the corporate quality is high, the number of these highly qualified enterprises increases, then the scale of social production will be higher with a higher standard, lots of high-quality products will be produced and the economic development will speed up; vice versa. This is the pattern as shown in Figure 7.2.

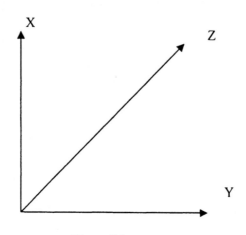

Figure 7.2

In Figure 7.2, X = quality of enterprises, Y = number of enterprises, Z = output. Z increases as the number of enterprises rises and quality of enterprises improves. Oppositely, Z decreases.

So, what are the decisive functions of corporate quality in economic growth?

First, corporate quality has a direct influence on the vitality of economic growth. In social re-production, the level and standard of productivity determine the overall level of economic growth, i.e. the quality and quantity of economic growth. Social productivity is not an abstract concept, but rather a material force accumulated in history. It comes from numerous enterprises in the society. The power of productivity is derived from the integration and coordination of enterprises. It is the ways of existence and function of social productivity that make up the structural cells and the symbolic levels of social productivity. The key factors for social productivity are the quality, the capacity, and the number of enterprises. Social productivity can stimulate economic growth. During the development of a modernized social economy, if there is the absence of new enterprises and enhanced corporate quality, social productivity will not be improved. On the whole, there will be a drop in the scale of economy. This clearly shows a direct correlation between social productivity and economic growth.

Second, corporate quality can increase the amount and quality of social wealth, because it's in essence the force of an enterprise's dynamic material and technology, and also it serves as a fundamental element for social productivity. If the number of enterprises increases with more complex composition elements, social productivity will be greater with a smaller structure of their material technology. Therefore, the total output and nature of product structure will determine the level of quality and quality structure of their products. Take the textile industry for example. The quality and quantity of cloth production will be increased in high quality textile enterprises with the advancement in textile machinery and a larger scale of production.

Third, corporate quality can influence the trend of economic growth. Under a modernized economy, there are altogether three levels of production with different kinds of industries among them. The output can be classified into two aspects, i.e., the annual total output of enterprises and the productivity of all labor. The summation of annual outputs increased in all enterprises is the total economic growth in a society. Hence, if the quality of all enterprises is high, there is a significant upward trend of social economic growth. The interdependence between quality of enterprises and economic growth can be shown clearly.

Fourth, corporate quality can generate a direct impact on the effectiveness of economic growth and the performance of social economy. Actually, economic growth effectiveness and social economy performance are an integrated indicator of labor productivity. The average labor productivity of enterprise is the source and the foundation of the social labor productivity. Effective economic growth relies on minimizing the amount of input. Thus, the annual wealth created can be increased years after years. However, if the increase of output is smaller than that of input, social wealth may not be increased and may even be reduced, and there will be no effective economic growth. From a micro point of view, if there is expansion in corporate investment, output and economic quality will be increased as long as the corporate quality is good. Enterprises can enjoy the scale of economy under this situation. We can conclude that a relationship between enterprises and the society can be traced, and the increase of the effectiveness and efficiency of enterprises may shrink the effectiveness and efficiency of economic growth in a society. However, the improvement on effectiveness and efficiency of economic growth in a society may bring positive impact to enterprises. Hence, corporate quality and labor productivity have a direct effect on the whole society.

7.3   Economic Growth Rooted in Technological Advancement

As mentioned above, corporate quality has a direct impact upon all aspects of economic growth. During the process of social and corporate production, output is determined by three main elements: capital, labor and technology. As the development of social productivity and technology, modernized economic growth attributed to technology has increased from 5%–10% in the early 20th century to 60%–80% or more now. Hence, emphasis shall be put not only on labor and capital but also on technology, especially on continuing technological advancements. Enterprises are the source of innovation and technological advancement. They possess the most motivational force for social technological advancement. Social technological advancement helps the transformation of the structure of technology and the development, industrialization, and commercialization of science and technology. As a result, economic growth and development of the whole society will be stimulated. No matter what kind of country it is, technological advancement cannot be isolated from economic strategy.

Developing countries and regions usually have a smaller scale of economy and lower levels of development. When compared with developed countries and regions, developing countries and regions have more economic problems. These countries pay too much attention to capital expansion, as they believe it can help to generate a larger scale of economy. This is understandable. However, as capital has been expanded to a certain level, the number and quality of enterprises have reached a desirable level; technological advancement of enterprises should be the main focal point. This can further promote corporate quality. Enterprises should establish a good technological foundation for intensive economic development. Otherwise, in the long-run, steady and healthy economic growth cannot be sustained.

The technological advancement of enterprises is a historical process, which can be neither too quick nor too slow. Enterprises need to develop strategies of technological advancement and actively implement them. Strategy of technological advancement refers to goal oriented strategies for planning an enterprise's research and development (R&D) and their implementation activities. For example, enterprises need to make decisions on choices of new building, rebuilding or expanding equipments or facilities, and technological investments. They need to choose a new technology or an appropriate technology in the technological category. There are some sub-level strategies on an enterprise's technology in which the strategies of technologic reforming, introducing, exploring and transferring are the most important ones.

Let's have a look at reforming the strategy of corporate technology. This strategy is about the technological planning and development, the implementation of investment activities, and the promotion of technological advancements. This process requires enterprises to have efficient allocation and adjustment of assets to enhance technology in existing situations. As we know, technologic reform relies on the foundation of asset management to achieve the optimum allocation of assets. As depreciation is found in assets, technology is required in the replenishment. This can increase the longevity of assets and the competitiveness of enterprises, as mentioned below.

(1) Increasing adaptability of resources to encounter changes. Utilization of resources will become efficient with changes in the existing production techniques and facilities, as well as with the integration of new resources to make production smooth.

(2) Enhancing adaptability to the market. This is another way to make enterprises more competitive in the market. Through modifying and improving production conditions, fine tuning the structure of products, exploring new products, and aligning production with market demand to increase short run production output so that enterprises can achieve their profit goals.

(3) Participating in international diversification to gain market competitiveness. Technological advancement like automation can reduce production costs to a large extent, increasing the quality and quantity of products, expanding production scale for export, and finally increasing the productive competitiveness in international markets. All these rely on the efforts of enterprises to explore their potential in technological reform and in saving time and materials. As a result, labor and material productivity will be increased for the whole society to achieve economic growth.

In addition, we are going to move to the strategy adopted by enterprises for technological introduction. This is a process of introducing overseas advanced technology to facilitate technological advancement at a low cost and in a short term. Generally speaking, there are three ways to improve technology, developing original technology; introducing it from local research institutions or other enterprises, and introducing it from advanced countries. Among the three ways, the second is a process of local technological diffusion. However, this kind of diffusion may be obstructed due to market competition and confidentiality of technology. Governmental intervention may not do any help in this aspect as undesirable forces may come from the market which often make the importation of technology difficult and impede economic growth. In order to save time, effort and capital for obtaining higher levels of advanced technology, labor productivity and economic growth, it is better to choose the third method of introducing innovative technology from advanced countries. During the years from the opening-up till 2004 in Guangdong, there was an average economic growth rate of 13.4% and a high growth rate of labor productivity. The reasons are the introduction of huge capital, $150.4 billion US dollars, and a large number of equipment and production lines which have had a great impact on technological reform; this ultimately brings a higher level of technology in many industries and lots of enterprises.

Technological strategy is a tool for transforming the results of research and development into new products, new materials, new facilities and new knowledge involved in developmental activities. Once production and technology have been widely spread, usage of new technology in a society will be increased. Technology changes along with time. Once new technology emerges, old technology will be replaced, forming a life cycle of technology. Enterprises cannot sit and wait for the emergence of new technology. They need to continue to explore new technology. Changes on economic value of products can be reflected in the market. Hence, enterprises should produce, explore, develop and store products at the same time. This is the way to make products stay in a competitive state with sustainable economic growth and efficiency.

The last thing that needs to be covered is the shift of strategy. This involves the decision making and the implementation process for enterprises to moving from an old field of technology into a new one. This is a change process for technology development. According to the theory of industry life cycle, industries, especially manufacturing industries, have to undergo the stages of input, growth, maturity and decline. When industries are at a period of decline, product demand in a society will fall down. This will become a production constraint for industries and consequently economic growth will slow down. In order to survive, and maintain or increase competitiveness, enterprises need to step into a new industry with new technology.

To conclude, technological improvement is a core issue for enterprise quality under modernized economic technological development, especially in making decisions and implementing technological reform, technological exploration and introduction for upgrading the quality of enterprises. Technological advancement is the only way to enhance labor productivity and guarantee an enterprises' efficient economic growth.

7.4 Enhancing Corporate Quality for Economic Growth Is A Tremendous Project in the Century

The global economy has entered into a new era with tremendous changes, constantly industrializing new technologies. As new technologies and new groups of industries have been emerging, the socialization of productivity in the world will enter a new stage. The 21st century is an age of transforming the focus of production from nationwide resource based manufacturing industries into worldwide information based service industries. In order to catch up with developed countries, developing countries need to make extra efforts to face the world, to face the future, to face the modernization stage in the 21st century, and in other words, to face the tremendous project of increasing corporate quality. If developing countries make fewer efforts, they will miss a historical opportunity as developed countries have already started to work in this area.

From the 1990s to the 21st century, advanced technology is the most important motivator for economic growth, because it speeds up the transfer of technology among enterprises and the emergence of high tech products in industries. This brings drastic social changes to all aspects of life as follows.

First, change comes from the trend of high technology. This trend is reflected in two aspects. On one hand, it has been shown in production and technological exploration tactics. A variety of areas have been involved with advanced technologies, such as technological exploration and innovation, introducing and reforming technologies, and upgrading technological facilities. The routine production of enterprises heavily relies on advanced technology, while management of production and development of technology rely on modern management tools, such as information management system and decision supporting system. On the other hand, for those enterprises running traditional products, their production will be reduced gradually while those that run high technological products will be increased. The sales volume ratio between traditional and high technological products will drop with a decrease for the former one and an increase for the latter one. The cultural and technological elements of all products will increase.

Second, change comes from the trend of integration. In the 21st century, production has been diversified among enterprises in the society. The scope of work of enterprises has been greatly enlarged, and single product operations can be no longer found. This is the result of economic development, multi-level social demand and an increase of high technology services. Hence, the core activities of enterprises have been changed from production into research, development, and other peripheral services, like the provision of informational services and labor related services for families and the society. The boundary between manufacturing and service industries seems not very clear as the primary, secondary and tertiary industries have been integrated.

Third, change comes from the trend of globalization. Transnational corporations will be a common form of operating enterprises. Transnational corporations have existed for more than 100 years since the end of the 19th century. They are economic giants in the world. In 1999, the number of multi-national corporations in the world has reached 63,000 with overseas subsidiary branches totaling 690,000. Their economic activities penetrate into countries all over the world making a total production of over 8,000 billion US dollars which takes up a quarter of the world's production.[48] The sales volume hits up to 14,000 billion US dollars, which comprises 48% of the world's GDP, with two thirds of the world's trade volume.[49] The business of some enterprises, especially of those transnational corporations, has spread across countries and has become an organization of economic activities beyond country's border. This is due to the rapid advanced development of informational systems. Otherwise, global economic activities in all countries, especially developing countries, would not be possible, not to mention the unification of worldwide markets and exploration of the future spaces, i.e., ocean space and outer space.

This is a big challenge for developing countries and regions as they need to develop both their traditional products and high tech products within a very short time. On one hand, traditional products in developing countries have not been fully developed. On the other hand, the development of high tech products driven by information technology needs to speed up in order to strengthen future economic growth and to increase their competitiveness in the international market. China is one of these countries which needs to face the challenge and makes a good use of the opportunity. They need to encourage medium and large enterprises to make more efforts in exploring and implementing the development of high technology so as to have more integrated, international and large scale economic development.

Deepening on internal reform and strengthening internal management are also needed. Therefore, enterprises should make themselves open, modern with high quality in all aspects to meet the demand of the 21st century. Economic development can be divided into two major parts, i.e., production and management. The core capability of an enterprise's production falls on automation and an efficient production process. This process is based on integrated advanced technological development. However, if the management system in these enterprises is old fashioned, advanced technology will not be taken advantage of. Hence, modern management theory, like those in operational research and behavioral science, shall be applied into enterprises in order to help them make correct scientific decisions. Thus, enterprises need to do the following things: 1) intensify internal management reform to establish a flexible, procedural management system and production mechanism; 2) make use of information technology and pay close attention to information and technological development both at home and abroad to ensure the right direction of future development; 3) acquire information of quality and customer feedbacks on products to improve products and production; 4) acquire market information to understand market trends and increase sales volumes in order to avoid blind production; 5) have economic information about the present situation of the operation such as, utilization of capital and materials, energy and labor; 6) obtain production information and apply them into new production in time with correct managerial techniques. All of the above rely on continuous efforts to improve management techniques. Currently, there are two stages of using information technology in enterprise management. The first is the initial stage for the execution of production schedules, management of finance, capital, materials, labor...etc. The second is the advanced stage for the actualization of research and development, experiments and product design, production and marketing, financial management, integrated management systems, analysis and forecast on economic development, and other strategic decisions of enterprises in order to meet the needs of the 21st century. Applying information technology can enhance corporate management, increase productivity of labor, and boost economic efficiency. The average labor productivity can be increased by 3% - 5% while managerial cost can be cut down by 15%-30% in enterprises of developed countries.

In addition, enterprises need to strengthen the education and training of their members and to establish a team of qualified top management staff for decision making. As there is a growing demand in intellectual development, the need for technological expertise is high. This has happened in the developed countries and they have been putting effort on education and training. For example, concepts of Total Employee Training and Life-long Education have been deeply rooted into the management system of Japan. Training has been provided to all levels of staff across all departments. This kind of training increases the cultural and technological levels of staff and builds a foundation for enterprise innovation and development. For the management of technical staff, a variety of methods have to be used to utilize their skills and increase their innovation. In America, creativity of advanced staff is stimulated through the use of "Salary Scheme for Researchers" and "Application for Research Funding". Based on the concept of "Salary Scheme for Researchers", money for researchers is not a salary, instead, it is treated as a kind of bonus. The term of research is usually 2-3 years. Within this period, researchers have to do independent research to make achievements. This can motivate researchers to use their strengths and creativity. "Application for Research Funding" is another way to stimulate researchers to reach fruitful achievements. This strategy is worth adopting in developing countries and regions, including China, as they need to learn from developed countries and regions to train their staff. A team of qualified staff in management can help enterprises make correct decisions and make their staff more efficient.

Chapter Eight

Industrial Construction: Fundamental for

Sustainable Economic Growth

The reasons why developing countries and regions are lagging far behind developed countries include: industries have not fully grown, industrial scale is small, industrial structure is simple and industrial level is low. In order to develop an economy and realize sustainable and stable economic growth, industrialization should be sped up, appropriate development strategies for industries should be chosen and established, and effective industrial construction should be undertaken.

8.1 The Selection and Determination of Developmental Strategies for Industries

History has demonstrated that productivity in a society is the process of formation and development of industries. The industrial structure forms a basis for both social productivity and national economic development. The formation and development of industries are the outcome of social productivity and are the motivators and material form of national economy growth. On the other hand, they also enhance the scale and the level of social productivity and generate national economic growth. In the social reproduction process, if there is large scale of industrial construction, there will be great development in social productivity which can help build a material and technological foundation for sustainable economic growth. Countries, either developed or developing, all need to make efforts to build industries, to define strategic economic goals, and implement industrial strategies. Through these efforts, they can have sustainable economic growth. Industrial construction is the base and the core for economic growth. Strategy of Economic growth determines the strategy and the implementation of industrial development while the latter is subordinate to and serves the strategic goals of economic growth.

In the process of social production, industries are dynamic economic activities based on the labor division of national economic sectors and systematically combine all kinds of production elements with business organizations as their basic units. This can be demonstrated in the following four areas.

First, the life cycle of a single industry. Any industry in any country during any historical period has a life cycle, which includes four stages: forming, growing, maturing and declining. After going through this cycle, it will be replaced by a new industry. The "sunset industries" transferred from the industrial adjustment of developed countries and regions are industries in the declining stage of the life cycle.

Second, the chronological cycle of industries. As social productivity keeps on improving, industrial development starts from primary industry, then to secondary industry, and finally to tertiary industry. The developmental sequence of industries moves along with economic growth and has a leading effect on a national economy. For example, primary industry used to dominate the national economy and fostered the industrial revolution to human economy, in return, which shifted the manual based agriculture to the machinery based agriculture. After that, the continuous development of machinery has allowed some advanced countries, like Britain, France, America, Germany and Italy, to achieve industrialization. Secondary industry, including manufacturing, coal mining and construction industries, starts to replace primary industry, and thus begins to lead other industries in the national economy. Today, from building on the foundation of high industrialization in developed countries and regions, tertiary industry have emerged and taken over secondary industries. This has a significant impact on national economic growth. Examples of tertiary industries are: the IT industry, education, commerce, finance and other service industries. The total output value of these industries in developed countries and regions takes up more than 60% of the national economy.[50] As a result, global economic power shifts from nationalized, resource-based manufacturing industries to worldwide, information -based service industries. Though this transition takes a long period of time, it undoubtedly pushes the social economy to move to a higher level. Social economic growth has been accelerated continuously which brings prosperity and improvement to the whole of society.

Third, the periodicity of industrial evolution and difference of industrial functions. Industries and industrial groups evolve with the change of their functions in economic growth. Based on this rationale, industries can be classified into strategic industries, leading industries, and supporting industries. Relationship among these industries is in essence the game between technical side and beneficial side as these industries often shift from one to another one. For example, strategic industries could shift to leading industries, and then eventually to supporting industries. This is not only an evolution process of industries' functions and positions, but also a demonstration of different stages in industrial development. Strategic industries hereby refer to those newly formed industries which may become leading ones for future economic growth. Leading industries are the most influencing ones that play critical roles in social productivity, which determine the direction, speed, quality and scale of national economic growth. The leading industries affect the location of industries in a national economy and represent the developmental stage of the economy in a certain country or region. Supporting industries are complementary with the development of leading or core industries.

Fourth, the evolution process of upgrading industrial structure. This process refers to that, along with the upgrade of human needs, industrial development begins from the industries for consumption goods, then moves to the industries for production goods, and again returns to the industries for consumption goods and services. In other words, industries evolve from the focus on material production into the focus on non-material production, i.e. spiritual production. The specific path can be described as: agriculture → light industries → heavy industries → high value added processing industries → service industries → knowledge industries. Moreover, manufacturing industries have been transformed from extensive ones into intensive ones and have become more advanced and more diversified.

The above four areas have investigated industries as dynamic processes in economic and technological development. Industries have to follow the sequence as shown in the first, the second and the fourth area. This means that industries cannot skip over the primary industry and jump into the secondary industry without having a foundation. Without the industries for consumption materials, there might not be the industries for production materials. Industries cannot enter the maturing stage and the declining stage without experiencing the growing stage. However, the period of maturity or transition time can be shortened. The third area is dynamic and flexible. In the third area, the span of a certain industry can be narrowed down or the sequence of industrial development can be reversed, while there is no fixed mode of industrial development. In terms of developing countries or regions, it all depends on the situation of the nation, geographic condition, and choice of strategies, such as choosing strategies or goals to improve the livelihood of people, to achieve social stability, or to reach a global level of advancement, etc. Developing countries or regions should realize: only with appropriate strategies and great efforts in industrial construction, can social productivity then be enhanced, sustainable economic growth be achieved, and strategic goals be obtained.

Based on the experiences of countries in the world's economic development, there are two ways to choose and make strategies of industrial construction.

The first is the typical way of industrial development. This has been used by traditional capitalist countries, like Britain and the United States, who followed a "gradual" strategy and started from light and transportation industries into heavy industries. In the U.S., the first industrial revolution started in about 1860 with the capitalist manufacturing system as its symbol. At that time, agriculture amounted to 63.8% of its total GDP, while industries, mainly light industries, took up about 36.2%. In 1900, industrialization was almost completed: industries amounted to 61.8% while agriculture was only 38.2%. Simultaneously, heavy industries were developed and accounted for 44.2 % of the total GDP. In 1860 the three main kinds of light manufacturing industries were shoe making, textile, and garments which then changed into two heavy industries and a light industry, iron and steel, machinery, and meat processing. Though heavy industries did not outweigh the light industries, they were already playing a leading role in the economy at that time. From the beginning of the 20th century till the outbreak of the Second World War, there was an unimaginable development in heavy industry. During the 20 years' period from1900 to 1920, heavy grew by 3.26 times and performed much better than other industry. In 1921, its percentage in the total output value of industries reached 50.6%, exceeding that of light industries for the first time, and went up to 55.7% in 1929. Since 1939, industrial modernization moved further, the percentage of heavy industries became even larger and reached 65.7% in 1975, while the percentage of light industries dropped from 44.3% to 34.3%. As a basic industry, transportation also developed rapidly. Especially in the 19th century, there was a trend to build railroads. The average length of railroads built during the 40 years from 1830 to 1870 reached 1,775 kilometers while the length built in the 10 years from 1880 to 1890 was 11,500 kilometers. With 50 years' efforts, the railroad network had covered 41,000 kilometers by the year 1920. This tells us that starting from transportation and light industries and then transferring to heavy industries, is the route that typical capitalist countries such as the United States have taken. In order to differentiate this developmental strategy of industries from others, we call this route the "Typical Strategy and Process". During this process, there was an average of 33.2 % - 49.7% growth in the national economy every 10 years in the U.S,[51] which has kept USA the strongest economic power in the western capitalist world.

The Second is the way adopted by Japan and the former Soviet Union, which can be called as "Catching-up Strategy" or "Catching-up Process". This kind of industrial development strategy is to emphasize heavy industry and increase its importance in the national economic structure. Though Japan and the former Soviet Union have adopted similar approaches, each has its own features, which makes the outcome different. Industrial development in Japan before the war was different from that after the war. Before the war and after Meiji Reform, as the main target of Japan was to catch up with European countries and USA, aggressive measures were adopted for external expansion, such as developing military industry. Later on, it became a militarized economy. After being defeated in the war, in order to expand the overseas market for its products, Japan adopted an "inclining" industry strategy, placing emphasis on heavy industries for economic growth. The proportion of heavy industries in GDP had increased from 44.2% in 1950 to 62.2% in 1970 with a rise in its national economy, and Japan became the second economy among the Western capitalist countries and the third in the world. A direct outcome of this kind of strategy was that the gaps among different sectors in the national economy were widened.

The labor productivity of the heavy industries improved quickly while the labor productivities in other industries improved more slowly, such as in light industry, commerce, service industry, agriculture and the fishing industry. The former Soviet Union is another example that adopted a "Catching-Up Strategy" to develop its industries. During the 50 years from 1928 to 1977, industrial output grew by 120 times, with an average annual growth rate of 10.3%, the highest in the world. In the 1950s, the output of industries in the former Soviet Union was equal to 30% of that in the United States and reached over 80% by the end of 1970s. Similar to Japan, such strategy also gave rise to some discouraging affects – light industries were suppressed and people were suffered with a long-term shortage of basic necessities. Only in 7 years out of the 50 years from 1928 to 1977 did light industries grow faster than heavy industries. The percentage of heavy industries in the total output value of industrial output increased from 39.5% in 1928 to 60.5% in 1940, and 74% in 1977, while that of light industry decreased from 60.5% to 39% and 26%, respectively.

The "Four Little Dragons" in Asia could also be categorized as typical examples of "Catching-Up" economic growth. Their successes was different from that of Japan and the former Soviet Union. Their industrial development and modernization started from light industries, progressed to heavy industries, and then to highly advanced processing manufacturing industries. They spent about 20 years to reach the economic level of medium developed countries in the 1980s. Now, they are making great efforts to develop high technology for industrial development.

As mentioned above, starting from the 1980s or 1990s to the beginning of the 21st Century, in order to maintain economic growth and reach global economic standards, developing countries and regions have to make good use of the "Golden Opportunity" provided by the world's industrial adjustment. However, the question is, how to make use of it? Does it mean increasing investment to expand the economy or speculation to create a "bubble economy"? No. The answer should be implementing the strategy of "catching up" to choose and make correct developmental strategies while expanding investment for economic growth. This is a matter of life and death for a developing country. Most of the developing countries and regions in the world all adopted the strategy of "catching up"; however, the results were not the same. There was a big difference between the former Soviet Union and Japan, as Japan preferred heavy industry development. Though there were some problems with this kind of strategy, it was generally successful as it balanced the acceleration of heavy industry development for economic growth with the stimulation of light industry and agricultural development, and in the end, the people reaped the benefits. The strategy of Asia's "Four Little Dragons" is different from that of Japan. That's why the expected results and actual outcomes were not the same. In the former Soviet Union, the volume of heavy industry output was already higher than in the USA and its weapon industry was of an advanced level. However, its industrial development was isolated from the basic needs of its people. Even home appliances in heavy industries were not developed and the agricultural and light industries were at very low levels. As people's lives didn't improve along with economic development, the Soviet strategy was not well implemented and finally collapsed. Even though the industrial development strategy of the former Soviet Union was a type of "catching up", and though it achieved temporary success when it became the second largest economic giant in the world, the imbalanced industry development, the unfulfilled basic needs, and the insufficient support from its people made this strategy a failure in the end. Hence, developing countries and regions need to remember a critical issue which is that: efforts should be placed on choosing and making appropriate industrial development strategy in order to improve industrial development and to achieve the goals of the "catching up" strategy. This can help the economy reach a high level and benefit the people so that stabilization can be maintained in the society.

So, how can an industrial development strategy be appropriately chosen and determined? This is a very practical issue that needs to be judged from a historical perspective. There are six guiding principles for this issue.

(1) Principle of strategic goals. Industrial development is the process of expanding reproduction for the society. Hence, it should serve and align with the long term economic and strategic goals to strengthen the capability of the nation and to improve the lives of its people. Hence, cohesion will be formed with enhanced spiritual and material power. Moreover, international competitiveness will be increased and the goal of catching up will be realized and maintained in the long run.

(2) Principle of making good use of the environment. The environment, on one hand, refers to the current situation and the developmental trend of global economy and technology. On the other hand, it also refers to the specific social and natural conditions of developing countries and regions. Modern society is both a highly open and competitive one. If the strategy of industrial development fails or technology lags behind, even developed countries and regions might lose their leading position in the global economic competition and their comprehensive national economic power might be weakened to the level of developing countries. In this case, even a developed country might lose its competitiveness in the world, not to mention developing countries and regions. Hence, the pattern of maintaining global competitiveness pushes developed countries to improve their industrial development. In such a global economy, developing countries and regions have "three low levels and one lagging-behind" because of their weak social and economic basis. The "three low levels" can be described as follows.

a) A low level of industrialization. An example of this can be found during the initial period of the opening-up policy in China. At that time, the output value of industries, including manual labor industries, was 30% that of the agricultural industry. There was not any modernized industrial foundation; the production material industry only took up 26% of the total industrial output and the mission of industrialization of all departments in a national economy could not be fulfilled by using advanced production means.

b) A low level of comprehensive quality in technology. Not only the physical facilities and management skills in industries, but also the quality of their people, including technical staff, was at low levels. Moreover, the industrial structure was incomplete with a low level of coordination among industries which caused a low level of industrial productivity.

c) A low level of capital and investment. The savings level in developing countries and regions was rather low as the average income level is also low. As a result, the savings of the whole society is also low without a wide channel for capital accumulation and investment.

The one lagging-behind refers to the weak basic industries and industrial foundation. However, it can yield a competitive advantage laid on its large labor supply and a low level of salary payment, which reduces production cost and broadens the potential market. This is a unique competitive advantage in the adjustment of industrial structure in the global economy. Facing an international competitive environment, with congenital disadvantages and acquired competitive advantages, developing countries and regions have to make good use of their labor advantages by choosing and establishing appropriate strategies. They need to "catch up" and "surpass" developed countries when undergoing the process of industrial development. This relies on technology application and innovation, application of strategy and a smooth transition among stages of industry development. In fact, adapting to the environment can only help a little for national economic development.

(3) Principle of the "advantage of latecomers" effect. Modernized economic growth is a historical theme around the world. Countries that started modernization were named "first comers" while those who did it later were called "latecomers". "Latecomers" are usually less developed with a low level of economic development. Their industrial infrastructure started rather late, with a smaller scale and lower standards. With the existence of a "dual economic structure", their values, social culture and labor quality lag far behind the "first comers". However, with pressure and influence from "first comers", the "latecomers" strive to complete nearly 200 years of development by the "firstcomers" in only a few decades. They need to construct industries while at the same time achieve modern economic growth. In the process of global economic development, "latecomers" may skip certain stages of technological development as they have already been exposed to a better technological environment that allows them to import mature technologies for development. A famous US economist Veblen called this kind of situation, as the "advantage of

backwardness". An example was Japan, a "latecomer" after the U.S., which only spent about 50 years to develop its secondary industry and made the population in primary industry drop from 50% to 20%, while the U.S. took about 100 years to do so. As long as an "advantage of backwardness" is found in developing countries or regions, they must not be bounded by traditional modes of development. They only need to have an open mindset of "catching up" for industrial development. Thus, economic goals can be achieved.

(4) Principle of giving priority to the development of fundamental industries, leading industries, and strategic industries. Fundamental industries refer to agriculture, infrastructure, and material industries which have holistic effects on the national economy. Working as "bottleneck" constraints, they affect the scale and quality of industrial development and even productivity. Leading industries perform a motivating role among the upstream and downstream industries. Their multiplying effect can be determinant in national economic growth. Judging as the name implies, "strategic industries" are used to build future leading industries and they indicate a continuous development of a country or a region. They accelerate industrial development, and determine its direction, scale, speed and even competitiveness of industries. Hence, developing countries and regions need to choose and establish their strategic industries, with the priority of "fundamental industries", "leading industries", and "strategic industries" in their medium to long term industrial development.

(5) Principle of considering coordination and efficiency as the first. Industrial coordination includes the coordination among industrial structures, organizations (among big, medium and small industries), and industrial quality. They indicate the coherence in industrial structures and are the source of efficiency improvement. The adjustment of industrial structure can enhance economic growth and economic benefits, which rely on the development of leading industries that are productive and flexible, as well as on the coordination and its efficiency of industrial structures. From a static point of view, coordination of industrial structures refers to the quality of industrial elements, with little difference in technological performance and labor productivity among industries. The relationship among industries is clearly identified and stratified, no matter whether they are single linked or multi linked. Industries can serve each other in a complementary way. From a dynamic point of view, it refers to the coordination among the growth rates of different industries, and the smooth transition in industry stages, such as the coordination of alternation among agriculture industry – light industries – fundamental industries – ordinary processing industries – advanced processing industries – modernized service industries. If the coordination among industries is in a good condition, better coherence and better structural outcomes can be achieved. Consequently, internal industrial technology, innovation diffusion, external economic efficiency,

and long term economic stability will be improved and maintained. As a result, economic fluctuation and the loss from economic friction will be avoided.

(6) Principle of openness and internationalization. Modern scientific technology and economic development in the world have narrowed down the distance among countries, and the "global village" has been formed. Economic exchange and co-operation have been expanded and intensified. International diversification has been transformed from vertical diversification into parallel diversification within industries. An industry in a country may be found across a number of countries. This makes industries more open and internationalized or even globalized. The industrial structure of a nation shall be in line with that of the world so as to adapt to the technological revolution in the world. This process cannot be undergone individually. Otherwise, competitiveness in the global market will be lost, imbalance of payments will appear, and the demand of international markets will not be fulfilled. Also, the economy will be deteriorated and ultimately industrial growth will decline, and political power will fall into the hands of others. Hence, industries must follow the principle of openness and internationalization. Hungary was a typical example of this in the 1970s-1980s. The economic reform of Hungary once brought great economic achievements and was an example for other socialist countries to conduct economic reform. However, as Hungary deviated from the principle of openness and internationalization in industrial development, its industrial adjustment was off track from the rest of the global economy and direction of industrial development. Not keeping up with advanced technologies, its industrial infrastructure remained the same within 20 years. Materials and technologies became outdated and exports were hindered. As a result, there was a deficit in foreign trade, and economic growth could not be motivated externally. People lost their confidence in the government and they began to believe that "we probably will have better days if we change the ruling political party."[52] Economic problems linked with other problems may turn into political risks; and the political power of a communist government may then be lost.

8.2   The Functions and Establishment of Infrastructure

Infrastructure or social overhead capital refers to departments, facilities and organizations which provide social benefits, public goods and public services to the people and the society. Infrastructure can be divided into three major categories: productive infrastructure, living infrastructure and social infrastructure. Productive infrastructure includes mutually used facilities or fixed assets in a productive process or an integrated department for organizing production. They can be transportation systems, energy provision systems, water supplying and discharging systems, material supply systems, telecommunication systems, information supply systems, business service systems, etc. Living infrastructure refers to the social departments creating general conditions for living and providing public social services, like residential and public facilities, services for daily life, public affairs, etc. Social infrastructure means public services for the society and its people, like education, research and development, hygiene, environmental protection, judiciary and public administration services. Among the three kinds of infrastructure, the first two kinds are micro-level infrastructure while the third kind is a macro-level one. Micro-level infrastructure is the focus of this chapter.

Infrastructure is the fundamental material condition for social economic growth. It has a determining effect in realizing modernized industrialization and the process of economic take-off. We can say that, without modernization of infrastructure and modernization of industries, sustainable economic growth in a society is impossible. The functions of infrastructure can be described in the following three areas.

(1) Improving the investment environment and facilitating diversification and coordination in economic development. Infrastructure is directly related to the establishment of production departments; its developmental level affects the cost and efficiency of production departments directly and indirectly, and the quality and quantity of supply. For example, developed transportation and information systems rely on coordination among production elements and conditions to lower the cost of transition; it can also help build a wide ' connection between production departments and the market, maintain a balance in demand and supply and lower the cost of exchange. Therefore, if infrastructure can be well managed in developing countries and regions, it can help investors reduce capital investment, shorten the time of production, and lower the cost of production to gain better investment efficiency. If living and social infrastructure are developed well they will be able to provide a good living environment for investors as well as managerial and technical talents. Hence, lots of investments and projects will be attracted for improving facilities, for establishing production and trade centers, for enhancing the development of leading and supporting industries, for obtaining a reasonable distribution of productivity and the development of labor division, for making production and operation professionalized and modernized, and for improving the economic structure, for market unification, and for increasing labor productivity and economic efficiency of the whole society.

(2) Ensuring a smooth social reproduction process and creating more job opportunities. In a market economy, there is an increasing interdependence and linkage among production units and related processes, which makes social reproduction and the process of economic growth rely on large scale and high levels of infrastructure, like transportation, energy supply, information delivery, material transfer, etc. Hence, infrastructure is an essential element to ensure the smooth operation of social reproduction. Infrastructure can create more job

opportunities than direct production departments, and large scale of infrastructure development employs increasingly more people. In the 1970s, the proportion of the infrastructure sectors' employment in the total population was around 45% - 48% in Western European countries while it was 60% or above in America and 28% - 35% in Eastern European countries. Hence, it is worth it to spend efforts on infrastructure for economic development as it can reduce the high pressure of employment in developing countries and regions.

(3) Motivating the reform of economic and social structures. This can help boost efficiency in the social economy and increase people's living standards. Globally, indicators such as average electricity usage per capita, the percentage of workers using electricity, water and gas, the level of mass communication, the number of telephones for every 100 people, etc., represent the developmental level of infrastructure and are also used to measure the social economic development level. These indicators form the fundamental elements of social economic development in a nation because infrastructure performs a holistic role in coordinating key production elements and in linking social and economic processes. Infrastructure provides more economical and safer conditions than those created by individual production departments. Infrastructure can accelerate social production, increase labor productivity and profits in all departments and the whole nation, and improve the efficiency of economic growth.

As infrastructure possesses such special features in the social economy, it becomes a fundamental condition for modern industrial establishment and development. The deficiency of infrastructure in developing countries and regions usually becomes a "bottleneck" in the process of industrialization. Also it might cause a huge waste in resources and delay development. Therefore, developing countries and regions need to emphasize the functions of infrastructure in actualizing industrialization and achieving economic take-off. However, another aspect of infrastructure results in a large amount of capital, the long cycle of return and building difficulties, which are determined by the special characteristics of infrastructure.

First of all, because of the large scale of infrastructure, the support of peripherals, and the intensive capital accumulation and the technology for construction are questionable. At minimum, a large amount of investment is required as initial capital. At the early stages of industrial development, limited capital is a problem in guaranteeing a large scale infrastructure investment. However, from a long term and holistic point of view, investment in infrastructure is unavoidable. If investment in infrastructure is insufficient or peripherals do not fit projects, projects will not be completed, real productivity will not be formed, and investment will be largely wasted. Secondly, compared with the direct production projects, the set up time for an infrastructure project is longer with a lower rate of investment return, and a lower rate of capital return. For example, it takes about 5 – 8 years to set up a large railroad project in transportation, and takes about 10 years altogether including preparation work. For the large scale of transportation network, it probably takes more than a few decades to have it completed. Third, there is a need to have infrastructure developed ahead of time. It is not only a matter of time, as it also needs to guarantee investment return and technology advancement. Recently, the steam engine, electricity, and wireless technology have emerged together with micro electronic technology, satellite communication and nuclear energy, which are the major parts of the modern industrial revolution. New requirements for modernized infrastructure have now appeared which has become the material foundation for a comprehensive national economic development. According to research done by a U.S. economist named H. B. Chenery (1918), in a developmental stage when average income per capita increased from $140 to $1,120, the overall output percentage generated from infrastructure elements was increased from 16% to 30%.[53] This demonstrates that developing infrastructure in advance has become an objective requirement in the early and middle stages of economic development.

Based on the above, the time sequence in handling the development between infrastructure and direct production industry is a big issue in motivating economic growth for countries all over the world. In other words, how to set priority among fundamental industry, leading industry and supporting industry is seriously worth exploring. This issue must be considered when determining the pattern of economic development and the strategy of economic growth for a nation or a region. There are three representative ideas for this issue from developmental economists and growth economists. The first is the "Theory of Prior Development" put forward by Nurkse and H. B. Chenery (1918). Though they also advocate the idea of "balanced growth", they still emphasize the prior development of infrastructure. The second is the "Theory of Big Forward" brought up by P.N. Rosenstren-Roden (1902). It is about a one-off capital input with a large scale and comprehensive investment into infrastructure for developing countries to get rid of backwardness in their economy. The third is the "Theory of Pressure" by A.O. Hirshman (1915). He mentioned that, in infrastructure development, a country has to maintain a high growth rate in economic development, to follow an imbalanced growth strategy of centralizing capital and resources on direct production sectors first, to make use of income generated from these sectors and make use of the "bottle-neck" pressure from insufficient infrastructure, and to enlarge investment in infrastructure to stimulate its development.

From the perspective of practice, there are three types of infrastructure development in the history of global economy. (1) Advance Type, the development of infrastructure is far ahead of direct production development for a certain period. Examples are Britain and other Western European countries which started their economic development at an earlier time and their infrastructure development is far more advanced than others. (2) Coordination

Type, infrastructure is aligned with the needs driven from production or consumption and the formation and expansion of processing industries are parallel with that of fundamental industries. Examples are those later developed countries in Europe and North America, such as the United States, Canada and Sweden. (3) Stagnant Type, infrastructure development lags behind direct production development or industrial development. This is the most common type found since the 1950s. For example, infrastructure in the former Soviet Union and Eastern European countries and most of the developing countries and regions including China, fall into this type.

The three types of infrastructure development are still found nowadays. The most important periods for global economic development are the 1990s and the first half of the 21st century. As mentioned before, there is a drastic change in developmental opportunities and the conditions for developing countries and regions: the source of foreign capital is increasing; the technological level of infrastructure is upgrading; various kinds of matured technology are advancing; and industrial structure in developed countries is being refined; manufacturing industries are being transferred to developing countries; and the outward shift of technology is accelerating. However, infrastructure has its own functions and characteristics which are complementary with an advanced technological level and complex peripheral support. In order to complete an infrastructure project on time, a huge amount of capital investment is required. This makes developing countries and regions have to carefully consider the selection of strategy in the decision process of building infrastructure.

To consider the priority sequence between the construction of infrastructure and the development of direct production departments, developing countries or regions will suffer a problem of insufficient capital, according to the "Theory of Prior Development". In this case, prior development of infrastructure will not last long. According to the "Theory of Big Forward", on the other hand, foreign capital is required. However, foreign capital also has its limitation: big investment in infrastructure without giving considerations to the level of direct production developments would go beyond a nation's ability. Hence, it may suffer the problem of repaying debt. According to the "Theory of Pressure", there are other constraints such as insufficient infrastructure for social production and people's living conditions, an unceasing increase of "bottleneck", and low economic efficiency. In these cases, social capital cannot be accumulated easily while the problems of "bottleneck" cannot be solved. These are the problems based on the theories. However, the problems may be interpreted from the practice perspective. Adoption of an "Advance Type" can boost economic development as a result of increasing economic efficiency. However, the efficiency of investment on infrastructure itself is not that promising. Developing countries and regions may not have strong financial support and availability of other related materials. If the "Stagnant Type" is used, infrastructure projects can be utilized in a better way, or even overburdened, and the result of investment itself is better off, but the macro level of economic efficiency may not be that good as developmental needs and social production needs have not been met. This approach will not be that desirable either. From a holistic point of view, "Coordination Type" will be a more desirable approach. The reason is that fundamental infrastructure goes parallel with social production and people's living conditions in the process of industry establishment. There is a balance between fundamental infrastructure and social production and people's living standards. This can avoid unnecessary waste in utilization of capability, while efficiency of infrastructure investment can be increased. On the other hand, it can satisfy the needs of social production and people's living standards; improvements can be seen in the development of production and people's lives, and efficiency of departments in national economy will be enhanced as well. Therefore, the "Coordination Type" of infrastructure development is the best as it combines the advantages of the "Advanced Type" and "Stagnant Type" while their weaknesses can be overcome. This is a more suitable type for developing countries and regions.

In order to build a good foundation for future economic development, infrastructure establishment was emphasized by all countries in the world in the 1990s. As for the U.S., in order to speed up economic development, it initiated the first wave of infrastructure establishment in the late 19th century, railroad construction projects. The second wave was started in the early 20th century, after the construction of the continental highways. The third one was a wave of information highways in the 1990s. If the first and second waves of infrastructure established belong to the "Coordination Type", the third one should be the "Advanced Type", to build a foundation for the U.S. to enter into a high level of growth in the service economy of the 21st economy. The term "information highways" refers to optical fiber communication used in information networks which is an important infrastructure element for social production and people's lives in the 21st century. It has crossed the boundary of countries and extended into every corner in the world and each level of social production and society. Not only the States, other developed countries are also aware of the establishment of information highways. As a result, fiber optics has been laid onto the roads and residential areas to actualize the concepts of "optic fiber office" and "fiber family". It is predictable that the whole world will be entering into an era of optical fiber communication in the early 21st century.

Developing countries and regions have also noticed this kind of trend and have spent great efforts on a large scale of infrastructure development than ever before. Entering into the 1990s, developing countries and regions in Asia and Pacific Regions have also initiated large projects in fundamental infrastructure to motivate speedy economic growth. For instance, the cost of infrastructure projects reached $29 billion in Malaysia in the sixth 5-year plan during 1991-1995. Thailand made an investment of $40 billion in developing electricity supply, skyway transportation systems and in enlarging harbors, etc. Indonesia spent 29 billion US dollars in broadening its source of energy, highway facilities, residential and township infrastructure, etc. It was forecast that the expansion of infrastructure projects in Asian countries in the 1990s will increase their economic growth rates at a range of 2% - 4%. This can help refine and upgrade the industrial structure of countries and enhance the overall competitiveness in all countries and all regions.[54]

China is a large developing country. Based on general experience, the amount of infrastructure investment makes up 50% - 70% of the total amount of fixed assets. However, in China's case, the amount made up less than 40% all the time as there was too much debt in infrastructure investment, like insufficiency in electricity, coal, oil, transportation, and telecommunication systems, which seriously constrained the development of national economy. For example, the capacity of railroad transportation could only satisfy 65% of the actual needs at the beginning of the 1990s, the rate of railroad utilization was low; tele-communication could only satisfy 50% of the total demand. Due to insufficient raw materials, about 25% production facilities could not function at normal levels, causing an annual loss of 100 billion Yuan. According to the mode of industrial establishment in the fast growth period in developed countries and the model of giant countries designed by the World Bank, in order to achieve an average national economy growth rate of over 7.7%, the infrastructure investment should increase at a rate of over 12.7% yearly, investment of fundamental infrastructure should take up about 52% of the total production value, investment in industries should take up about 38% of the total investment in infrastructure, and investment in fundamental infrastructure should take up 40% or above. Based on the trend of high technology and heavy investment in infrastructure development, China should put over 50% of its investments into fundamental infrastructure from implementing the Eighth Five-Year Plan, and make optical fiber telecommunication a part of its fundamental infrastructure projects, and develop ahead high technological projects in appropriate balance. However, China is a large country with vast land and huge population, there is big gap in the developmental conditions in different regions. Hence, the mode of infrastructure shall fit with developmental conditions in a specific region. The "Advanced Type" can be used by those provinces with a higher level of economic development. For those provinces with better economic conditions but a medium level of economic development, they can adopt an "Advance Type" in certain areas to satisfy the needs of social production and people's living standards. For those provinces which have undesirable economic conditions and stagnant economic and industrial development, their infrastructure development can be slowed down to allow some adjustment, and large scale infrastructure development may not be appropriate for them.

8.3   The Selection and Establishment of Leading Industries

Rostow, a famous US economist, stated that economic growth is a process of the economic "take-off", a drive to economic maturity, and also a process of quick economic development with sustainability. During this process, appropriately selecting and develop leading industries is the second fundamental condition for developing counties and regions to realize economic "take-off" and sustainable economic growth (Rostow considers a capital accumulation rate of 10% or above as the first condition). This is determined by the role played by leading industries as core elements in the whole process of economic growth in a country or a region. Within the development of industry and economy, leading industries have their own unique positions and characteristics which enable them to achieve innovation in technology and organization in a country or a region. Such industries enjoy quicker economic growth and higher labor productivity than other industries. As the core of social production chains, leading industries have a stronger direct and indirect economic technological connection with other industries. They can stimulate the formation and development of many other industries. The function of leading industries can be illustrated as the effect of an inter industry connection. According to the viewpoint of Rostow, the functions of leading industries can be classified as three effects: "backward effect", "side effect" and "forward effect".[55] Leading industries can demonstrate more usage through the functions of these three effects, and can also bring a comprehensive economic growth for a country or a region. Because of this, if developing countries and regions intend to develop faster than advanced countries, they must highly emphasize the selection and establishment of leading industries.

So, how do they choose and determine the leading industries or what principles do they need to abide by? The following principles should be considered.

(1) The principle of maximizing income elasticity. Income elasticity, also called income elasticity of demand, refers to the relationship of the increase in demand for a certain product along with an increase of national income. This relationship is the ratio of the growth rate of demand for products and that of national income, assuming the price remains unchanged. In other words, income elasticity of a certain product in an industry equals the growth rate of demand for the product divided by the growth rate of the national income per capita. If the elasticity is greater than 1, the "income elasticity of demand" of a society will also be greater, and vice versa. As mentioned before, human need is an eternal motivator for social production and for enlarging social reproduction. It is the highest principle of social economic growth. In a market system, a country needs to have currency for making their payments, which represents the real needs of a society. Under the condition of a market economy, the human needs of a society are the greatest and the most direct motivator for industrial development and the change of its structure stimulates the change of the industrial structure and

development. Industries with a greater "income elasticity of demand" will create greater income for their products thus creating a higher level of need. Hence, these industries can have a greater motivation effect to the society, i.e., more opportunities of development and a higher efficiency of development. It is undeniable that industry development will be faster, the scale will be greater, and the rate in national economic growth will be higher. Therefore, "income elasticity of demand" should be taken into consideration while choosing and determining leading industries. That is to say, products chosen should have an "income elasticity of demand" greater than 1. Only these industries can act as leading industries, and improve income levels and consumption structures, as well as strengthen the potential of economic growth.

(2) The principle of maximizing increase in productivity. This refers to the extent of increase in a certain industry or a certain department. Here, productivity does not mean the productivity of a certain element, but is referred to as the productivity of integrated production elements, including labor productivity, capital productivity, energy productivity and average productivity of all the production elements. Under the social production and expansion of reproduction for industries with a higher increase in their productivity average, their technological advancements will not only be higher but their cost of production will also be lower. Hence, these industries will attract all sorts of resources to ensure a sufficient supply of technology and will then develop much faster, and produce cheaper and better products with a much higher productivity. The competitiveness of these products will be much higher within the international market and they will make greater economic contributions to the country. Therefore, these kinds of industries will have better conditions for development and stimulate other related industries to expand complementarily. In this way they will become the backbone of a country.

(3) The principle of having the greatest degree of inter industrial connections. Inter industry connection means the technological structure and the demand structure of products existing among different production departments and different industries. It is a special structural condition for social production development. The degree of inter industry connection refers to the degree of this kind of relationship, technological structure and demand structure of products, and their interdependency and inter-motivation. A development economist, Hirschmann, claims that the inter industry connection among industries should be a main principle for choosing and determining the kinds of leading industries. There are two kinds of connections, forwards and backwards. An example of a forward inter industry connection is that automobiles and machinery departments will have a forward connection with the iron and steel industry. An example of a backward inter industry connection is that coal mining and other similar kind of departments will have a backward connection with the iron and

steel industry. The inter industry connections is shown in Figure 8.1.

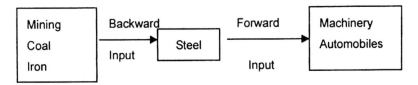

Figure 8.1

Generally speaking, the backward connected industries are those that produce agricultural products, primary products, raw materials, semi-finished products, while the forward connected industries are manufacturing departments. There are some special departments which can be considered both backward and forward. For example, machinery manufacturing provides the steel industry with capital goods, like machinery facilities (a backward connection), and also absorbs steel industrial products (a forward connection). In economic development, the stronger the interconnection among the forward and backward production departments, the greater they can stimulate the development of other industries and have better conditions and more opportunities for economic development.

(4) The principle of industrial coordination. Industrial coordination is the result of fine tuning industrial structure, representing a reasonable, coherent and efficient structural condition. This refers to the complementary function and relation among different industries in the structure of material technology. Under the process of industry establishment and social production, coordination of industries is a kind of holistic coordination which includes the coordination among production, technology, benefits, distribution, etc. When departments in industries are all in a coordinated state, they will bring a result of $1+1 > 2$ in the whole structure of industries of a society and a higher level of structural productivity with better coherence among industries. Then economic efficiency in industries will be increased, more wealth will be created in production and social economic development will be faster, healthier and more sustainable.

(5) The principle of the "advantage of backwardness". It has been mentioned in previous chapters that the "advantage of backwardness" is found in developing countries and regions. Compared with developed countries, they have rich natural resources, labor resources, mature technology and other combined resources which can generate efficiency in economic development. Through market mechanisms, its function as a core competitive advantage for industrial development can be further strengthened. Moreover, from the viewpoint of choosing and determining leading industries, we need to choose

those with greater "advantage of backwardness" for a better industrial establishment, to create more social needs through increasing income, and to provide a variety of products with low prices and high quality to make the social economy prosperous.

(6) The Principle of maximizing growth potential. Maximizing growth potential has two meanings. First, there is a certain renewable pattern in the operation of leading industries in the everlasting social production. After the decline of old leading industries, newly developed strategic industries will replace them and take up the role of helping the national economy to grow. This kind of replacement and interchange will continuously happen between old leading industries and new strategic industries. Second, both the growth rate of certain industries, and the industrial groups' contribution and impact to the society and the economy, will be taken into full account in the picture of economic growth. The prime focus is to choose those industries with profound and long lasting impact. Therefore, growth potential means that certain industries can have great impact in the society. The more direct the impact is, the greater the potential of growth will be and vice versa. Based on this rationale, industries with the most meaningful outcome shall be selected to develop as the leading industries. Though these industries may not have a high productivity rate, they can support continual economic growth. Hence, in order to maintain stable economic growth, developing countries and regions should pick those industries with great growth potential as their leading industries.

The above six principles have an interdependent relationship. Developing countries and regions shall follow these applicable principles to choose and determine their leading industries. The above mentioned principles judge the quality of industries themselves and the outlook of future development from different perspectives. The first principle concerns the motivating power of industrial development; the second one concerns the integrated development ability of industries; the third one concerns the expansion ability of industrial development; the fourth one concerns the self-adjustment ability of industries; the fifth one concerns the ability of using industrial advantages; and the sixth one concerns the potential motivation of industries for economic growth. Judging from all six principles, leading industries should be strong and powerful. They have made great contributions to economic growth. Developing countries and regions have to select and decide their leading industries for national economic growth first before concentrating on utilizing resources for industrial establishment, and ultimately for generating great synergy of economic take-off and material and technological foundations.

However, choosing and determining leading industries are at a preliminary stage in economic practice. There will still be a long way to go to put the principles into action. For developing countries and regions, economic take-off and sustainable economic growth are the processes of transforming their leading industries of agriculture into industries, a process of industrialization, an adjustment stage for social material structure and spiritual structure, the structure of different concepts, views and ideologies, and a phase of change and revival. During the whole evolution process, it takes a long time to build up leading industries, to foster and develop the whole social economy, and to reform social material structure and spiritual structure. This, in return, enables leading industries to integrate with the establishment of the whole industry mechanism. Judging from the economic modernization of most countries, the initial stage of developing leading industries usually took about 30 years. Though the time was shortened later, the minimum has to be around 20 years. For example, Britain spent about 30 years on it after 1783; France and the United States spent about 30 years after 1830; Germany spent about 20 years after 1850; Japan, Canada and the former Soviet Union respectively spent about 20 years in the late 19th century and before World War I; Brazil spent about 20 years from 1940 to 1960; Asia's "four little dragons" also spent about 20 years during the 1960s and 1970s. This process was indeed a revolution of industries. Because of the acquired advantage of backwardness, the time required for establishing leading industries may be shortened. That is to say, developing countries and regions cannot be too hasty for economic take-off, even though they may really want to enhance the development of their leading industries. They still need to foster and develop their industries in an objective way and build a good foundation for leading industries.

In addition, choosing and determining leading industries is a natural historical process. Starting from the first industrial revolution in contemporary world history, every country needs to understand its own economic context, technology, and the level of productivity development in the whole society before choosing and determining their leading industries. The result of the first industrial revolution is that social productivity has been transformed from a manual labor period into a machinery period. Britain and a few of other countries entered into a phase of modernized economic growth from their traditional one and formed the first leading industry, the textile industry, and the first leading industrial group that made up the textile industry namely the iron , coal industry, primary manufacturing and transportation industries. Though there were not any further revolutions in industries after that, a series of related industries emerged along with the extension of the first industrial revolution, including the development of railroads and automobiles. The expansion of railroad construction in the mid 19th century formed the second leading industries, the steel, railway, and machinery industries. The second leading industrial group comprised of the iron and steel, shipbuilding, textile, machinery, railway transportation, shipping transportation industries, etc. From the end of the 19th century till the beginning of the 20th century, the invention and application of electricity and the second industrial revolution was thus formed and led to the establishment of the third leading industries like electricity, the automobile, chemical, iron and steel. In the first half of the 20th century, with the deepening of the second revolution, the fourth leading industries emerged, such as the industries of the automobile, petroleum, chemical, iron and steel, and durable consumer products. People predicted that there would be a fifth cycle of economic boom from the end of the 20th century to the beginning of the 21st century, and a fifth group of leading industries would be established.

However, it might still be a long time before there is an economic boom in more developed countries. The fifth group of leading industries will be the information industry and will include new materials, new energy, biological engineering, aerospace, and other new industries together with those industries included in the fourth leading industrial group. During the industry development process, the evolution of leading industries and industrial groups is from low level to high level, from simple to complex while the volume of production is from small to large. In this process, the gradualness of development can be shown, – human need shall be fulfilled and its development stages should be in an order of low to high, the development of technology in social production is not interruptible. This order of development forms a basis for developing countries and regions in selecting and determining their leading industries and industrial groups. Should the gradualness of development be violated, the required potential for growth will not be accumulated for a quick, stable and healthy economic development. In fact, some areas may allow the "bouncing" development with the combined advantages of leading industries and industrial groups to shorten the time of industrial establishment. In the condition of late development with a low starting point, a shorter time may be used to complete the 250 year journey of industrial advancement and modernization of leading industries and industrial groups in more developed economy.

The following Table 8.1 shows the five major leading industries and their corresponding industrial groups over the last several centuries.

So, how to handle other basic relationships in regard to the establishment of leading industries?

Table 8.1 The Five Main Leading Industries and Industrial Groups

Project Sequence	Leading Industrial Sectors	Leading Industrial Group
First	Textile Industry	Textile Industry, Metallurgical Industry, Coal Mining Industry, Early Machinery, and Transportation
Second	Steel Industry, Railway Industry	Steel Industry, Coal Mining Industry, Shipbuilding Industry, Textile Industry, Machinery Industry, Railway Industry, and Transportation, etc.
Third	Electricity, Automobiles, Chemistry and Steel Industry	Electricity Industry, Appliance Industry, Machinery Industry, Chemistry Industry, Automobile Industry, and Second Leading Industries
Fourth	Automobiles, Petroleum, Steel, Durable Consumption Goods Industry	Durable Consumption Industry, Air Space Industry, Computer Industry, Atomic Industry, Composite Material Industry, and the Third Leading Industries
Fifth	Information Industry	New Material Industry, New Energy Industry, Biology Industry, Aerospace Industry, and the Fourth Leading Industries

(1) The relationship between agriculture and industry. As mentioned earlier, the process of social economic growth is a transformation process from a traditional agricultural economy to a modernized industrial economy, emphasizing industrialization and modernization for the national economy. Because of changes in the developmental phase, the pace of industrialization in developing countries and regions is fast, the importance of agriculture as a foundation may be overlooked. A critical issue about ways of treating agriculture in the process of industrialization is worth considering. The relationship between agriculture and industry, especially the leading industries, should be considered in the process of industrial development. Marx made a good point, "agriculture under a certain developmental level, whether abroad or at home, is the foundation for the development of capitalism."[56] It means that agriculture is a foundation which can be established locally or overseas. Without a high level of agricultural productivity which is more than just to satisfy the needs of agricultural laborers, industries cannot be developed independently and take off, not to mention developing leading manufacturing industries. Therefore, in the

process of establishing industries in developing countries and regions, agriculture has to be developed as a foundation when choosing and determining leading industries. When industrialization reaches a certain level, for example the GDP per capita is about US$1,000–$3,000, industry can nurture agriculture by increasing investment to promote the development of agriculture from irrigation farming to machinery farming, chemical farming and biological farming, and to strengthen the foundation of well developed agriculture for the modernization of social production and people's living standard.

(2) The relationship between leading industries and strategic industries. Leading industries help actualize economic growth in a society and can be a foundation for social benefit. Undeniably, they play an important role in a society. However, strategic industries, as only the possible potential leading industries in the future, have some uncertainties, including a huge amount of input, high risk and many other unpredicted factors. Therefore, making a correct decision is not easy. But this point often be ignored. If strategic industries do not receive enough attention in the developmental process, there will not be any motivation or support for national economic growth. We need to be aware that innovative technology and newly developed industries are not equivalent to leading industries, and the strategic industries that we choose should meet the requirements stated in the above six principle. Meanwhile, they should have an innovation mechanism, an emergence of new production variables drawn from integrated technology, a sustainable growth quicker than that of the total economic output, and a great impact on the entire economic growth. All these elements are critical for transforming strategic industries into leading industries. As a result, efforts shall be put onto predicting and developing some potential leading industries of the next phase when establishing leading industries of the current phase. Theoretically, this can be possible. In fact, there may be some constraints from the society. Strategic industries may not have enough government support, as the government has to handle declining industries and maintain political stability. The outcome is that there may be an imbalanced industry structure or wrong judgments in executing policies. This may potentially lead to poor economic growth and widen economic distances with developed countries. For example, when facing a drastic change in the global economy, the French government failed to make a right decision to focus on high technological departments in the industrial development of the late 1970s and created a wide technological gap with American and Japan. Developing countries and regions may be distracted by goals of catching-up or the political aspiration of leaders, so they may not consider economic standards and conditions before making great efforts in developing strategic industries from isolation. As a result, structural imbalances among industries and tremendous waste might occur.

(3) The relationship between leading industries and supporting industries. In developing countries and regions, both of these industries are part of the social industry. As described earlier, leading industries have a strong motivation in social economic growth which tightly links backward, middle and forward industries together. All the industries that work closely with leading industries are called supporting industries. The relationship between leading industry and supporting industries is the relationship of the controlling and the being controlled, or the determining and the being determined. On one hand, the development of supporting industries should comply with the development of leading industries and support and serve them. On the other hand, supporting industries may not be completely subordinated to leading industries. They can promote the development and improve the productivity of leading industries. If leading industries are being isolated from supporting industries, their function in economic growth will be weakened.

(4) The relationships among leading industries, backbone enterprises and leading products. Leading industries play a leading role in a national economy. The basic and key components of an industrial chain in leading industries are the backbone enterprises and its links to consumers in the market by products, especially leading products. Without the existence of backbone enterprises and leading products, especially large and medium enterprises and their leading products, the function of leading industries cannot be executed. Hence, developing countries and regions should spend substantial efforts on establishing large and medium enterprises, and on the exploration and production of branding products, in order to build sustainable industrial development for economic take-off in the long run.

8.4 The Historical Trends of Industrial Development
There are definite rules and historical trends in industrial development. Developing countries and regions should recognize and grasp the rule and trends when catching up with developed countries so as to have a higher level of industrial development and industrial structure, to link the fostering and developing of industries with the global economy, and to make industry establishment more international and modernized.

Under the social production and reproduction process, industries have been developing from low levels to high levels, from simple to complex, from a small scale to a large scale. The rule of development can be demonstrated as the following trends.

First, the diversification of industry and the upgrading of industrial structure. In the process of social economic growth and development, human beings are the main body to integrate the power of nature into production and further, to transform it as social productivity. It is a process of intensifying social production and reproduction. Based on this process, people start to explore more about the regularity of social production and reproduction. Industrial establishment and industrial development form a process of unifying themselves together. For industrial construction, there are four features needed to be mentioned: 1) the sequence of industrial development is the first industry, the second, the third, the fourth, and then the fifth; 2) manufacturing industries start from light industries, to fundamental, then to heavy manufacturing, and finally to advanced processing industries; 3) production techniques change from ordinary machinery systems to automation systems and then to intellectual automation systems; 4) the industrial space moves from the earth to outer space. Along with advancements in aerospace technology, developed countries, like the United States, are now exploring a new industrial field, outer space commerce. It includes five areas of services and products which are related to space: space transportation, satellite communication, satellite remote sensitivity, collecting information regarding the earth in the areas such as agriculture, harvest, climate, mineral resources, geology, forestry, ocean pollution, etc., space material research and processing, and facilities related to space industry. Some experts in this field predict that satellite commerce, from 1985 – 2010 will reach $600 - $1,000 billion, with an investment return ratio of 1:14.5. The form of product develops from natural material product to synthetic material product and to service product. This can demonstrate that industrial structures change along with the advancement of scientific technology and social productivity, from among the industries to within an industry, from industry produced means to industry produced products, with continuous industrial diversification and structural upgrade. This trend is a result of and is a symbol of technological advancement and development of social productivity. It can also promote the world's economy to transform from a material-product economy to a service-product economy and from an earth economy to an outer space economy.

Second, the internationalization of industry. This refers to the internationalization of technological and economic connections among industries which can be demonstrated by the performance of transnational corporations and the expansion of international trade. Correspondingly, international trade has extended the scope of the world; linking markets of all different countries to form a world market. The total volume of world trade has increased at an annual rate of 11%, which directly drives the development of transnational corporations. Transnational corporations are global economic entities with a fundamental network linking up all industries for organizing production and business operations across the world. They have become true "Global Factories" and "Global Industries" with "Global Products". American scholars investigated a US based automobile called Pontiac LeMans in 1989 and found out that, their design was finished in Germany, but last installation work was done in Korea, with the engines produced either in Korea or Singapore and oil pumps manufactured in the US and batteries made in Korea. This is to show that national boundaries are only for politics but not for production or consumption.

This kind of global economic development has pushed more and more countries, developed or developing countries, Western capitalist or socialist countries, to intensify their reform, to continue to open up, and to increase their participation in international investments in activities of production, trade, and finance. The industrial establishment has pushed industrial development internationally and extended the economy into the global cycle.

Third, the high tech trend of industry. Though the term "High Technology", with short form as "high tech" in English, was originated in the United States, there is not a definite meaning for it until now. Generally, it refers to those new technologies with their fundamental theories built on latest scientific achievements. It can promote a higher economic efficiency and higher value-added production, and can penetrate into all the economic and social areas. Currently, with the continuous developments in global scientific technology, with different kinds of explorations and applications, with advanced technologies commercialized and industrialized, the development of industries has certainly been motivated. On one hand, new industries based on the explorations and applications of high technologies emerge, such as information industry with microelectronic based technology, new energy, new materials, aerospace industry and bio engineering industry. On the other hand, advanced technologies are applied to the restructuring of traditional industries in order to make them more advanced and integrated. Since the establishment of the first high tech development zone, the Stanford Industrial Zone, in US in the 1950s, there have been over 300 similar kinds of zones in the world with about 200 zones that achieved a certain scale economy and one third of which located in the USA.

High-tech zones have become an important form for technological advancement of industries in every country. During this trend, the microelectronic industry has become a symbol for comprehensive capability of a nation or a region. It is predicted that the IT industry which is built on micro electronics would become the largest industry by 2,000, and the core area of industrial competition in the 21st century will be in the IT industry. Looking back at global economic development from a holistic point of view, we see that starting from the 1970s, with a boost of new technologies, almost all countries put emphasis on electronic technology to improve economic efficiency.[57] The microelectronic industry is a new industry that has more vitality and potential than the iron and steel, electricity, automobile and other traditional giant industries. The electronic information industry has become the largest industry in the United States, and knowledge production possesses a significant proportion in the total output value, reaching 8% or above in the year 2000 which has already gone beyond that of automobile industry. The annual growth rate of the sales volume of integrated circuits has reached 68% in the world, that of calculators have soared to 52%, and the annual growth rate of the microelectronic industry is over 20%. Based on statistics, two thirds of the total output value in developed countries is currently related to the application of microelectronics. The profits of IBM, the largest computer producer in the world, and that of Microsoft have already exceeded that of ESSO, the largest international oil company, in 1990s. Up till the end of the 20th century, the electronic industry was the second industrial department, just after energy.

According to a research report conducted by the US government, up to the year 2000, the sales volume of 12 items in the four high tech areas of the material industry, information systems, manufacturing systems, and bioengineering reached 356.6 billion US dollars. The development of all these new products and new industries symbolize not only high technology in these industries, but also the technological advancement of industrial structures which brings profound economic and social changes. Within the 10 years of 1980 - 1989, the annual growth rate of the US electronic industry was 8.2%, while that of Japan was 10.8%, Korea 28.2 %, and Taiwan 18.6%. The developmental speed of the electronic industry in these regions was almost 2 - 3 times of the average speed of development in their national economies. Similar phenomena can be also found in developing countries and regions like China. The average growth rate of the electronic industry within the 10 years of 1980 - 1990 was 23.6%, the total output value of the electronic industry reached 67.32 billion Yuan in 1990 and 86.6 billion Yuan in 1991, which was 26.9% higher than in the previous year. The 1990s were a critical moment for China, as the annual growth of its electronic industry accelerated really fast, at the rate of 25% -30% which was 2.5 - 3 times the average annual growth rate of the total output value. It is predicted that the industrial establishment in almost all countries in the world, developed or developing, will be moving towards a developmental path of technological advancement in the 21st century. Otherwise, they cannot actively participate in the diversification and competition of the global economy.

Fourth, the flexibility of industry. The term "flexible" may be meant "hollowing out" to some westerners. Because of the development of scientific technology, industry has become more flexible. As the results of the first and second industrial revolutions, machinery replaced and extended the reach of human limbs and enlarged the space of activities, and production systems like machinery facilities, which became the main determining factors in production and rigid physical systems. As the results of development in modernized scientific technologies, for example the third industrial revolution, and the emergence of the electronic information industry, computers or "intellectual machineries" replaced human brains, and they can complete all kinds of repetitive labor work and operate and control production machines in a fast, precise and stable way, which make factory production, office work, and housework "automated" and "informationized". Besides this, they also extend production into every corner of ocean, land and space, and make production to be a "three-dimensional" production. They change production gradually from material-based into informational-based, from intensive and large scale into dispersed and small and even individualized, from standardized, specialized into multi diversified, personalized, popularized. Along with all the above, as well as achieving "to supply enough in time", they make intelligence and knowledge replace machinery as a decisive role in the process of social production and economic growth. These changes in the social production system are what we call "to have the production system flexible", which is in fact to make industrial development flexible. This is the highest level of production development.

Fifth, being a human oriented industry. This trend goes along with the technological advancement and flexibility of industries. It integrates the intellectual and knowledge factors into the process of economic growth and changes the labor force to be intellectual worker dominated rather than physical laborer dominated. It also changes the production process from being controlled by laborers to being controlled by robots, causing more and more laborers to break away from material and machinery production; so, "unmanned factories", "unmanned hospitals" and "unmanned shops" appear in developed countries like UAS and Japan. Similarly, people start to use innovation in management activities, in learning, in conducting scientific experiments, in product exploration, and in other kinds of mental activities involved with creativity. It makes learning and education play a decisive role in the social production process and gradually become an independent department with a more important and decisive impact on industrial structure and economic development.

Because of these changes, the development of a modernized economy depends on the involvement of technology, intensity of knowledge, and the composition of science, technology and knowledge. Based on related information, the increase in science, education and knowledge have played a dominant position in the national economy since the 1980s, contributing 60% - 80% of the total output value. E. F. Denison, a famous US economist, predicted that the contribution of US education to the US economy was 23% from 1929 - 1957 and its contribution to the growth of US income per capita was 42%. At the same time, Schultz also estimated that education's contribution to income per capita was 25% - 45% in the USA.[58] We also need to notice that this trend will be further intensified. Hence, social economy becomes based on knowledge and information. Therefore, education, especially higher education and professional technical education, and technology become independent industries in modern economic development. Quality of laborers in social production and reproduction becomes a key element and represents the competitiveness in industrial development. As a result, in industrial establishment and development, investments are mainly made in education and technology instead of on material facilities, to produce high qualified laborers instead of material products, and industries then transform from the objective oriented into the subjective oriented. From this subjective trend of development, "it is predicted that the 21st century will be the era of education."[59]

Chapter Nine

Technological Advancement: The First Driving

Force of Modern Economic Growth

The development of human society - the development from a traditional economy into a modern economy, in fact, is a developmental process of social productivity, which is in essence a process for technological improvement. Without developments in science and technology there will be no development or improvement in social productivity, not to mention the development of social economy. In today's modernized global economy, the gap between developing and developed countries is actually a gap of technological advancement, which is a reflection of the competition in science and technology, especially in high technology. Science and technology serve a prime function in modern economic development and economic competition. If a country possesses the advantage of high technology, it will have greater economic growth and greater competitiveness in development. Without high technology, countries will not have economic growth but if a country can overcome the hindrance of slow technological development, it can catch up with or even surpass developed countries. Otherwise, the gap between developed countries and regions and underdeveloped countries and regions will widen. Even for developed countries and regions, if they do not pay sufficient attention to the development of technology, they will be degraded to developing countries and regions.

9.1 The Meaning and Fundamental Patterns of Technological Advancement

From the perspective of productivity economics and managerial economics, technology basically means experience from production practice (for example, techniques, know-how, labor skills of people, etc.) and the sum of material and knowledge elements drawn from the applications of science in the production process, including "hard techniques" from an engineering perspective, such as physical production facilities, scientific knowledge in production techniques, etc., as well as "soft techniques" from a management economy perspective, such as management techniques, decision-making techniques, etc.. From the economic perspective or a broad perspective, technology advancement means that, because of the improvement in tactics of labor and workflow, and the development of new technology and new facilities, new products, new techniques, new materials and new energy, as well as the enhancement in scientific decision-making techniques and economic management techniques, labor productivity can be increased with the same or less input, but with more output.

From a historical point of view, technological improvements are a unified process of gradual and dramatic improvements. A gradual development of technology means that a society, under the social production process, will be able to create more wealth to survive and develop. People carry out reform and innovation in current technology or the technological system, or come up with new principles or new methods in some fields or systems on the basis of existing principles of technology and organization. This kind of technological improvement happens frequently and is characterized by not breaking the existing scope of technology, technology and management systems, and management technique system, and is displayed as the evolvement of technology, so it is therefore called "gradual" technological improvement. "Dramatic" technological improvement means to have a new revolutionary breakthrough based on existing technology and the accumulated knowledge about the natural objective system as well as to promote changes in labor tools, in machinery facility systems or production systems. Therefore, new technology and systems will emerge; new industries will be formed; economic structure will experience re-engineering and reform and labor productivity will be greatly enhanced. Typical examples of "dramatic" or revolutionary technological improvement are the several technological revolutions since the farming revolution in the last phase of the Primitive Society. This kind of technological improvement is also called technical innovation or innovative technological improvement.

Based on the nature of this process, there are two types of technological improvements, gradual or evolution and dramatic or innovative. However, as the aim of our research on technological improvement is related to economic growth and development, especially the speeding up of development, which bears the aim of satisfying the growing needs of a nation, to achieve the multiple goals of a nation, to making a better society between man and man, and an more harmonious environment between men and nature. Hence, there is a need to further investigate the fundamental patterns of technological improvements to find out the relationship between technology and economic growth or economic development.

(1)   The Pattern of Technical Innovation.

Technical innovation is a kind of leap, a kind of revolution, and a kind of qualitative change. In other words, it is a vertical development or accumulation. So, it can also be called the pattern of vertical technological improvement. The concept of "Technical Innovation" was first put forward by a western economist named Joseph Alois Schumpeler (1883-1950). He established the theory of dynamic development with innovation as its core in his book *The Theory of*

Economic Development in 1912. Based on his viewpoint, "innovation" refers to the setting up of a new production function, that is, a composition of elements in production, like $P = f(a, b, c....., n)$. It mixes a new kind of production element or condition into the existing production system. The newly introduced production elements include: 1) introducing a new production; 2) introducing a new technology or new method; 3) exploring a new market; 4) acquiring a new source of materials; and 5) implementing a new organization of industry.[60] These five elements can be grouped into two main areas: 1) new facilities, new materials, new product development, and new invention and application of technique; 2) update and improvement in organizational management methods in social production. From the perspective of epistemology and technical innovation, it is a process of deepening breakthroughs, continuous development and unceasing revolution in the understanding of nature and social economy under social production. The initial knowledge of the scientific element is undeniable. The new concept is based on existing scientific elements, yet has surpassed the old principles and mechanisms. Therefore, a holistic view of technical innovations in human social production shows that it is a process of continuous breakthrough, continuous accumulation, continuous take-off and continuous application of scientific knowledge, as well as a process of continuously exerting revolutionary impact on economic growth and economic development. The integration of all these processes is a pattern of vertical technological improvement. It's mainly reflected in the following forms. First, the level of technology is upgraded along with the scale of social production and the complexity of structure. For example, the development of machinery materials: stone – copper – iron, and natural materials – synthetic (modernized advanced material); the development of machinery power: wind or water – heat – electricity – nuclear energy; the development of information processing capability of machines: material and energy systems without the capacity of handling information but with manual operations of its control and management – information and control systems based on material and energy systems; the development of products: material products – intellectual products, natural products - manufactured products, coarsely processed goods – finely processed goods, single category – multiple categories, single function – multiple functions. All in all, technical innovation brings a process of evolution, that is, a process to extend the reach of our human limbs and brains. Second, the more developed an economy, the higher the labor productivity. Some statistics shows that, Bessemer converter (invented in 1855) and Siemens-Martin open health process (invented in 1857) were two huge technological innovations in the late 19th century that in the 50 years from 1900 to 1950 increased the output of iron almost five times from 4 million tones to 200 million tones, and increased the output of steel almost seven times from 2.8 million tones to 208 million tones.[61] The growth of the output of iron and steel in the second half of the 20th century relied on three kinds of technological innovations – continuous hot-striping in 1923, continuous pouring in 1952 and oxygen steelmaking in 1950. Before 7,000 B.C., society was primitive with stone as the means of labor with the growth rate of productivity labor about 1% ~ 2% per 1,000 years. After 2,000 B.C. there was the slave/feudalist society with copper and iron as the means of labor and a growth rate of labor productivity at about 4% per 100 years. During the 200 years after the first industry revolution in 1760, means of labor developed from manual tools to bulk machinery, and, the growth rate of labor productivity was about 1.5% -3% per year. Since 1950, with the emergence of the third technological revolution, means of labor was transformed from machine automation to intellectual automation with social productive forces upgraded from machinery into science, and the growth rate of labor productivity was 4%-5% per year.[62] This tells us that from a historical point of view, technical innovation is a process of continuous accumulation, continuous revolution and continual development of social productive forces, and a process of acceleration of productivity improvement. This reflects not only the nature of technical innovation pattern, but also the basic functions of technical innovation in social economy and in the theory of economics.

(2)   The Pattern of Technological Diffusion

Technological diffusion refers to diffusion and application of new technology through market or non-market channels to expand the application scope of technological achievements. This motivates economic growth for a region, a country, or even the whole world. During this process, though there may not be any major fundamental changes in technical innovation itself, its diffusion can actually insert a greater power than technology itself in motivating economic growth. It is true to say that the pattern of technological improvement is rooted in innovation, as its nature is a reflection of past accumulated innovation. However, it is different from vertical expansion and take-off of technical innovation, as it is a horizontal movement of innovative technology, which is being copied, promoted and dispersed in the social production process. Through the upgrade of products, the improvement of technological process and the expansion and enhancement of industries, this pattern of technology innovation can improve the quality and quantity of products, increase productivity growth rates of industries and enterprises, and speed up the economic growth of a society so as to achieve a lot more than the pattern of technical innovation. A Chinese scholar named Dr. Lam stated in his book *Technological Innovation Economics* that, "diffusion contributes more to the economy than innovation", which can demonstrate that "the economic growth rates in semi-industrialized countries during the period of 1960 - 1985 were greater than those of highly industrialized countries", because "those countries have made use of copying and diffusion" to obtain the benefits from the pattern of technological diffusion while "industrialized countries get the benefits mainly from innovation."[63]

9.2 Technological Advancement – the First Driving Force for Catching-up in Modern Economy

Technological advancement is the source of development of a social economy. The economic competition among developing and developed countries is, in fact, a global competition of technologies. In modernized global economic growth, technological advancement has become the first driving force and essential element in developed countries and regions, which stimulate their sustainable economic growth. Meanwhile, it will also become a decisive element in developing countries and regions as they try to catch up with developed countries. The main functions include: 1) saving the amount of input, while increasing the volume and the quality of output; 2) reducing the reliance on natural resources while increasing stability in economic growth and competitiveness in the international market; 3) enhancing diversification and advancement of industry structure and growth rate of labor productivity; 4) motivating the formation of new industries, expanding the associating effects among industries, stimulating new needs of labor in the society, creating new channels for employment, and improving the livelihood of people.

In the 1950s, the economy of the United States was developing at such a fast pace that it eluded the explanation of traditional economic theory of capital and labor factors. A well-reputable US economist R. Solow has conducted a large scale of statistical analysis with practitioners and economists and presented his results in a masterful paper, entitled "Technological Improvement and Production Function" in 1957. In this paper, he created a scientific method to predict contributions of technological improvement in economic growth. This model was based on a formula of growth speed, using "residual method" to measure the contribution from technological improvements. The general form of production function is as follows:

$$Y = F (K, L; t)$$

Here K and L represent the input of capital and that of labor respectively, and Y is the volume of output while t is a variable for time, and $f (k, l, t)$ is a differentiable function. Based on this method, Solow analyzed the doubled labor productivity in non-farming departments in the U.S. during the period of 1909 – 1949, of which 87.5% was attributed to technological improvements and only 12.5% came from the increase of capital per labor. Though this kind of figure was not widely accepted at that time, almost all economists later accept that technological improvements have made a tremendous contribution to economic growth. In this century, the ideas of Solow and other western economists can be further proved correct. Some statistics shows that, the contribution of technological improvements to economic growth in industrialized countries has reached 50% -70%, some even have reached up to 60% -   80%. In the U.S., the output of private non-farming industries increased 216% during 1909 – 1949, in which the increase of labor input was 54%, capital was 102%, and technological improvement was 146%. Based on calculation, contribution from technological improvement was 68% while that of labor and capital was 32%.[64] After 1949, the contribution rate from technological improvement soared along with an intensified scientific revolution; up till now, it has reached 80%. The annual growth rate of total output of the former Soviet Union in 1965-1975 was 8.18%, in which 5.03% was generated from technological improvements, and the contribution rate was 63%; the annual growth rate of total output of the national economy in Japan during 1952 – 1966 was 9.5%, and the contribution rate of technological improvements was 65%; the annual growth rate of total output of the national economy in Korea during 1966 – 1976 was 10.47%, and the contribution rate of technological improvements was 22%. The annual growth rate of total output of the national economy in China during 1952 – 1982 was 10.67%, and the contribution rate of technological improvements was 19%, which increased to 24% in 1992, and even more in 2004. This shows that in modernized economic growth, technological improvements are the main motivation for national economic growth and labor productivity. Reasons for economic lagging behind found in developing countries and regions like China are the slow speed and low level economic growth, and small contribution rates of technological advancement. In developing Countries, the motivation effect of technological improvements has not been fully exerted.

In the process of modernized economic growth, because of the results from technological advancement and diffusion, technological improvement has become the first motivator. Technological improvements not only extend but also replace the reach of human limbs and brains. Owing to "extension" and "replacement", there are repetitive revolutions in social productivity. Technological improvements are playing an even important role in economic growth, and hence becomes the first motivator and powerful lever for economic growth. There is a challenging issue to be faced by the governments of developing countries and regions: what are the things required to do in order to escape from poverty and economic laggard? Most economists believe this relies on technological improvements. According to the history of economics, if traditional human-based strategy with increment in facilities for expanding production are used, then the under developed countries will need 746 years to catch up to the advanced levels of developed countries. Therefore, only intellectual exploration and technological improvements can shorten the process. During its Song and Yuan Dynasties, China used to be a leading power in the world. But due to the Renaissance, British people widened their minds and quickened their technological improvements so that they shortened the catch-up process to merely 400 years. It took the Germans about 70 years to catch up with British while it took the Americans only about 40 years to surpass the Germans. Due to intellectual exploration and technological improvements, the Japanese only spent 15-20 years to reach the status of a developed country. Technological improvements are the only way to improve economic performance for developing countries and regions in the late 20th and early 21st century. This is an objective pattern independent of people's will. Presently, most developing countries and regions are suffering the constraints of human resources, material resources, financial resources and natural resources, so that economic development cannot be sustainable though a large input of labor and capital. Only through the use of technological improvements can natural and labor resources be fully utilized in developed countries and regions for saving input, increasing output, improving quality of output and minimizing the gap between developed countries and regions. As a developing socialist country, China has adopted a three step catch-up strategy to development. China has doubled its total output value by 2,000, half of which was due to technological improvements. This goal could not be achieved without technological improvements.[65] Therefore, to rely on technological improvements is a fundamental belief for modernization and boosting an economy. The prime position of technological improvements can be demonstrated in these elements and is actually reflected through the process of actualizing modernization in developing countries and regions. This is the first rule for an economy to catch up.

The functions of technological improvement patterns are different at different stages of economic development. Developing countries and regions need to fully recognize, grasp and apply these ideas to catch up with the advanced levels of the world economy.

Developing countries and regions need to make use of technology diffusion, and the introduction, absorption and imitation (for certain innovations) of advanced technology from developed countries in the stage of economic catch-up and take-off. They need to adopt the "taking and using" strategy to nurture and develop their industries, to expand the scale, to improve the structure, and to enhance their quality and productivity. This can minimize the amount of investment, shorten the time for speeding up economic growth, and narrow the gap with developed countries. A Chinese scholar Dr. Liu Yulin has used the data of foreign technology diffusion, local knowledge increase, and the ability to utilize technology in 25 semi-industrial and industrial countries and regions during 1961-1985, to explore this issue. By using the formula of $Y=ZQ^aT^bC^c$ [66] and designing three types of models for experiment, he has proved that "technology diffusion, technological improvement and the ability of applying knowledge locally are the three main elements for economic growth", and "diffusion makes more contribution on economic growth than innovation"[67]. Because of this, the speed of economic growth in semi-industrialized countries between the years of 1960 -1985 was faster than that in industrialized countries (see Table 9-1).

Table 9.1 Division Growth

Year	1960-1968	1968-1973	1973-1979	1979-1985	Changed Volume
	I	II	III	IV	V-I
Contribution from	Model I				
Pervasion	1.9	2.0	1.8	1.7	
Innovation	0.8	0.4	0.1	0.3	-0.2
Investment	2.0	2.2	2.3	1.8	-0.5
Growth (Estimated)	4.7	4.6	4.1	3.8	-0.2
Growth (Actual)	5.2	5.8	3.5	2.4	-0.9
Difference	0.5	1.2	-0.6	-1.4	-2.8
Contribution from	Model II				
Pervasion	2.0	2.1	1.9	1.8	
Innovation	0.4	0.2	0.0	0.2	-0.2
Investment	2.3	2.6	2.7	2.1	-0.2
Trade	0.4	0.0	-1.5	-0.5	-0.2
Growth (Estimated)	5.1	4.9	3.1	3.6	-0.9
Growth (Actual)	5.2	5.8	3.5	2.4	-1.5
Difference	0.1	0.9	0.4	-1.2	-2.8
Contribution from	Model III				
Pervasion	1.8	1.9	1.7	1.7	
Innovation	0.5	0.3	0.0	0.2	-0.1
Investment	2.2	2.3	2.4	1.9	-0.3
Demand	0.6	1.3	-0.9	-1.2	-0.3
Growth (Estimated)	5.1	5.9	3.3	2.6	-1.8
Growth (Actual)	5.2	5.8	3.5	2.4	-2.5
Difference	0.1	-0.1	0.2	-0.2	-2.8

Note: this form comes from Section 7.3 on p. 146 in *Technology Innovation Economics* by Liu Xielin.

However, along with the application of technology diffusion in economic growth in developing countries and regions to shorten the economic distance with developed countries, some changes are found as illustrated in Table 9.2.

Table 9.2 shows that the contribution of technologic diffusion is greater than innovation in newly-industrialized developing countries (or called semi-industrialized countries); however, the role of technological innovation as the first driving force in developing countries and regions, which intend to develop economically, is becoming more and more important as the distance between developed and developing countries is shortened and the level of technology is enhanced.

Table 9.2 The Differences between Actual and Estimated Growth

Compared with Advanced Countries (1973-1983) [68]

	Actual Growth Differences	Estimated Growth Differences	Explanation Elements			
			Pervasion			
A Team	–	–	–	–	–	–
B Team	0.5	1.0	0.4	0.4	0.3	-0.2
C Team	1.0	1.0	0.2	0.2	0.5	0.1
D Team	3.0	3.1	1.4	0.9	1.0	-0.2
Japan	2.4	3.5	0.5	1.0	2.1	-0.2
Latin-America NICs	1.9	2.3	1.5	-0.1	0.8	0.1
Asia NICs	6.0	5.7	1.6	2.9	1.7	-0.4
Europe NICs	1.3	1.2	1.0	0.0	0.5	-0.3
All Countries	1.5	1.7	0.7	0.5	0.6	-0.1

Note: NICs mean New Industrial Countries and Regions

This implies that technological improvements play a critical role in developing countries and regions if they intend to catch up to the level of advanced countries and regions, to align with international levels, and to compete against the U.S. Because of this pattern, Japan invested a lot in technology in order to obtain great achievements in technological improvement. In the 1960s, Japan followed the diffusion pattern, adopted a strategy of "Introduction of Technology", introducing a great deal of technology from overseas, and insisted on integrating technology introduction, reformation and development to motivate economic growth. After its comprehensive national strength caught up with advanced countries and ranked second among western capitalist countries and third in the world, following the pattern of technological advancement, Japan turned to the strategy of "building the nation with science and technology" in the 1980s, which was to explore the latest technology and undergo technological advancement initiatively, rather than introducing technology. This pushes up the cost for research and development to 14.6% which is higher than the level of USA (i.e., 8.8%), and reaches an international level. In 2001, the cost of research and development took up 2.98% of the total output, which was higher than that of USA – 2.8%. The same thing has been found in some countries and regions in the "Four Little Dragons" in Asia. For example, in the 1950s and 1960s, Korea entered into an age of economic take off which lasted for about 30 years. In the 1980s, Korea adopted the strategy of "building the nation with science and technology". The cost of research and development from 1981 – 1991 increased 10 times, and its percentage in the total output rose from 0.6% in 1981 to 1.91% in 1991, and to 2.92% in 2001, close to that of the United States. The reason for executing a change in economic strategy in Japan and the "Four Little Dragons" is that, they intend to compete with developed countries to be the best in the world, in which technological innovation, the basic form of technological advancement, plays the critical motivating role.

China is a large developing country with 10 times the population of Japan. Is it possible for such a large country to follow the pattern of technological advancement and realize catching up as its driving force? History and reality can give us a definite answer: yes. As mentioned earlier, since the reform and opening-up, China has obtained a strong driving force for economic growth; the annual increase in its national output value reached 9.3% in 1993, and the productivity of labor hit up to about 6%; thus, China has become one of the most economically active countries in the world. This is the reality. At the same time, history has showed that Chinese people possess invaluable creativity. Back to the 6th-7th century, China was one of the three most powerful countries in the world and maintained its technologically advancement and economic development at advanced world levels until the 14th-15th century. According to the publication *Chronology of Great Events in World Natural Science* in 1975, before the Ming dynasty there were about 300 great inventions in the world, of which 175 came from China, and accounted for 57% of the total, while inventions from the rest of the world only accounted for 43%. Hence, a UK scholar R.G. Temple stated that, "almost half of the fundamental inventions and discoveries for world modernization came from China". "Modernized farming, modernized sea transports, modernized oil industry, modernized observatory, modernized music, ten-digit mathematics, currency, umbrellas, fishing rod thread, the trolley, fireworks, gunfire, torpedo, poisonous gas, parachuting, fire balloon, highflyer, whisky, brandy, Chinese chess, printing, and even the basic design of the steam engine, etc., all come from China". Besides, "The typography was not actually from J. G. Gutenberg but from a Chinese. The blood circulation of human beings was discovered by a Chinese not by W. Harvey. Newton was not the first one to discover the First Law of Motion, a Chinese was".[69] Temple claimed that, if there were no modified techniques and facilities in sea transportation including compasses imported from China, then the great discovery of the New World by Europe would not have been realized, Columbus would not have sailed to America, and Europeans would not have established their colonial empires. Consequently, he drew the conclusion that, "Most of the world's innovative power came from Chinese people instead of Europeans, but we (Europeans) do not need to feel frustrated." Hence, the west owes a lot to China, and "now it is time for the West to appreciate the contributions the Chinese have made."[70] This British scholar deeply understood the history of China and the history of the world, and made fair comments on things that happened in the past. People can be assured that, with innovative capability and a history of epoch contributions to world technological advancements and modernized global economic development, and with great economic performance and its reform and opening-up since the last 20 years of the 20th century, China will surely be a tremendous driving force, revive itself, and even make immense contributions to the world economy in the 21st century.

9.3 High Technology – the Symbol of Competitiveness in the 21st Century

High technology possesses a tremendous driving force for modernized social development. It is a catalyst for changes in the world structure and the symbol of competition in the 21st century. Since 1980, both developed western countries and developing countries and regions have been busy launching strategies based on high-technology to create modern economies. For example, "Star Wars" (also named as SDI – Strategy Defensive Initiative) and "Re-industrialization" in the USA; the "Euroka" plan in Western Europe and "Revitalizing Industries" in France; the strategy of "Building the Nation with Science and Technology" and "The New Scope of Human Science" research plan in Japan; "Speeding Up Strategy" and "the sketch for science and technology development till 2000" for the countries of the Council for Mutual Economic Aid in the former Soviet Union; the "863" high technological research development strategic plan in China; and other developmental strategic plans made in the mid 1980s by the "Four Little Dragon" countries in Asia, Brazil,

Canada, India, etc. Moving to the 21st century, every country places emphasis on increasing their input in high technology. In 2001, 83% of the world's research expenses was from that of the OECD, of which 44% was from America, 28% from Europe, and 17% from Japan. It was predicted that the development budgets of the USA and Japan would go up at a much faster rate than the increase of total output. The research expenses of developed countries are approaching 3%.[71] These are no coincidences or simple copies of strategies from one country to another. It is the result of the first driving force from the technological advancements of developing countries and regions to catch up and to obtain a position in the world economy, and it's particularly the result of the strategic impact of the development and application of high technologies in the world economy and the society.

Up till this moment, the competition of high technologies has been the most profound one among countries in world history. Evidence and statistics have showed that competition and breakthrough of high technologies have brought tremendous benefits with new ways of production and new patterns of economic development. Some people thought that almost all the major changes found in social production, economy and social life in the past few decades were actually attributed to the invention, exploration and application of advanced technologies. As advanced technologies are already at the highest strategic point of technological advancement, they can be comparable with armed forces for a country or region or national corporations in the competitions for benefits in the aspects of economics, politics, and military. If a country wants to be the strongest one in the world or maintain its position, like the USA or Japan, it needs to develop high technologies in order to possess the advantages in these areas. Otherwise, one scenario will appear in such a developed country as USA. That scenario has been described by US scholars Humter Lewis and Donald Allison in a book titled "Global Economic War". According to Fell, a former president of a US correspondent bank, "If the position of having an advanced technology industry is going to collapse, then the United States will be degraded to a developing country within 10 to 15 years".[72] This implies that not only developing but also developed countries are facing great challenges and they have to rediscover the trends of world development. In this aspect, the analysis and viewpoint of a famous Chinese scientist Qian Xuesen are correct. He pointed out that the 21st century is a science and technology-based century, a century of "science and technological wars" or "intellectual wars" instead of military wars. During "war", advanced technology has become the symbol of competition among countries, the symbol of their economic, political, and military power, as well as a symbol of comprehensive national strength, and also the symbol of the capability of a country or region to stand tall in the world. Only with advanced technologies, can a country control "brains", obtain the strategic initiative in "science and technological wars", acquire the golden key of the present and future, and win in world competitions.

Presently, a large scale war like technology fight has been going on all over the world. During this high technology war, every country has already left the starting point, and they have been developing at dramatically different paces. America is playing a leading role with Japan as a competing partner. Initially, Russia used to be a leading competitor too. However, the power of Russia deteriorated in 1991 when the Soviet Union collapsed. America is now facing strong competition from Japan. According to the military report "Plans for Important Technologies" by the US Department of Defense in June 1989, among the 22 high technologies items that the US is concerned with, there are 14 items in which the US is stronger in than Japan, while there are 2 items in which both USA and Japan are equally powered, and 6 items that Japan has stronger than the US. These areas are military aspects where the US only maintains a competitive advantage in software exploration. Japan is good at civilian technology. Western Europe is in the second tier when it comes to possession of high technology and cannot be compared with the US or Japan. The third world countries, like China, India, Brazil and Asia's "Four Little Dragons" are mainly in the third tier, though some of them may develop faster and can be classified in the second tier. Because of the weak economic strength or comprehensive national strength, the rest of the countries in the world that still remain near or even lag behind the starting point of technological advancement belong to the forth tier. This is the current situation of the technology war.

So, what is the basic driving force to form such a situation in the world? Some people say it is the economic growth in order to actualize or maintain strategic goals, others consider it is the need of national security. Both of these views make some sense. However, the basic driving force should be the need of maintaining the position of a strong economic nation, because the national economy is the foundation of national security. This is determined by the economic function of advanced technology in industrialization, which can be demonstrated as follows.

First, industrialization of advanced technology can greatly enhance labor productivity and boost economic growth. Deng Xiaoping pointed out that, "science and technology are the first elements of productivity." The increasing of labor productivity leads to an increase in national income and the overall wealth of a nation, is a determining factor to ensure the sustainable growth of a national economy, and to improve society and the living standard of its people. Evidence has demonstrated that there is a parallel relationship between the adjustment of industry structure and the enhancement of labor productivity. Under modernized economic development, drastic changes in industry structure and labor structure coincide with the development, commercialization, industrialization and internationalization of technologies. The employment of intellectual labors has kept on expanding with the reduction of employment in traditional industries and the increase of employment in industries like electronics, space technology, biology, new materials, etc. This makes the factor of intellect, rather than the factor of physical labor, a determining function in the holistic production process. Because of this, advanced technology has become an impetus for economic growth and a main source for strategic national economic development.

Second, high technological competition can also motivate market competition. It allows a country or a region to reach the highest point in market competition and obtain advantages. After the Second World War, competition among countries and regions has become more intense along with technological development, and industrial wars unceasingly occur where technology itself becomes the product of fierce competition and even the most important product. Since 1990, competition in the world economy has been reflected by the content of technology in various products and by the level of technology in competition. Exploration and application of technology were production-oriented and market-oriented with a minimized cycle of commercialization and industrialization of the achievements, or even with a zero distance in the cycle. During this process, the shorter the cycle, the more the products with high quality. This makes international market competition even fiercer. If a country or a region possesses the advantage of advanced technology, the market competitiveness of that country or that region will be much stronger in the international market. External needs will then help motivate the economic growth of a nation to reach a larger scale at a faster pace with a higher quality of development.

Third, the development of high technology itself is becoming the foundation of victory in the competitions for all major production elements in the world economy or in the political and military contests in the 21st century. As we know, there are six major technology clusters which are getting increasingly commercialized and industrialized in the development of modern economy and technology. They are: information technology, new material technology, new energy technology, biotechnology, marine technology and space technology. Among these technology clusters, the first three clusters form three objective elements (information, materials and energy) which are the material foundation and knowledge foundation for other kinds of technology and industries; the forth cluster is a new technology cluster formed by the application and exploration of the achievements of the first three clusters; the last two clusters are the new industrial technologies by which people boost production both intensively and extensively in order to expand the space of survival and development. All these researches and explorations can widen the horizon of human beings and improve their ability to remake the nature, to enhance social productivity, and bring about drastic changes to the lives of people. Under the pressure of world economic growth and the steady increase in population, constrains in natural resources for social production have become more obvious while production per capita and livable land has been reduced. High technology is the only outlet to increase natural resources and to enlarge social re-production, productivity per capita and livable land. From a worldwide perspective, the more technological advantages that a country possesses, the more production elements and social wealth it will receive. This country will therefore be able to enter into new spaces in the universe ahead of other countries and regions to make social production, to create new living space, and to establish its own empire.

Based on the aforesaid reasons, exploration and development of high technology are called for and considered to be a good solution to the problems of slow economic development by people everywhere in all countries, especially developed countries and regions in the 21st century. In the competition between the United States and Japan, Japan tries to have a higher productivity per capita than that of USA, with a high technological output value of up to 60% -70% in the total output value. It seeks this in order to become a strong economy in the world and realize the Japan-centered "Century of the Pacific" and hold a leading position in the world just as the US. Based on export volumes of high technological products in OECD members, the proportions of US and Japan in 1970 were 25.8% and 20.2 % respectively, 24.6 % and 17.2% in 1975 respectively, and 31.1% and 26.9% in 1980 respectively. It seems that the US still has a competitive advantage over Japan in the 21st century.[73] Although the technological level of Western European countries are still below that of the US and Japan, they want to do something to change this, as Europe has always held a significant position in the history of civilization. In order to reach the levels of the US and Japan, they have spent great efforts to utilize their economic strengths and advantages in some technologies (like high-energy physics, aerospace technology, fusion energy, etc.) to stand together to establish a unified Western European market with exploration and development of high technology for civilians. So, what about a developing country as China? Deng Xiaoping claimed that, "The coming century (the 21st century) will be a century of high technology development", and "China needs to develop its technology in order to claim a prime position in the world".[74] This is a reflection of confidence and determination of the Chinese people in the 21st century, and is also an inevitable trend of the development of world history.

9.4 The 21st Century - A Century of Human Resource

As mentioned earlier, the development of industries is an outcome and a symbol of social productivity development. Looking back on the history of human society, labor tool-based social productivity has undergone three phases of development in accordance to the enhancements in science and technology (i.e., the first phase, manual tools; the second phase, generic machinery; the third phase, intellectual machinery or science production). In the first and second phases, labor tools were developed to extend the reach of people and increase their physical power. People in these two phases did not receive any formal education or training, but learned through some kind of apprenticeship; the third phase, on top of performing the functions of the first and second phases, also replaces and extends human brainpower, which allows most laborers to move away from material production processes, and provides more people the opportunity for more formal training and education. Thus, when they go back to the production, they can take more brainwork in the forms such as research, invention, exploration of technology, experiment, marketing, etc.. This forces the direct production process to change from a material product production process into a non-material product production process, thus widely extending the scope of production. Because of this drastic change in social productivity development and the trends of advancement, internationalization, high technology-orientation, flexibility and subject-focus in industrial development, and quality of labor have all become more and more important in the establishing and development of industries. This means education, an independent department in the economy that produces human resources, plays an even more important and decisive role in economic growth and development. US scholars John Naisbitt and Patricia Aburdene have predicted in their book *The Big Trend of Year 2000* that, "In the next 1,000 years, human resources will become a more competitive advantage in our global economic competition."[75]

The advantage of human resources in economic development and its function in making education an independent department in the development of economy are based on advanced technologies in industrial development and informationization. The world is becoming smaller and smaller where a nationalized economy is becoming an international economy and the material production economy is becoming a service economy and information economy, and the international society is becoming an information society. This leads to an all around open world with a unified global market and multi-level competitions. Simultaneously, continuous exploration and industrialization of technology have helped establish a global network of capital, raw materials, technology, etc. Within the process of economy growth, if a country can make the best use of this network, then it will outweigh others in competition and quickly develop its leading industries, which include high-tech industries like information technology, new material technology, new energy technology, biotechnology, marine technology, and space technology. These industries have an established developmental mode of "three intensiveness" in technology, knowledge, and intelligence, where human resource has become the key issue in industry development. A famous US scholar Thurow L. C. stated in his book *The Competition of 21st Century* that, "the fate of development (of these industries) depended on the advantages of people, i.e., the advantages of intellectuals and techniques."[76] The 21st century is a century when "people-based advantages are going to replace the advantages of traditional economic development. Green revolution and reform on material science make raw materials no longer an advantage, computers and telecommunication make accumulated capital no longer an advantage. From now on, only technology and human resources will be real advantages. When comparing these two elements, human resource is even more invaluable as new technology can be easily copied. Those enterprises and countries which have entered into the global economic competition can achieve success only by placing lots of emphasis on education, on quality of people, and on enhancing workers' skills.[77] Hence, all those leaders who are facing the challenge of and bearing the responsibility of leading their countries or regions onto global levels should acknowledge the new mindset that, education is to produce and re-produce human resources and productivity. Education is a special industry standing for the economic competitiveness of a society, and they should discard the traditional idea that education is just for inputting cultural or political beliefs. Without a right mindset towards the industry of education, these countries will not have the capability of moving towards the 21st century. As a result, their advantages will be lost, and their countries and people will fall behind others. This can be applied to both developed and developing countries and regions.

During the process of modern economic growth, education is a critical symbol for the potential of the economic development of a country, especially a developed country. With advanced education to continuously produce and re-produce human resources of high quality for economic and scientific development, industrialized developed countries enjoy continuous development with improvements in labor productivity and enhancements in technology. The US is a good example. Since 1979, the enrollment in US universities has been doubling every 20 years; from 1960 to 1970, the enrollment in its universities tripled 2.4 times, increasing the number of people with master degrees or similar qualifications. The percentage of students entering universities at the right age was 27% in 1955 and 40% in 1965, and has kept going up since then. D. Bell predicted in his book The Arrival of Post-Industrial Society that, America would become a group-based knowledge society in the year 2000, and then there would be 10 times more enrollment for higher education than that in 1940.[78] According to the overview of the trend of international science and technology development in 2003 described in the "Report of International Science and technology Development in 2004", till 2003, the percentage of receiving higher education in young people in the countries of OCED reached up to 45%, while the percentage of employees with university degrees was 28.2%, and 36.8% of these employees were Americans. Besides this, America has also been taking in international students to complete undergraduate, master and doctoral degrees or engage in science research. In this aspect, Americans are smart in that they are paving a way for their future. They realize that developing the education industry will help them boost American economic development and keep their economic competitiveness and maintain their superpower status in the world.

As human resources are critical to the growth of an economy, education will be a leading industry in the 21st century. Toffler claimed that, the informationization of a society would make industry, commerce, and finance further rely on the information of the market and technology. Information is the most important element for every country and region. With knowledge and information, the chance of standing out in the coming century will be much higher. Knowledge and professional skills are the focus of competition among people, as the production in a society has been transformed from being dominated by blue collar workers to being dominated by white collar workers. Winning or losing, it all depends on the multitude of knowledge and information that a country possesses, and they are the source and symbol of wealth and also the symbol of power of a society. This gives education a historical mission that education together with information will become a leading industry which is critical to the economic growth and survival of a country or a region.

Along with the development of education and information industry, social economy operates quicker and quicker. Under economic development in the 21st century, capital will turnover at a unprecedented speed with high growth rates in wealth, and time will be a decisive production factor as it can shorten the time of economic turnover greatly, and there will be a historical transformation in social economic development. This is a good opportunity and a challenge for developing countries and regions. If a country can take this invaluable opportunity to integrate traditional industrialization with modernized industrialization to achieve a parallel development with developed countries, it will be a successful country. If not, it will have to retreat from the world stage. As knowledge capital is different from money capital and other kinds of visible capital, it can be utilized by lots of countries at the same time. Hence, developing countries and regions have to pay extra attention to their educational industries and the production and re-production of high quality human resources, and strengthen their capability in the application of knowledge and all kinds of innovative technologies, so that they can have speedy economic growth.

However, there are more difficulties in the development of an education industry and the production and re-production of human resources than in the development of other industries, and it takes more time for the former to develop, especially in developing countries or regions. The reasons are that: first, the value of knowledge and human resources are not popular enough to arouse sufficient attention; second, the formation and development of the education industry should have the foundation of an advanced development of material-producing industries, and should be based on the strong needs to develop an information industry. Unfortunately, these two conditions are not mature in developing countries and regions, and therefore the education in these countries falls far behind that of developed countries and regions. Developing countries and regions should be aware of this if they intend to catch up with world economy levels.

Though China is a developing country, its education industry has been greatly developed since its reform and opening up at the beginning of 1980s. There are certain bases and some barriers in establishing education as an important foundation of the economic industry. Based on information provided by UNESCO in 1984, the illiteracy percentage in China's total population in the 1980s was 23.7% with an entry rate of 98% in primary schools but with only an entry rate of 37% in secondary schools. In 1984, the number of high school students was 1.396 million with only 1% of the population enrolled in universities. There was a wide difference when compared with developed countries. The difference was not small even when compared with India. The number of high school students in India in 1984 was 3.442 million with an entry rate of 9%. Even though there was an adjustment in the national high school education structure in 1991, the growth was still slow. The number of new graduate students enrolled was 30 thousand which was the same as in 1990, while the number of graduate students was 88,000 which dropped by 5.4% compared with that in 1990. The number of enrolled undergraduates and junior college students was 620,000 which increased by 1.8% compared with that in 1990, while the number of students at school was 2.044 million which was a bit lower than that of the previous year.[79] Such a slow growth in education is alarming and really needs to be paid close attention to. Otherwise, China will lose great opportunities due to a gloomy development in education, which will further hinder the 3-step strategic goal and lead to failure in the 21st century.

A conclusion can be drawn when summing up the above. Under the process of modernized economic growth, especially after entering into the 21st century, human resources are a unique and the most important resource of all economic resources, it represents the developmental level of modern social productivity and the direction for world economic developmental. Education which produces and re-produces human resources will be the most important industry and exerts great influence on the future growth of economies. We can say that, from now on, whoever possesses a well developed education and a number of high quality talents, especially the talents in entrepreneurship, management, technology, economic education and administration, and qualified labor, will be the one that has the most efficient capital to create wealth, and a bright future with a leading position in the coming world. This country will be the one who also makes impressive contributions to human kind. No matter whether the countries and regions are developed or developing, their leaders should fully realize the importance of education and talent development in economic development and competitions of all countries from a historical perspective. Otherwise, the spirit of the future will be lacking as there are no leaders with such an ambition. China has a tradition of education. The leaders of China clearly realize that the key of the realization of four modernizations lies in the modernization of science and technology, which is based on education. It is forecast that, in China, education as an economic industry shall be vitalized and be the base of power for China to take part in world economic competition.

Chapter Ten

Opening-up: A Definite Rule for Modern

Economic Growth

It has been well covered in previous chapters that the world, with the development of modern scientific technology and economics, is shrinking into a "global village". From the aspect of the operation of economics, as social productivity development has become highly advanced and the economy in every country has been internationalized, the operation of every economy is on a global track, and globalization has been strengthened through the interdependence and close interaction of economic activities of countries. The economic growth of a country greatly affects the economic growth of others. Actualization of economic growth depends on the international mobility of production elements and the enlarged needs in international markets and the economic growth of other countries. Economic bonds among countries will form a global economic operation mechanism for stimulating economic growth, where no single country will be able to undergo speedy economic growth or actualize economic take-off by itself. The development of the world economy has witnessed that survival comes from an open-mind while failure is caused by stubbornness, a definite rule of modern economic growth. In a modernized world, any country or region, especially the developing countries and regions, all need to insist on keeping themselves open to the outside world, to enlarge the multitude of their openness, and enhance the level of their openness if they intend to have speedy economic growth, and to realize economic and societal modernization.

10.1 Modern Economic Growth - A Process of Opening-up

The result of economic growth is the increment of total material products and labor services produced by a country and a region; it is the increment of the total sum of production and average productivity per capita; as economist Rostow stated, economic growth is a dynamic process, that transforms a farming economy into an industrial economy, into a service economy, and from a traditional economy into modernized economy. Within this process, the farming industry not only needs to make itself more open and coordinated with regional or federal markets, but also absorbs technology from countries all over the world and applies them into its production process for industry revolution and economic take-off, to make industrial production a leading position in social production and economic growth, and to reach a mature stage of sustainable economic growth, a new stage of modernization and internationalization. This matches what Engels said 120 years ago that, "the time for the economic sector to survive individually and silently has ended, and that they are now interdependent. They rely on the improvements of countries both near and far away, and even the whole changing world."[80] This is to show that in modern economic growth, no country can escape from exchange and competition in international markets, no country can survive without using the economic resources from other countries during internationalization and globalization of the economy, and no country can live by themselves without touching the global economy for growth. Openness is an attribute for the process of modern economic growth.

Looking back on the history of economic growth, we can reflect back to the days when Europeans escaped from the "Dark Age" into prosperous times, and the days when Britain initiated the industrial revolution to actualize their economic take-off. Based on a research done by British scholar R.C. Temple, the introduction of Chinese inventions enabled Europeans to establish a modern culture and achieve modern economic growth. Examples include: modernized farming, modernized sea transport, a modernized oil industry, modernized cosmological observations, modernized music, 10-digit mathematics, manual trolley, all levels of fireworks, firearms, torpedoes, poisonous gases, parachutes, hot air balloons, aircraft, brandy, whisky, printing techniques, textile technologies, basic design of the steam engine, paper making, shipbuilding, navigation technology, etc.[81] Among all these, textile technology and the design of the steam engine have directly affected the formation of the first industrial revolution in Britain, with manual production replaced by bulk machine production, leading to the first industrial revolution in social productivity, paving the way in Britain for a breakthrough from a traditional farming economy into a modernized industrial economy, creating a big leap in the global economy, where capitalist societies enjoyed an improvement in social productivity and created more wealth in less than 100 years time than what had been created before in all of human history. The diffusion and mobility of the results of the first British industrial revolution gave rise to the economic take-off of France, America, Germany, Italy, Spain, Belgium, Switzerland, Sweden and other European countries, and led them into a new age of modernized economic growth. With cross-regional influences of new technologies in the 20th century, countries like Japan, Russia, the "Four Little Dragons" in Asia, Brazil, Mexico, China, and Malaysia also enter into the age of modernized economic development, some of which even have moved into the stage of developed or medium developed countries. That is to say the first industrial revolution, the British "Global factory", and the economic take-off and modernization in economic growth in certain countries and regions, all relied on the horizontal diffusion and mobility of technology and the opening-up of countries.

Apart from a technology-driven economic boom and modern economic growth, international mobility of products and connections among countries has also been strengthened to promote global economy progress. Economic history tells us that 85 years after the birth of the world's first railroad in 1825, there were hundreds of kilometers of railroads across the world in 1910. At the same time, the dominant position of the steamship in world transport was also recognized, and other results of modern technology like the exploration of sea routes, the telegraph, and the railroad systems in America, Asia and Africa merged every national market into the world market and extended the scope of openness and formed centers of world trade. Before the "Great Geographical Discoveries" at the end of the 15th century, the Mediterranean Sea was the center of world trade. However, after the "Great Geographical Discoveries", the center shifted to the Atlantic Ocean which became a center of the world economy, especially for capitalist countries. This is due to a number of factors, such as the various industrial revolutions in Britain, France, Germany, Italy, Russia, and America in the mid 18th century. These revolutions helped to push world productivity to a higher level and embedded countries into the economic mechanism of capitalism, turning Britain into a "Global Factory" whose total industrial production output accounted for half of the world's production output. In the middle of the 20th century after the Second War, a peaceful development age emerged in the world's economy. This occurrence moved along with the third science technology revolution initiated in America and spread across many countries. The most active countries were in the Asian Pacific region, achieving impressive economic growth rate.[82] As the growth in one region stimulated the development of another, the development of Japan helped that of the "Four Little Dragons", and even that of South East Asia, eventually leading to the great development of China. This wave of economic growth caused the global trade center to start to shift from the Atlantic region to the Asia-Pacific region. Thus, it is predicted that the 21st century will be "the Century of Asia-Pacific".

Taking it a step further, the enlargement of international trade volumes and the expansion of international markets are always hand in hand with the growth of the world economy. This is a fundamental rule in the highly-developed modern market economy and also an attribute of the production expansion. For a country or a region, an increase in international trade volume is a symbol of its broadened openness to the external world. Openness reflects an economic aspect of the relationship between a country or a region and the rest of the world. This is the proportion of the total volume of imports and exports of a country or a region to its GNP. When expressed in a formula, openness = total volume of imports and exports/total output value. This implies that the higher the percentage of the total volume of imports and exports, the greater degree of openness there is, and vice versa. In normal situations, small countries are more open during their economic take-off and sustainable economic growth, but the degree of openness in large countries is smaller. However, a general rule of openness is that in the process of economic growth, countries, big or small, all need to engage in international trade for diversification and competition with other countries and regions in order to utilize their comparative advantages. Because the value of their products need to be realized in the market and they want to earn the greatest amount of profits possible, they have to go beyond their boundaries and undergo a process of exchange. Since the first industry revolution in the mid 19th century, the speedy growth of the world's economy has stimulated the growth of international trade. The most impressive performances can be found in the following two periods. In the First Period (1840 – 1860), because of the first industrial revolution, the growth rate of world trade was double of that of the world economy. Until the period of 1880 – 1913, the growth rate of world trade was still greater than that of the world economy. Hence, American economist I.B. Kravis named international trade as the "handmaiden of growth".[83] His viewpoint was correct from the perspective that production determines circulation, and that the growth of the world's economy requires and enhances openness of every country and motivates the development of international trade. However, we also need to realize the accumulated negative side-effects that international trade can have on world economic growth. During the Second Period (1955- 1973), the annual growth rate of world trade volume was 7.3% while the average growth rate of the world's industrial production was 6.3%. Even though the growth rate of international trade volume and that of the world's industrial production both dropped after 1973, the former one still outweighed the latter one. The average annual growth rate of world exports between 1973 and 1981 was 3.6% while that of the world's industries was 2.7%. According to the analysis drawn from Section 2 of Chapter 13 in Ji Zhu's *An Introduction to Global Economy*, there was a tremendous growth in the world's trade volume after 1981: it was 4.3 % during 1980 – 1990 and 6.9% during 1990 -1999. The above illustrates that modern economic growth is the result of the diffusion of global technology which enhances the development of industries and products; while the speedy growth of world trade and the shift of world trade centers are the objective requirements of modern economic growth. Under modern economic growth, the repeated but expanded cycle of the process from production to exchange and back to production is a process with an increasingly strong requirement of openness which extensively pushes the economy of a country and a region more open to the world. The shift of the world's trade center and speedy economic growth reflect the opening of countries under modern economic growth.

10.2 Openness Promotes the Mobility of Production Elements and the Development of Industries

Most developing countries and regions have the similar problems of a poor economic foundation, low levels of national income and education, so that they are severely short of capital, technology and talents in economics and administration. Hence, it is difficult for them to develop their industries and to have fast economic growth. In the development of a modern world economy, as the economies of countries become more and more interdependent and open, international factors have greater impacts on economic growth, production elements move increasingly more frequent among countries and become the great motivating force for economic growth in developing countries, regions and even the world. In the cycle of international economy which is continuously open, low labor costs and great market potential in developing countries and regions attract inputs of surplus capital, shifting industries, and inflows of experienced management staff from developed countries and regions. Combining their own advantages with the inputs of foreign capital, technology and management experience, developing countries and regions can form their own comparative advantages, speed up their infrastructure development, develop their leading industries and industrial groups, enlarge the scale of their social productivity, enhance the level of social productivity, and create the conditions for economic take-off and the foundation for sustainable economic growth.

Let's take a look at the impact of international capital flow on the solution of insufficient capital in developing countries and regions.

The fundamental elements for quickly developing industries and actualizing economic take-off in developing countries and regions are to have an increase in investment rates, to expand the scale of investment, and to undergo a large scale of production investment and infrastructure development. However, with low income levels and low saving rates, developing counties and regions cannot meet the needs of a large amount of investment. The concept of the "Two-Gap Theory" was put forward in 1960 by two US economists, H. Chenery and A.M. Strout, and offers a solution to these issues. The main idea of this theory is that: there is a gap in developing countries and regions between the efficient supply in savings, foreign currency and absorption, and the demand of resources for actualizing economic development goals. An effective tool for making up this gap is to attract and utilize external resources.

A formula for the "Two-Gap Theory" can be expressed in the following way:

$$I - S = M - X$$

in which, I represents investment while S stands for saving; M stands for imports while X for exports; $(I - S)$ on the left hand side of the formula represents the difference between investment and saving, which can also be called "gap of saving"; (M - X) on the right hand side of the formula is the gap between imports and exports "gap of foreign currency". This formula tells us that in open economic conditions, the greater part of investment demand than local savings can be filled by of the greater part of import and export, and the latter can be filled by the inflow of external resources.

In the "Two-Gap Theory", the balance of saving gap and foreign currency gap is a kind of posterior balance, like the balance between total supply and total demand in the national income balance formula. The reason is that investment, savings, and imports and exports all change independently with the individually planned volume before the adjustment. In practice, the gap between investments and savings may not equal to the gap between imports and exports. Developing countries and regions have to make adjustments if this scenario occurs. If the gap of savings is greater than that of foreign currency, i.e., $(I - S) > (M - X)$, balance can be achieved by reducing local investments or increasing local savings. On the contrary, if the gap of foreign currency is greater than that of savings, i.e., $(M-X) > (I-S)$, balance can be achieved by reducing the amount of imports or increasing the amount of exports.

This kind of making up derived from the "Two-Gap Theory" is a pessimistic solution, as it's a self- balanced method without utilizing external capital. Although in the situation of $(I-S) > (M-S)$, balance can be achieved only by reducing local investment or by increasing local saving, the former method will affect the development of industries and the conditions for economic take-off, and will reduce the rate of economic growth in developing countries and regions. The latter method is not practical for the short run. Under the situation of $(M-X) > (I-S)$, the balance can be achieved by reducing imports or by increasing exports. However, reducing imports will slow down economic growth while increasing exports is hard to actualize in the short run. Therefore, the "Two-Gap Theory" is in fact dilemma and does not provide us with a radical solution for the deficiency of capital in developing countries and regions. But it makes people realize the importance and necessity of using external resources in the dilemma. It reminds developing countries and regions that increasing the use of external resources is a better way to balance the two gaps and enhance sustainable economic growth, such as enlarging their investments, developing their industries, realizing their economic take-off, and quickening their economic growth. During the opening, the introduction and utilization of external resources to balance the two gaps can produce dual effectiveness. From the perspective of supply, the inflow of the capital of machinery from overseas into developing countries and regions can be regarded as a kind of import of resources, and this type of import does not need to pay by increasing exports, and thus releases the burden of insufficient foreign currency. On the other hand, from the perspective of demand, this kind of import is an investment and it does not need to pay by savings. It also reduces the pressure of deficiency in savings. This effect is in fact to expand local investment by introducing and utilizing foreign resources, which is a good choice for developing countries and regions to solve their problem of insufficient capital and to improve their economic performance.

The "Two-Gap Theory", has another meaning that economic reform must accompany with opening-up in developing countries. Although utilizing external resources can enhance economic development, it is not a long-term solution. The "Two-Gap Theory" demonstrates that developing countries should make use of external resources efficiently to develop their production, increase their exports, increase their ability of accumulating savings, balance the two gaps by utilizing internal resources, gradually reduce the constraints imposed from external resources on local economic development, establish their own power or capabilities, and rely on themselves to achieve sustainable economic growth. In order to achieve this goal, economic structures need to be fine-tuned and economic systems need to be reformed, in order to make their economy more open and more parallel to the world economy. This is to say that, they need to make the development of their industries adapt to the adjustment of industrial development in the global economy and the trend of becoming more internationalized, more advanced, more hi- tech, more flexible and more active, so that the economies can be more competitive and open. If not, the two gaps will exist, the economy will rely on external resources, and will continue to face an imbalance of international payments, and debt crises will occur as in Brazil and Mexico. Many other economic hindrances will also emerge during the process of economic modernization.

Anyways, it is very clear that expanding, opening, and utilizing the mobility of international capital can promote economic growth in countries or regions. This can be demonstrated in the following two areas.

First, the function of introducing foreign capital during the initial periods of economic take-off and development in developed countries. For example, foreign capital accounted for 40% of the total capital of Canada during 1870 – 1914, and 37% in Australia during 1861 – 1900, and 29% in Norway during 1885 – 1914. Though the percentage was rather low during the Civil War in America and Meiji Reform Japan, the impact of foreign capital introduced to these two countries was still tremendous.

Second, the function of introducing foreign capital in economic growth of developing countries and regions since World War II, especially in Asian countries. Table 10.1 demonstrates that there has been a wide gap between investment and savings in countries or regions located in Asia since the economic take-off in the 1960s. The average economic growth rate in Korea reached around 10% with a wide gap between its investment and savings. The average national savings rate was 11.3% in the 1960s while the investment rate reached up to 19.1%, a difference of 7.8%; in the 1970s the national saving rate climbed to 21.8% while the investment rate reached up to 25.2%, a difference of 3.4%.; during the early period of the 1980s the saving rate was 26.9% while the investment rate was 32.1%, with the difference soaring to 5.2%. Singapore experienced a similar phenomenon, where the difference between investment and savings was as high as 9.2% and the lowest point was 3.1%. This reflects that, in a situation of insufficient national capital, foreign capital, as a long-term and stable inflow of capital can be an important source of capital to expand

investments and to maintain a higher level of economic growth in the above
countries and regions.

Table 10.1 The Investment and Savings
in Asian Developing Countries / Regions

Nations/ Regions	Savings Rate(S)			Investment Rate(I)			S-I		
	1961 - 1970	1971 - 1980	1981 - 1985	1961- 1970	1971- 1980	1981- 1985	1961 - 1970	1971 - 1980	1981- 1985
South Korea	11.3	21.8	26.9	19.1	25.2	32.1	-7.8	-3.4	-5.2
Taiwan	17.4	31.8	38.9	18.4	26.2	26.4	-1	5.6	12.6
Hong Kong		26.5	30.8		19.6	28.9		6.9	1.9
Singapore	12.8	28	42.4	22	224.5	45.5	-9.2	-6.5	-3.1
Malaysia		29	27.6		24.2	31.8		4.8	-4.2
Thailand	20.2	23.5	21.4	20.8	22.6	22	-0.6	0.9	-0.6
Indonesia		21.1	21.9	10.2	19.1	23.2	-5.7	2	-2.2

Source: *Outlook on Pacific Economic Region's Development* (in Chinese), edited
by Japanese Trade Association, October 1985, p. 161.

The source of foreign capital indicates that, due to geographical and
historical reasons, the amount of Japanese investment is quite significant
amongst all other Asian counties. Table 10.2 illustrates that up to 1986, of all
foreign direct investments, Japanese investments ranked number one in Korea,
Thailand, Indonesia, and ranked number two in Hong Kong, Singapore (in 1984),
Malaysia (in 1985) and the Philippines.

Table 10.2 Foreign Investments Constructs in Six Asian Countries/Regions

Countries/Regions	Japan	America	China	U.K.	Others
South Korea (1986)	51.6	28.6			15.5
Hong Kong (1986)	20.5	41.2	15.2		23.1
Singapore (1984)	23	29.7		13.1	34.2
Thailand (1986)	20.5	19.1			54.1
Malaysia (1985)	27.5			28.6	24.8
Indonesia (1986)	33.2	7.7			47.2
Philippine (1986)	15.7	54		(HK 6.2)	24.1

Note: this table was made on some statistic data published in China

China is a large developing country with a population of 1.3 billion. In order to solve the problem of insufficient capital in the process of economic take-off, the country must expand the introduction and utilization of foreign capital. Since the fundamental opening-up policy in 1979 until 1993, the actual amount of foreign capital used in China was 145.4 billion US dollars. During the same time debt in the international capital market totaled $83.5 billion, direct investment of foreign capital totaled $61.9 billion, and registered foreign enterprises accumulated to 174,000. The annual foreign capital accounted for 10% of the investment of social fixed assets, with most of them being infrastructure projects. In 1993, the total value of imports and exports in China took up 38% of its GNP, and 34.3 % of the total national imports and exports came from foreign funded enterprises; in 1994 the percentages of these two areas increased to 45% and 37% respectively.[84] Up till 2004, utilized foreign capital totaled up to $561.2 billion which was 10.56% of the total investment in social fixed assets. This shows that foreign capital has played an important role in economic growth since the opening up of China. In China, Guangdong was the first province to open up to the outside world, so it has a significant effect on Guangdong's economy: the foreign capital actually used was almost 30 billion US dollars from 1979 - 1993 which was about 25% of the total fixed asset investments, and in 2004, the accumulated foreign capital utilized was 150.4 billion dollars with a percentage of 29.8% in social fixed asset investments. The foreign capital in Guangdong came from 59 countries and regions during 1979-1995, and from even more countries in 2004. The source countries during 1979-1995 are shown in Table 10.3.

Table 10.3 Source Countries of Foreign Investment in Guangdong (1979 – 1995)

Nation (Region)	HK/Macao	Taiwan	America	Japan	Singapore	Europe	Other
Percentage (%)	82.3	6.1	1.5	1.3	0.8	0.9	7.1

The above form shows the importance and necessity of utilizing foreign capital, with a precise review of developing countries and regions utilizing foreign capital for economic growth from a practical and historical point of view. In order to have a better utilization of foreign capital, there is a need to further understand external resources. Generally speaking, external resources can be classified into two main groups: 1) loans or aids from international organizations or foreign governments, or"Foreign Support" in short; 2) investments from overseas, or "Foreign Investments" in short. "Foreign Support" is a mutual international agreement of support among countries. This kind of support is without any repayments or any certain kinds of debt under privileged conditions. For example, food donations, medical services or aid after natural disasters offered by international organizations or charity organizations to developing countries; or some interest-free loans, low-interest loans or long-term debts offered by some countries or organizations. "Foreign Investment" is also called "Foreign Private Investment" or "Foreign Direct Investment", which refers to the activities of obtaining investments and assets from other countries. This kind of investments can be stocks, securities, debts or tangible assets like machines. Foreign debts are involved with repayment of principal and interest while foreign investment needs to remit profits earned. Therefore, in receiving foreign capital resources one has to consider the ability to repay interest. From a long term perspective, if the use of foreign resources cannot efficiently promote economic growth and exports, there will be debt crisis' which can accelerate the imbalance of an economy, and economic lag or recession will occur under certain conditions and in a certain period, as the "Latin-American Phenomenon" in Argentina and Brazil. That is to say, the use of external resources can both promote and hinder economic growth. Hence, developing countries and regions must seriously consider how to make use of external resources in an efficient way in the process of international capital flow.

Let's move on to the functions of the inflow of some other key production elements for developing countries and regions. "Scarce Production Elements" refer to the critical resources of operation, other than capital, in developing countries and regions. Operation resources are the comprehensive resources used to run business, foster industries and make production, which include techniques or specialized knowledge in production or sales, operational management knowledge and experience, information, mechanisms of technology exploration, purchase of raw materials, sales of finished products, and financing networks, etc.. Introducing foreign investment of billions of US dollars would be a big success for a developing country or region. However, operational resources brought by direct investment even exert more effects on the development of industrial quality and the enhancement of economic and technical levels and productivity than investment itself. According to a quantitative study done by a reputable Japanese research organization on the factors affecting the growth of developing countries and regions in Asia,[85] the direct contribution of foreign capital to the economic growth of "Four Little Dragons", the Philippines, Indonesia and other Asian countries, was less than 1%. However, the contribution of such operational resources brought by foreign capital as advanced labor and technology to economic growth was 50%. For example, the national economic growth of Korea from 1975 – 1980 was 7.6% with 3.7% of the economic growth coming from an accumulation of capital while 0.9% of the growth formed by foreign capital. The greatest contribution of foreign capital was found in Singapore during 1970 -1975. During this period, the national economic growth in Singapore was 9.5%, of which 1.8% directly came from the utilization of foreign capital while 2.7% from operational resources related to foreign capital. The average economic growth in Korea in 1970- 1975 was 9.5%, 6.9 % of which came from employment and enhancement in technology, and the contribution rate was 69%. Thailand, which had an undeveloped economy and lower levels of technology, its average national economic growth from 1975 – 1980 was 7.5% in which 3.5% came from the improvement in labor and technology, i.e., these two kinds of operational resources accounted for 46.7% of its economic growth. Surely, the structure of operational resources is rather complex. It is a result of direct foreign capital, and more importantly it's the result of the cohesiveness of the people in developing countries and region. However, it is undeniable that operational resources related to foreign capital has played an important role in economic growth. As the technology level in developing countries is quite low without much capital for research and development, the enhancement in their industry structure and industrial technology equipment relies on the utilization of foreign capital, and the introduction of technological facilities and operational or management experiences in certain periods, especially in the probation period for economic take-off. Hence, this reflects that foreign investments have a stimulating effect on economic growth in developing countries and regions.

Finally, we are going to look at the motivating effects of the shift of industries in developed countries on the industrial development and economic growth in developing countries. Economic industries possess a miraculous power for stimulating economic growth. Industries have to experience different stages such as formation, growth, maturation and decline, and they transfer from one country/region to another country/region with declining industries replaced by new ones. All these lead to the fluctuation of economic growth in countries and regions all over the world. Tracing back the process of global economic development, the adjustment, shifting and changing of industries are actually the adjustment, shifting and changing of integrated production elements. During this process, due to the effects of the basic laws of a market economy, like the production elements, industries usually transfer to countries or regions with the best development conditions and with the highest return rates. In the development of a global economy, if a specific industry enters the stage of decline in a developed country, new production elements have to be added into this industry to promote its shift into developing countries, in order to gain new life and success, which would quicken the economic development in developing countries. This kind of international transfer impacts the industrialization and economic take-off in developing countries/regions. This phenomenon was especially evident in some Asian countries after the two world wars.

In Asia, firstly, the industrial structure adjustment and industrial transfer in America enhanced the economic take-off of Japan in the 1950s and the 1960s. At the end of 1960s and beginning of the 1970s, economic improvement in Japan required the similar adjustment and transfer of industries as in America, which helped to boost a more mature economic development of Asian countries, especially the "Four Little Dragons". The transfer of industries in Japan was parallel to its direct investment to other countries in Asia. In this process of industrial transfer, the upward movement of three different industrial groups appeared. The first industrial group included fiber, home electrical appliances, dyeing products and other labor intensive industries; the second group contained iron and steel, shipbuilding, oil refinery industries, and other capital intensive industries; the third group included motor accessories and their installation, electronics, and other industries with advanced technologies. These three industrial groups are of different levels and there is mutual promotion among each other. By 1972, investment made by Japan in other Asian countries, had primarily concentrated in the first group of industries, which made up 58.9% of the total investment amount; the concentration shifted to the second group of industries which accounted for 41.5% of the total investment amount in 1982 and increased to 43.9% in 1984. Simultaneously, though the third industry group has not held a leading position, there was a gradual increase year by year, 21% in 1972, 23.7% in 1981, and finally climbing up to 26% in 1984. Parallel to this, the industrial establishment and development in the Asian "Four Little Dragons" started with the fiber industry, and then iron and steel, shipbuilding, and oil refinery followed and are now moving towards developing the motor industry as well as some other high advanced industries. The gradual shift and enhancement of industries created conditions for the economic growth. The international transfer of industries in the open system of "Four Little Asian Dragons" helped them to realize industrialization with economic levels reaching that of developed countries. In 1991, Singapore had the highest average productivity per capita,

1.447 thousand US dollars followed by that of HK at 1.32 thousand US dollars, next was Taiwan at 0.8597 thousand US dollars and the last one was Korean at 0.626 thousand US dollars.[86] The international transfer of industries in the open system of a global economy helps Asian economies perform well. As Japanese economist Okita Saburo mentioned, the first wave of Asian economic development was found in Japan, the second wave was with the "Four Little Asian Dragons" while the third wave will be the economic take-off of China and ASEAN countries. These waves happened one after another which has made Asia the most active economic region in the world.

Based on the above, in the development of the world economy, because of the mobility of international capital and operational resources, and the shift of some industries in the process of industrial structure adjustment from developed countries to developing countries, developing countries can combine their own advantaged resources with international resources to speed up industry development, to create conditions for economic take-off, and to enhance their sustainable open economic growth.

10.3 Foreign Trade – An Accelerator for Economic Growth

International trade is the earliest and most basic form of interaction among countries in the global economy. From the perspective of production (supply), international trade is the result of cost differences among countries, which stimulates product and service exchanges for comparative advantages; from the perspective of value realization of products and services, international trade can expand the market from a nation to the world, create better conditions for realizing and increasing value, enlarge the national income, and expand demand which is the motive force of production. Because of this, the global economy has developed, especially with the economic growth of developing countries and regions. This moves along side with the development of social productivity, the transition of a traditional economy to a modernized economy, the increase in demands and actualization of needs, and the speedy expansion of international trade. In the 1930s, D.H. Robertson claimed that foreign trade was "A Engine for Growth".[87] A famous French historian D. Mantou stated in his book *Industry Revolution in the 18th Century* that foreign trade was the catalyst that enhanced economic growth.[88] The former Commerce Minister of the United States at the beginning of the 20th century believed that the function of foreign trade in economic growth was just like the pendulum "controlling the whole part of this machine".[89] In the 1950s and 1960s, Japan brought forward and successfully implemented the economic strategy of "establishing the nation with trade", which helped to actualize economic take-off and enhance a speedy economic growth.

Economic theory originates from practice. Looking back to the process of economic development experienced in the main countries with an earlier and faster economic take-off and sustainable economic growth in the global economic development, foreign trade has played the role of "accelerator".

Britain is the first country to have this kind of experience. In 1688, exports from Britain accounted for 5% of its total national income; after 100 years, the percentage increased to 15%; in the 1980s, it climbed further up to 30%. It is undeniable that the increase in exports strongly motivated the development of related industries in Britain. For example, the export of wool in Britain took up 30% of the wool production volume at the end of the 17th century, and soared up to 50% in 1771 - 1772. Other industries, like textiles, also experienced a similar kind of trend. According to the book *European History of Cambridge*, the expansion of overseas markets and overseas raw materials of manufactured products from Britain in the 18th century, and the exploration of food supply sources, had a tremendous strategic impact on all stages in industrialization. The rapid growth of British manufactured products distinctly stimulated its economic growth, which is shown in Table 10.4.

Table 10.4 Growth Rate of British Economy in 18th Century

Year	National Income	Export Industries	Domestic Industries	Agriculture
1700	100	100	100	100
1760	147	222	114	115
1780	167	246	123	126
1800	251	544	152	143

Another example is America whose promising economic growth was driven by foreign trade at the end of the 19th century and at the beginning of the 20th century. During the years of 1895 – 1914, the volume of the manufacturing industry doubled in the US, with its manufacturing exports increasing by 5 times in the same period. The major sales channels for its products were in the international market and raw materials also came from the international market, such as plastic, leather, fur, silk and fiber. International market demand and supply drove rapid growth in the manufacturing industry in the US. At that time, while Europe faced sales problems with their products, the US however maintained the continued growth of their manufacturing industry and squeezed into the European market through the strong competitiveness of its products. This upset most of the European countries who called this phenomenon the "US Invasion by Exports".[90]

Next is Japan. After the two world wars, in order to achieve its strategic target of surpassing the US and Europe, Japan executed the strategy of "Establishing the Nation with Trade" to integrate their local rich labor resources with external natural materials to enhance its comparative advantages, and increase its labor productivity. This strategy was implemented for a long time and has motivated comprehensive economic growth. A few stages of growth have been experienced during this period of time: in the 1950s, a protective strategy for local maturing industries and for increasing their export competitiveness was implemented; in the 1960s, export and competition were encouraged, and a certain level of open policy on foreign trade was implemented, which increased the free export ratio from 40% to 93%; in the 1970s, the trade policy emphasized on coordination and competition, to open its local market, to make overseas investments, to expand external markets and to reduce international conflicts for better economic growth. During the years of 1950 – 1972, the average export growth rate of Japan reached 17.5% which was higher than twice the average level of the world at that time. Compared with 7.4% in the US, 15.4% in Germany, 6.5% in Britain and 10.3% in France, the rate in Japan was the highest amongst capitalist countries. Simultaneously, in the international trade volume of all capitalist countries in the world, the exports of Japan accounted for 1.4% while its imports accounted for 1.6% in 1958; the percentages increased to 7.9% and 8.6% respectively in 1981. Exports motivated the growth of imports and the growth of the whole economy. During the years of 1950 – 1980, the total foreign trade amount of Japan increased by 149 times and its GDP increased by 93 times, and the percentage of foreign trade in GDP increased from 16.3% to 26%. Presently, Japan is the third largest trade empire in the world after the US and Germany, and the second largest economy after the US.

The fourth countries are the "Four Little Dragons" in Asia. They were newly industrialized countries that experienced economic take-off in the 1960s - 1970s. Their annual growth rate in foreign trade was much greater than that of the total output value with a significant motivation effect on their economic growth during this period as shown in Table 10.5.

Table 10.5 Economic Growth Rates and Export Rates of Asian "Four Little Dragons"

Type/ Countries	GDP Growth Rates (%)					Growth rates of Export during 1965-1975 (%)	
	1963-1973	1973-1980	1981	1982	1983	Total	Industrial Products
South Korea	9.8	7.8	6.6	5.4	11.9	40.1	44.5
Taiwan	11.1	8.1	5.7	3.3	7.9	28	25.9
Hong Kong	9.1	9.5	9.4	3	6.5	18.1	18.9
Singapore	10.1	7.7	9.6	6.9	8.2	18.5	22.2

Source: World Development Report 1986, by World Bank; UN, Yearbook of International Trade Statistics.

The fifth country is China, a developing country with its national economy greatly improved through the expansion and growth of foreign trade in the 10 years after its opening up policies. From 1979 – 1991, the annual average growth rate of its GNP was 8.6%, and its total industrial output value was 12.2%. The average growth rate of its foreign trade was 15.6%, and its exports were 16.8% while that of imports were 14.6%, 7%, 8.2% and 6% higher than that of GNP. The average growth rate of the export of manufactured products was 21.3% which was 9.1% higher than that of the industrial output value. The Ratio of Dependence on Foreign Trade, or the ratio of foreign trade in GNP, increased from 9.9% in 1978 to 36.4% in 1991, and reached 37% in 1993, with the ratio of dependence on exports and that of imports increasing from 4.7% to 16.7% and from 5.2% to 17.1% respectively in 1991.

From the perspective of global economic development, foreign trade also promoted the development of the economies of all countries from 1965 – 1985. Based on statistics done by the World Bank, the growth rates of production and exports of manufactured goods in countries by groups during the years of 1965-1973, 1973- 1985 and 1965-1985 indicate that, in the last 20 years, except for those low income countries which have not actualized economic take-off, the export growth rates were higher than the growth rates of production in market economic industrial countries, and high-income oil exporting countries, and developing countries. This was especially significant in those mid-income developing countries. This is shown in Table 10.6.

Table 10.6 Growth Rates of Production and Exports in Country Groups (1965-1985)

Type/ Countries	Growth rate of production (%)			Growth rate of export (%)		
	1963-1973	1973-1985	1965-1985	1965-1973	1973-1985	1965-1985
Market Economic Industrial Countries of	5.3	3	3.8	10.6	4.4	6.8
Developing Countries	9	6	7.2	11.6	12.3	12.2
Mid-income Countries	9.1	5	6.6	14.9	12.9	13.8
High-income Petroleum Exporting Countries	10.6	7.5	8.4	16.2	11.7	16
Low-income Countries	8.9	7.9	7.5	2.4	8.7	6
Total	5.8	3.5	4.5	10.7	5.3	7.4

Source: *World Development Report 1987* (In Chinese), by World Bank. Beijing: China Finance Press, 1987, p. 47.

To sum up, the economic development histories of Britain in the period of industrial revolution, and US at end of the 19th century and the beginning of the 20th century, and Japan after World War II, and the new industrial countries in the past 20 years all show that, no matter whether the global market is developing or not, no matter whether the percentage of foreign trade in GNP is high or not, there is a definite motivation effect of foreign trade on modernized economic growth, especially in developing countries. The question is: as a channel for global economic growth, why and how does foreign trade exert influence on the economic growth for a country or a region?

There have been tons of theories trying to answer this question in recent times, such as the theory of absolute advantage put forward by the classical British economist Adam Smith, the theory of comparative advantage by David Richado, the theory of "engine" by US economist Robertson in the 1930s, the theory of resource endowment by the Swedish modern economists Heckscher and Erling, the theory of the product life cycle by the modern American economist Vernon, and the theory of "Flying Geese" by the Japanese modern economist Trisong, etc. Summarizing the ideas of these scholars, there are five ways for the high growth rates of exports to enhance the economic growth of a country or region, so foreign trade can have accelerated effects on modern economic growth, especially in developing countries and regions.

First, to form the comparative advantages of elements and benefits. Through participating in international division of labor and competition, a country or a region can expand exports and increase its foreign exchange reserves for imports. In foreign trade, through importing products, especially capital products, a country can obtain comparative advantages from international divisions of labor, greatly reducing the amount of production inputs and form its comparative advantages in key production elements, comparatively increase labor productivity, output, and efficiency.

Second, to improve investment and economic structures. Led by its exports, a country can improve its industry structure by allowing more local capital to flow into the industries with better export profits and comparative advantages. Social economic structure will then be improved and productivity will be enhanced especially in those industries with comparative advantages and the whole society.

Third, to expand markets and obtain economies of scale. The increase of the exports in a country or a region indicates the expansion of its market. This helps extend the local market's products into the international markets. It is definitely helpful for enterprises and the society to enlarge production scales to gain more economies of scale.

Fourth, to improve product quality and lower production costs. In the global market, product competition is key, and there exhorts great pressure on the exporting and importing industries in that specific country, and pushes them to fine-tune their product quality and lower production costs and eliminate those industries with low efficiency, especially the sunset industries. This kind of pressure from imports and exports transforms into a stimulus for development, which strengthens the competitiveness of products, enterprises and industries in a country or region, and speeds up their economic growth by expanding market demands.

Fifth, to obtain a multiplier effect from investments for the development of other industries. The multiplier effect theory was put forward by the famous American modern economist Keynes. He claimed that if there is an increase in investment in an industry, this industry will increase its expenditure on purchasing means of production and livelihood from other industries whose income will then be increased, which will further expand the consumption and promote the development of consumer goods. Therefore, the increase in investments will force income levels to increase by several times and the size of the multiplier effect is determined by the ratio of consumption and savings. In an open economy, the unceasing expansion of exports in a country or region will certainly encourage investments both domestically and internationally, which can have an multiplier effect to stimulate the development of processing industries or ancillary industries and transportation and power industry, etc., and to enhance the introduction of overseas advanced technology and management knowledge. This not only expands the scale of social productivity, but also improves the level of social productivity, and creates a better material and technical basis for further sustainable economic growth.

Chapter Eleven

Policy System: The Adjustment Tool for

Economic Growth

Modernized economic growth is a complex social economic process. It includes the social production and circulation, such as the production, exchange, distribution and consumption of production elements, material products, spiritual products, and service products in both local and international markets. In addition, it also includes the impacts of other economic factors and non-economic factors on production and circulation, and the influence and impacts of international economic and non-economic circumstances on economic processes. Therefore, as for modern economics, a historical perspective is required when analyzing a holistic economic growth issue in developing countries. It is important to take into consideration the process of social economic growth and all other related social factors and their impacts. It is important to consider how to adjust and control the process in a smooth manner by policy instruments, and to ensure sustainable economic growth. Aligning with the complexity and diversity of social economic process, policy instruments have complex and diverse features. The integration of all the policies involved in the social economic process is the policy system we need to focus on. In order to facilitate the study of the economic growth issue and to smooth the operation of the economic growth process, we will mainly analyze the policy system with economic theories, and the controlling functions of policy systems on economic growth. Other non-economic policy instruments are not included here.

11.1 The Meaning, Target, Structure and Economic Functions of Policy Systems

During economic growth, the policy system consists of various policies which reflect a series of constitutive relations or main relations and have an adjustment effect on economic growth, especially an integrated adjustment system combined by economic policies. Since economic growth is a complex process with lots of economic and non-economic conflicts, there are problems that need to be resolved between the motive of a nation and its associated behaviors, and problems between the economy and the objective economic process. As a result, the government needs to overcome all these conflicts to make necessary adjustments to minimize negative impacts, therefore the government makes and releases various rules, regulations and policies, which all together constitute the policy system.

It is necessary to realize that every policy is designed for problems in a particular economic growth process at a specified stage or for problems of a specific aspect. Therefore, these policies have some specific goals. However, the goal of each policy cannot be isolated from the overall goal of economic growth and needs to have some restrictions for the actualization of the overall goal. Hence, the goals of a policy system should reflect the goals of all related policies and the overall goal. As for the internal demands of the adjustment process of economic growth in developing countries and regions, polices should offer help to solve the main problems in economic growth or a healthy economic process, such as employment, price stability, equal allocation of resources, international balance of payments, social stability, national security and spiritual development, etc.. Under normal situations, an effective policy system, as the adjustment system of economic growth, should have the following eight fundamental goals: 1) achieving sustainable economic growth; 2) maintaining sufficient employment; 3) emphasizing on a fair distribution without wide income gaps; 4) stabilizing prices in a society; 5) achieving international balance of payments; 6) obtaining social harmony; 7) ensuring national security; 8) exploring spiritual and cultural development. Among all these eight goals, the first five are basic economic goals while the last three are non-economic ones. With these two groups of goals, goals strictly related to the economy are the main part of the policy system while non-economic goals do not directly reflect the development of productivity or the change in economic indicators. However, they are necessary for the realization of national economic growth. For example, the security of a nation, the harmony and stability of a society, and a certain level of spirit and culture, etc., are all needed to guarantee a stable economic growth of a nation and a region.

A policy system is a system of structural relations. It includes pluralistic structural relations and multilevel structural relations, which are the basis for a policy system, and periodic structural relations of a policy transfer, which run through the whole practicing processes of structural systems and policy systems. Due to the limitation of the study and the size of the book, a detailed description of all structural relations of the policy system will not be covered. Only six aspects are going to be discussed in this chapter. They are the main and fundamental components of the system, including industrial policy, investment policy, financial policy, monetary policy, income distribution policy, and consumption policy. These six areas are used by a country or a government as an administrative tool with two hands, visible and invisible, to interfere with the market under market economy conditions. They are the basic adjustment tools to control the behaviors of economic subjects, resource allocation, development speed, fluctuation in prices, income distribution, etc.. Other policies are not going to be covered in the following chapters.

In order to simplify the contents of the chapter, a holistic description of economic functions derived from the policy system will be illustrated. Economic functions of the policy system refer to the combined effects of all kinds of policies in the system of economic growth processes and its related areas. There are both positive and negative effects on their economic functions. Under normal situations, positive effects, rather than negative ones, are induced in the formulation and execution of a policy and the policy system. As long as the positive effects outweigh the negative ones, a desirable function still can be achieved from a holistic point of view, enhancing economic growth. The following are the economic functions of the policy system.

(1) Function of guiding investment and development. In the above mentioned policy system there are detailed regulations for all policies, such as policies from industry to investment, finance, currency, income distribution and consumption, and for all aspects of investments, such as from investment directions to investment profits and the stimulation of capital formation. These regulations, as policy instruments, focus on actualizing economic goals of policy systems and have a stimulating effect on the subjects of an economy, which can guide reasonable consumption, increase savings, expand investments, and enhance development.

(2) Function of benefit coordination. Every policy is a reflection of a beneficial relationship. Economic policies reflect the beneficial relations among economic subjects, that is, the beneficial relationship among the government, enterprises, and individuals under market economy condition, or relationships between enterprise and enterprise, individual and individual. The adjustment of policies and the changes in the internal structure of the policy system, in essence, reflect the adjustment of beneficial relations. Under the development of a market economy and the process of actualizing economic growth, a policy system is an adjustor for regulating benefits, for realizing benefits, and for changing benefits. For example, financial policy is to adjust allocation of funding and taxes, and monetary policy is to adjust the volume and structure of money issued, and the interest rates of deposits and loans. In addition, income distribution policy and consumption policy are to adjust salaries and prices, etc. A policy system has a fine tuning effect on the benefits of all economic subjects, which then forms a benefit mechanism to encourage advancement and innovation, and creates passion in the grass root levels of a society and promotes sustainable economic growth.

(3) Function of adjusting economic operations. Sustainable economic growth relies on the smooth operation of a national economy. Through various

economic policies, the policy system controls the input of currency, controls the scale of investment and adjusts the structure of investment, controls the demand scale and adjusts the supply and demand structure in order to coordinate the social benefits and individual benefits, the long-term benefits and short-term benefits. This helps to achieve a state of balanced structural operation in the national economy, and then forms a synergy, which can enhance an ordered operation of social economy with high quality growth. Otherwise, economic functions will fail without enough adjustment of policy to withhold the input of currency. As a result, "overheating" will appear along with uncontrolled investment and an inflated currency. This will side track the national economy from healthy development into a disordered state with fluctuations. Ultimately, economic fluctuation will cause social instability.

(4) An indirect economic function. Economic policies need to be aligned with the process of national economic operation. Besides, as the operation of a national economy and economic growth process are social processes, they must be coordinated with many non-economic social factors. Therefore, economic policies should be paralleled with social policies, and have an indirect economic function. This kind of indirect function of a policy system in economic growth is to create a stable social environment to promote and guarantee sustainable economic growth, through aligning with social policies.

As we know, in the economic growth process, economic policies within the policy system must be agreed to by members in the society in order to get their recognition and actions so as to actualize the adjustment functions in the process of economic growth. During the process, the psychological reaction of each economic subject or member in the society, from the view of attitudes toward economic policies, is actually a kind of social psychological stress. If the whole policy system or individual economic policy cannot reflect the nature of the social economic process, imbalance will occur in the economy, psychological over burden will be created with chaos in the society, and there will be failure of policies which will hinder economic growth. Oppositely, if a policy can release psychological burden and gain support from the people, a stable society with continuous economic growth will be formed. This kind of indirect function of a policy system can only influence the economic process through the mediation of people's psychological states and the social environment. That's why it is called the indirect economic function.

11.2 Industrial Policy and Economic Growth

Industrial policy is an important component of the policy system. It is a reflection of objective demands for policy adjustment in modernized economic growth and is a critical tool adopted by the government to compensate for the deficiency of the market from a macro perspective based on the objective rules of the economic growth process. If the law of value and market mechanism are an "invisible hand" for adjusting the operation of the economy, then the industrial policy is a "visible hand", which can demonstrate the intervention of a nation or the government in economic growth to keep the market economy on the right track.

The process of modernized economic growth is a shift from a traditional economy into a modernized economy and from an undeveloped state to a developed state. From a global perspective, this started in the middle of the 18th century in some countries like Britain and then became worldwide. Therefore, the theory of economic growth should not only be for developed countries as mentioned by western economists, but also be for developing countries and regions. Generally speaking, economic development goes with economic growth. Both developed and developing countries need to encounter the problem of economic growth rate and need to maintain a certain levels of growth rate. Otherwise, there will not be a material foundation for the resolution of social problems and the building of a harmonious and stable society. Hence, economic theories shall also be applied to developed countries and regions. This book mainly concentrates on studying the economic growth in developing countries and regions. The modernized economic growth process in developing countries and regions goes parallel with the issues of a high economic growth rate and a high rate of change in industry structure, an emergence of newly formed industry groups under technological revolution, and strengthened mutual reliance among countries. The demands of having economic growth accelerated cannot be achieved merely by a spontaneous allocation of production elements in a market mechanism for industry establishment. If developing countries and regions intend to develop their industries at a greater speed to create conditions for economic take-off, they need to enhance their macro level adjustment and concentrate production elements on leading industries so as to form support for speedy and continuous economic growth in industries with high technology, and to rapidly fine tune the structure of industries. As a result, they can realize sustainable and stable economic growth and coordinate growth in their national economies. In order to adapt to the objective needs of modernized economic growth, developing countries and regions have to select some economic policies, i.e. industrial policies, which are helpful for the enhancement of industry structure and national economic growth. However, industrial policy cannot override other economic policy in an unrealistic way. It should be treated as a macro level adjustment tool adopted by a nation and the government. It is more important than other economic policies as it is highly integrated and is a means for administrative intervention adopted by a nation and the government to make up the defects of the market. Industrial policy itself cannot solve any economic problems without the help of other economic policies. All levels of government, especially the central government, should pay attention to this.

So, what should developing countries and regions pay attention to when selecting and making industrial policies?

First, is to determine the aims of industrial policies. Industrial policies are used to serve the highest aim of economic strategies. Hence, their aims should be: 1) enhance the formulation and development of strategic and leading industries, coordinate their relations with supporting industries, and improving industry structure; 2) avoid the down-turning of industries, make necessary adjustments to recessionary industries, and improve the international relations during the organization and establishment of industries to form a condition with desirable public relations; 3) achieve a well balanced allocation of resources to improve labor productivity.

Second, is to fix the contents of industrial policies. Generally speaking, industrial policies include industry organizational policy, industry technology policy, industry structure policy, industry location policy and industry policy instruments, etc. There are two main functions of these polices: (1) to promote the increase of total volume and to ensure the supply of the total volume to satisfy the needs of a society; (2) to enhance the fine turning of the supply structure and the coordinated development of regions to make sure that the supply structure in a society fits well with its demand structure. The idea of these two functions is to ensure a sustainable, stable, speedy and coordinated economic growth.

The following is a brief description of the contents of industrial policies.

(1) The industry organizational policy. This is a part of the industrial policy with the key function of ensuring an efficient increase in supply of volume and settling the conflicts between supply and demand. In other words, it means selecting a highly efficient industry organizational format to ensure a fair allocation of resources for balancing supply and demand when devising industrial policies. There are three main parts of industry organizational policy. A) Choosing an efficient organizational format of industry. Based on the requirements of a scale economy, the units of the organizational format, enterprises should choose a reasonable organizational format for a certain production scale in order to fully utilize all kinds of resources, to establish a system for supplying products, to enhance technological improvements, to lower production cost, to increase social efficiency and to increase social wealth. B) Selecting an industry organizational format with a fair distribution of resources. That means finding an industrial relationship among industries and among enterprises which can have an equal allocation of resources. Every industry and every enterprise should be equal in the market without abusing comparative advantages or prohibiting other industries or enterprises to enter the market. Only with this kind of fair operational relationship can price mechanism utilize its function properly so that resources can be distributed fairly within industries or among industries and move to efficient industries and enterprises in time. Therefore, under a market economy system, there is a need to devise such an industry organizational policy that can help establish a fair operational

relationship and avoid monopolies. C) Picking an industry organizational format without wastage. From a macro point of view, this is to establish an efficient and reasonable price mechanism with fair competition within industry or among industries. In order to enhance continuous economic growth, when devising industry organizational policy for industry competition, it is necessary to ensure normal price competitiveness with focusing on competition among industries through industry organizational policy. Unfair competition should be restricted. This is to avoid wastage and to maintain order in competition and to guarantee an increase in efficiency.

(2) The industry technological policy. Its basic purposes are: a) making industries highly advanced; and b) ensuring that industry development is reasonable. Innovation and coordination should be regarded as the guideline in industrial policy if we want to achieve these two purposes. In industry development, advancement and rationalization are actually a technical issue. Innovation mainly refers to technological innovation, that is, the nature of industry development is that the level of technology, the level of productivity, and the types of industry that will adapt to the changes of social demand. It should be an evolution process, from a lower level to a higher level, from smaller to larger, from less to more. During the development process, the core parts are innovation and technological advancement while industrial policy should reflect, enhance, and adjust its condition. That's why devising industry technological policy is a must and should be a major part of industrial policy. The main elements of industry technological policy for developing countries and regions are: a) encouraging integration of research and production; b) promoting introduction and absorption of overseas advanced technology to increase product quality and levels of technology; c) stimulating a gradual increase of inputs in research and development with plans of developing critical technical projects and digesting foreign technology comprehensively to speed up technological innovation; d) speeding up advanced technological research and development to make technology commercialized, industrialized and internationalized; e) implementing and promoting internationalization of production standards to enhance the internationalization of the local market.

(3) The industry structural policy. This is another critical part of industrial policy. The nature of this policy is to find out the direction and process of industry change in a specified time according to the internal linkage of economic development, to determine the position and function of industry departments in social economic development according to the development pattern of the industry structure. It is also to bring up a reasonable ratio for the internal structure of industries to ensure a coordinated industrial structure and smooth industrial development. Hence, the main purposes of an industry structure policy is to ensure a proper structure and balance of supply and demand by adjusting

industrial structure, to avoid losses arising from conflicts of supply and demand under the market mechanism, and to maintain stable growth in the economy. This is an objective requirement of industry structure policy itself. If there is something wrong in the selection of the industry structure policy, the adjustment of supply and demand will not be fulfilled and the economic operation will be deteriorated. Therefore, two points need to be focused on when devising an industry structure policy. A) Fully utilizing the function of the market mechanism. Industry structure is affected by market demands, so the adjustments and changes in leading industries should truly reflect the changes in the structure of demands and develop along with the development trend. Simultaneously, industry structural transition is actually a process of re-engineering production elements in an enterprise under a market mechanism. During this transition period, a nation usually makes use of a variety of tools to enhance the transition abilities of enterprises, rather than adopting mandatory administrative tactics. It should be led by the behavior of enterprises to motivate the move of resources from long term to short term. B) Choosing certain kinds of leading industries within a certain period of time. Developing countries and regions should consider their national conditions (resources, demands, capital, technology etc.), their own strategic goals of economic development, and the trend of industry structural changes in the long and medium term, when selecting the leading industry departments and groups in different stages of development to ensure a coordinated development of all departments in the national economy.

(4) The industry location strategy. Surely, the core parts of industry establishment and development are technological innovation and advancement and the formation of technological structure which aligns with the demands in a society. However, the geographical location of industries for developing countries and regions is a crucial issue for sustainable and coordinated economic growth. Hence, industry location policy shall be also covered in industrial policy. The very fundamental nature of the policy is to reflect and adjust differences in the levels of development in different regions in order to realize the ultimate aim of national economic growth. The main principles of this policy are: a) to positively support economic development in less developed regions when facilitating and enhancing the privileged advantages of developed regions in order to narrow down their economic gaps; b) to take the privileged advantage of natural resources and that of the economy to promote different kinds of specialization in different industries based on their level of economic development. The reason for this is   to form a reasonable location of industries, such as in coastal regions, in areas along rivers and roads, in areas near large cities which lie within the reach of a transportation network, to motivate regional economic development.

(5) The industrial policy instrument. Developing countries and regions have to consider two main basic goals when devising and implementing industrial policies: the development of leading industries and the development of all industries. Industry administrative instruments are solutions for achieving these goals. If there is a fixed goal for industrial policy without peripherals to support it, it will be like crossing a river without a bridge. Goals cannot be realized just as crossing the river cannot be done either. In average, the industry policy instruments include: a) fiscal tools, like reducing tax; b) financial tools, like lowering interests of loans, government guaranteed loans, rationing credit loan amounts, etc.; c) direct control, like limits on the import amount of products, capital and technology, control on foreign trade, constraints on investment and production; d) establishment or abolition of systems like issuance of permits, or the setting up or abolition of some temporary regulations etc.; e) administrative guidance, including general notice, advice, coaching etc. There is some freedom in choosing all the aforesaid instruments. Under normal conditions, choosing the best method is rather difficult, but choosing the second best is more practical as long as the following two criteria are well considered. A) The cost of industry policy instruments. There are two types: economic costs and non-economic costs. The former one refers to the cost of labor, capital and raw materials to actualize the determined goals of industry polices while the latter one means the cost in the aspects of social, political and cognitive thinking, that is, non-material costs. These two types of costs need to be well considered as non-material costs can be changed to material costs under certain conditions. For example, the inappropriate use of policy instruments can cause chaos in a society and increase economic cost; or dependency can lower labor productivity under inappropriate protection. These are examples of having non-economic costs transformed into economic costs. As a famous Dutch economist Tinbergen mentioned, "which kind of instrument to adopt is not important in terms of welfare. Under any condition, cost is included in the welfare function of policy executors".[91] Generally speaking, we should choose methods which can actualize the goals of industrial policy with minimal cost. B) Appropriateness of policy instruments packages. Normally, one policy goal can fit one policy instrument, but in some conditions, a few polices can fit a single goal or vice versa. Under industrial policy, using a number of policy instruments for one single goal is called a package of policy instruments. That's why the policy instruments are effective, as a package of policy instruments can be more efficient than the sum of isolated instruments. From the perspective of total policy cost, the more reasonable the package is, the more efficient the policy is, and the lower the cost is. Therefore, when choosing instruments of industrial policy, losses caused by the inappropriate use of instruments and the unreasonable combination of instruments should be avoided.

11.3 Investment Policy and Economic Growth

Investment policy refers to the basic principle of a nation in determine the scale and structure of investments so as to adjust the total supply and demand. As mentioned earlier, investment is the first motivator for developing countries and regions to have their economic take-off and to have speedy economic growth. In order to actualize the strategic goals of economic growth, to go beyond the advanced global economic level, new investment should be added to social production and re-production under the condition of a coordinated development of the total supply and total demand. In the short run, the expansion of the investment scale, the increase of investment rates, and the drastic change in investments will have a decisive effect on the total social supply and demand and their structures through the change of total investment demand and its structure. If the scale of investment is small with a slow investment growth rate and inappropriate investment structure, the driving force for economic growth will be affected, and social supply will be in a shortage. If the ability of the nation, the material structure of social products, and the constraints of market capabilities are ignored while expanding the scale of investment lavishly with an unreasonable speed and unreasonable structure of investment, there will be a booming demand, and an "overheated" economy. Prices will all soar with economic fluctuation, and an imbalance of departments in the national economy will occur, which will influence the continuous, stable and coordinated economic growth. Hence, there should be appropriate investment policy for making necessary adjustments on fixed asset investment for forming reasonable investment scales and structures, for forming appropriate volumes and structures of social supply and social demand, and for enhancing a sustainable, stable and coordinated economic growth. Investment policy can fine tune the national economy in a more direct and holistic way. Besides, it can adjust the amount and structure of fixed asset investment in social production, control economic growth, and help to actualize the adjustment functions of income distribution policy and industrial policy. Therefore, investment policy is crucial in a macro level of adjustment and is an important part of the policy system.

Investment policy includes the following two main parts.

First, policy of investment scale. Generally, there are two types of this policy: a) tightening policy to suppress the expansion of demand; b) expansion policy to stimulate demand which is insufficient. From the perspective of global economic development, developing countries and regions generally seek for speedy growth to catch up with the global level but with a constraint of insufficient resources. The problems that developing countries and regions encounter in economic development include: insufficient resources with expanded demand; the scales of investment are constrained by the amount of resources. Hence, investment shall be limited within an appropriate scale to suppress expanded demand so as to reduce investment. Controlling the amount of investment appropriately is also very important. In order to implement the investment policy more efficiently to control the investment scale, there are three critical steps for strengthening the adjustment of investment activities. Usually, the process of investment has three stages: demand for investment, the starting stage, acquisition of investment capital, the middle stage, and implementation of investment, the ending stage. Any of these three stages can give rise to investment expansion. Therefore, investment scale policy should focus on controlling these three stages; otherwise, "overheating" will appear with economic fluctuation and affect the economic stability of a society.

Second, policy of investment structure. This refers to the principles, rules and regulations guiding the adjustments of allocation proportions of fixed asset investments in different departments of a national economy. Under social production and re-production with other conditions unchanged, there is an interrelated but independent relationship among investment structure, production structure, and supply structure. For the interrelated relationship, normally, investment structure determines production structure while production structure determines the structure of supply; on the contrary, supply structure constraints investment and production structures through affecting investment demand. These three structures are closely intermingled with self adjustment and upgrading of the initial production structure which motivates adjustment and changes on supply structures; on the other hand, investment structures can greatly affect social demand. The latter is due to the demand investment activities place on social products. From the starting point of production, investment structure is a kind of demand structure of investment, and is an important part of social demand structure. During the process of investment, changes on the structure of investment demand should strongly and effectively affect the changes on the social demand structure. Therefore, on the whole of the social production and re-production process, the structure of investment affects social demand structure strongly in a short term, and it also affects and determines social supply structure in the long run. Investment structure policy acts as a necessary moderator to fine tune the balance of social supply and demand structures to ensure the smooth production and circulation and stable growth of an economy.

The above has illustrated two main aspects of investment policy. So, how to make use of investment policy to macro control the economy in developing countries and regions in order to enhance a long-term stable and coordinated development?

(1) Control the currency supply appropriately. Based on development needs and possibilities, countries and regions should control the total amount of currency input according to economic development needs. Reasonable needs of economic growth and changes on prices determine the annual currency supply volume. The influence of foreign currency reserves on local currency supply is also worth considering. At the same time, special attention should be put on the

ratio of currency spent on purchasing production materials and consumption materials. If the former volume is over or under a certain level, prices of production materials will be raised or the materials will be piled up in storage; if the latter volume is over or below a certain level, consumption materials will have good or poor market, and their prices will soar up or there will be poor demand and poor sales. Besides, there should be different levels of control for a variety of currencies. Take savings as an example, an increase in savings should be consistent with the increase in actual wealth so that the growth of savings can reflect the growth of actual wealth. Otherwise, if the increase in savings is just superficial, it will not reflect the real increases in wealth. Oppositely, if the amount of savings is too low, it may indicate that either the savings absorbed by the bank is not enough or there is not a big increase in actual wealth. Hence, banks should control the input of currency through obtaining enough information about the mobility and sources of all currency in every department of the national economy.

(2) Control credit availability appropriately. Most of the time, overheating in investment found in developing countries and regions comes from inappropriate control of credit availability. When the credit control is insufficient, the investment is over-expanded, and the economic growth is hindered, thus the operation of national economy tends to rely on increasing the input of currency. As a result, an undesirable situation will appear. This kind of situation will last until social instability is found and the government make some intervening actions, such as adopting administrative tightening policies to control the volume of credit. The consequences of tightening policies are discontinuing projects, lengthening cycle times of projects, lowering investment efficiency, weakening the market, overstocking products, staggering productivity of enterprises, which all lead to bad results for the economy. Until the situation goes to an unbearable level, expansionary policy will then be used to enlarge the scale of investment for the recovery of the economy. This is a kind of administrative monitoring policy illustrates that the controlling of credit input is very important in devising and implementing investment policy. However, under the condition of a market economy, strategic and commercial banks operate independently, so currency as a special commodity should follow the law of value. Strategic banks are under the direct administration of the government for the management of currency volume and structure. Commercial banks follow the management format of enterprises and currency enters into market like ordinary products and the decision on interest rates is based on the demand and supply of currency. Interest rates and saving reserves act as leverage to adjust credit volumes and structures. Normally, marketization of interest rates should be insisted, instead of the adoption of the above mentioned administrative policies.

(3) Control the investment structure during the whole investment process. The mentioned investment and credit control are based on the control on supply to monitor the investment volume. In order to make the investment policy a desirable one, the whole investment process should be monitored structurally with a certain level of total investment volume. As mentioned before, the need of a nation is one of the greatest principles in economic growth. Therefore, social production development and economic growth all rely on the satisfaction of the total needs of a nation and the structural needs at different levels and even the needs of different individuals. If focus is only placed on the total needs in social production and economic growth instead of the structural needs of a nation, a shortage or surplus in structural supply will occur together with a insufficient total supply. In the end, this will lead to the dissatisfaction of people as part of the economy growth is inefficient and the lives of people are difficult. Therefore, overall control and structural control should be conducted at the same time during the process of investment. Looking at this process from a short term point of view, enhancement of investment structure is achieved through adjusting social demand structure to improve social supply structure, and solving the conflicts between supply structure and demand structure. When there is an expanding demand on non-productive investment in the social demand structure with a low demand on productive investment, the government can adjust the structure through suppressing the non-productive investment and expanding productive investment to change the investment structure; the social demand structure will then be fine tuned and aligned with the social supply within a short period of time. From a long term perspective, investment structure policy shall be carried out through the adjustment of the production structure to fine tune the structure of supply so as to reduce the structural gap between social supply and demand. If there is overproduction in processing industries with a severe shortage of energy, transportation, and other fundamental industries, then a nation needs to make adjustments on the investment structure, contracting currency and credit investment in processing industries while to expand investment in energy, transportation and fundamental industries. Through changes made on the structure of incremental assets, production structure can then be improved with the balance of the supply structure and social demand structure.

When adopting a comprehensive investment structure policy during the whole process of investment, great attention should be paid to structural adjustments in the short and long term, as they have different transmission mechanisms and different depths and breathes of influence. The former aims at short term ease while the latter aims at long term solutions. The short term transmission mechanism is an adjustment on investment demand structure, using the adjustment of investment demands as a means to ease the imbalance situation of social supply and demand structure. The policy produces a precise, direct, and fast effect. The deficiency is that it is only for easing rather than solving the imbalance problem. In order to have the problem thoroughly solved and to realize a stable and coordinated economic growth, the long term effect of investment structure policy should be utilized, and adjustments on investment structure should be executed at a certain level of the total volume of supply and demand. As this kind of structural adjustment is complex, time consuming, multi-leveled, and needs to go through several stages of investment structural adjustment, the production structure adjustment – supply structure adjustment – balance of supply and demand structures, thus the effects will take time to manifest. Leaders and governments of developing countries and regions need to realize this, and need to have persistence to execute the policy. Otherwise, the structural conflicts in economic development will be lengthened without a definite solution for fine tuning and enhancing the structure, the economic efficiency cannot be achieved, and the style of economic growth cannot be changed from aiming at speed to aiming at both speed and efficiency.

11.4 Financial Policy and Economic Growth

Financial policy is one of the policies for the intervention of the economy in developing countries and regions. It is called a "built-in stabilizer" by Western countries in economic growth. From a narrow point of view, financial policy refers to a series of policy instruments related to national finance which use the revenue and expenditure of a country to control total consumption and total investment in order to obtain a balance in total supply and total demand. Besides, it also helps a country to actualize some specific strategic goals. From a broad point of view, financial policy generally includes the policy of taxes, policy of government bonds and national credit issuance, policy of financial allocation and financial investment, policy of financial subsidy, policy of social security which is based on financial expenditure, policy of financial balance and policy of financial mechanism management, etc.

The main purpose of financial policy for a nation is to support and enhance economic growth, to realize a sustainable, stable and coordinated growth in a society, and to serve the highest strategic goal of the strategic police system, through financial revenue and expenditure control. In order to actualize the aim of financial policy, certain kinds of tools need to be chosen. This is going to be covered from two aspects as follows.

First is the government's expenditure policy that includes investment policy, consumption policy, and financial subsidy policy.

(1) Government investment policy is also called a financial investment policy. This is the strongest tool used by the government and one part of the expenditure policy. Two problems need to be avoided when devising this policy: a) traditionally treating government expenditure as a tool for supplying capital for the nation; b) placing the focus of financial policy on fulfilling human need - "public consumption", putting economic establishment investment on

enterprises and banks while ignoring the investment function of the government in economic establishment. In fact, developing countries and regions, especially in socialist ones, the role of government is still important under the condition of the market economy. Government investment is a main source of investment in large infrastructure projects, monopolist projects, public service projects, and national defense projects. Government investment policy is powerful as it is used to adjust economic structure and proportion relations in the development of the national economy, i.e., adjustments on industries, products, resources, technology, labor structure, the relationship of accumulation and consumption, and the proportional relationship in different government departments; it is used to implement comprehensive industrial policy to support the establishment of leading industries and to motivate other general economic establishment projects for a sustainable, stable and coordinated economic growth. It is also used as a macro tool to adjust the economic cycle into a more favorable way to align with the development of the national economy and social planning projects with a rationale of priority and persistence, to select projects according to the importance, to ensure sufficient financial capital support, to effectively control the operation of the economy, and to ensure a healthy and stable national economic growth. Also, it is used to improve the condition of supplies and increase the sources of finance, and concentrating the necessary capital to solve the conflicts between supply and demand in the short run.

(2) Government consumption policy. This is a critical economic strategic tool to adjust consumption by the government intentionally under a certain economic condition. Among the government expenditure, a large amount is spent on maintaining national safety, conducting administrative activities, and paying labor services and salary/wages for civil servants etc. The main means of government consumption are government purchases. The main functions include: a) to directly affect the production of some key departments, to stimulate the development of government focused products and labor to enhance the implementation of national industrial policy; b) to promote employment through increasing government purchase, especially in situations of insufficient employment; c) to fine tune economic cycles, stimulating the recovery of the economy during recessionary periods; d) to support some specific economic strategies, like offering subsides to farming products in some western countries or buying in bulk overstocked farming products at low prices.

(3) Government subsidy policy. This policy bears a strong administrative function in reaching political and economic goals through the allocation of financial capital. This is to give support to those failing enterprises and those enterprises with the nature of social security in production activities. The methods are: a) selecting different kinds of targets with different kinds of intentions to create subsidies for a variety of enterprises, products or projects to

stabilize prices of some specific products or services which affect the livelihood of people, to support new product testing, to promote new technology and develop high technological industries, and to increase the competitiveness of national products in international markets; b) choosing appropriate methods for compensation. There are two kinds of subsidy methods, "Straight-forward" and "Hidden". "Hidden Subsidy" refers to offer subsidies to those enterprises with higher production costs and purchasing costs in certain kinds of products under a condition of "no change" in prices of the products, as these enterprises suffer losses in cost increase. There are no obvious subsidies to consumers as no changes can be found in prices, therefore, so it is called "Hidden Subsidy". Countries having executed a planned economic system usually adopt this kind of subsidy. "Straight-forward" subsidy refers to subsidies offered to consumers. When there is an increase in costs of production or costs in the purchasing of specific products, the prices of these products will rise and the government will offer subsidies to consumers to release pressure. There are two kinds of "Straight-forward" subsidies: welfare-type subsidy and wage-type subsidy. The former type will be given on a per-head basis after prices increase on consumer products while the latter one is used directly to increase people's wages after prices increase on consumer products. Since people know the exact amount of the subsidy, it is therefore called a "Straight-forward" subsidy. No matter whether the subsidy policy is straight-forward or hidden, the main purpose of the government is to: stabilize prices, comfort people psychologically, secure the social environment, and ensure a desirable environment for economic growth. Along with the development of the market economy, the subsidy format will be changed and its amounts will be reduced to focus on price stability and maintain social equality.

Second is the financial revenue policy. The main tool of this policy is the policy of taxes. From the perspective of economic theories, in the past years, people only concentrate on its fundamental role as financial policy, and treat it as a tool for guaranteeing financial income. Along with the development of an open modernized economy, people start to realize that financial policy also affects their social economic activities by adjusting the direction and the level of economic development. Under modernized economic growth, as a tool for adjusting economy, taxes have the following characteristics: 1) Coerciveness. Individuals or legal entities have to fulfill the tax obligations imposed by the government, or they will suffer legal punishment. 2) Flexibility and diversity. Tax collection is an administrative tool to manage conflicts or solve problems in economic activities through imposing or discharging tax regulations, changing tax rates, and increasing or deleting tax credit, etc. 3) Regularity and generalization. Under modernized economic growth, tax adjustment has been changed from temporary and short run to regular and long run with all areas of social production and all aspects of the national economy involved. Surely, there are other characteristics of tax collection, but they are all derived from the above three characteristics. Hence, this will not be illustrated in details here.

11.5 Monetary Policy and Economic Growth

Monetary policy is one of the main policies government uses to adjust the total volume and quality of capital in the currency and capital market, and conduct   systematic and administrative control over these two markets, so as to intervene the national economic activities for actualizing the economic growth. It is an important part of the policy system used for adjusting economic growth.

In market economic operation, monetary policy is implemented by the central bank within the banking mechanism which represents the government. The banking mechanism is an organizational system for utilizing the function of monetary policy. Within this system, the central bank is the authority for devising and executing monetary policy on behalf of the country and the government to monitor commercial banks and other monetary organizations. The main functions are: to adjust and control commercial banks, to manage monetary mechanisms of the whole country, to control currency supply and credit issuance, and to align the monetary policy with the macro level goals of the economy. The central bank is a government bank and also the bank of all commercial banks. It is the only authority and the last resort with power to issue notes and coins, to act on behalf of the government to buy and sell their bonds, to collect government taxes and other revenues, to keep accounts for the government, to balance its revenue and expenditure, and to submit all the profits over a certain level to the government as financial revenue. Commercial banks handle current deposits and offer credit loaning services to most industrial and commercial enterprises. The more developed the countries and regions are, the larger the system of commercial banks will be. The number of commercial banks that handle current deposits all over the world total around 14,000 to 15,000. In 2002-2003, America possessed three of the ten largest banks in the world. In 1999, the assets of the top 50 banks out of 6,800 banking organizations assumed 74% of the total assets of all banks in the world, and 10 of them assumed 49%; and 8 out of the 10 assumed 78.6% of the total assets of all banks in America. However, the commercial banking system is rather weak in developing countries and regions as their economic level is low and their ability of colleting savings and accumulating capital is not strong. The primary services of commercial banks are taking current savings and issuing short term loans with a function of currency issuance and withdrawal. For these credit activities, commercial banks have to put a reserve in the central bank for the withdrawal of money by account holders. This has turned into a tool to control commercial banks for limiting currency supply. The amount of reserve put in the central bank is determined not by the amount of withdrawals, but by legal regulations. Commercial banks will not put the whole amount of the reserve in the central bank. Instead, they will keep part of it as cash reserve.

Under the operation of the national economy, commercial banks control the currency supply through savings and lending activities in order to intervene in the economy. This function is achieved through expanding or contracting the amount of current savings. In the banking mechanism, the amount of initial savings and lending can be multiplied several times through financial activities and means. This is what the Western monetary theory called the ability of creating money by the banks. It appears in the following two ways in economic activities.

(1) Through issuing loans to or withdrawing loans from individuals or enterprises to increase or reduce the amount of current savings. For example, a person A applies for a loan of 10,000 Yuan from a bank and gets approval. However, A does not take the money out immediately, instead, the approved loan is deposited into his bank account. If commercial banks are expanding credit loans through current savings, the currency supply in the whole society will be increased. Oppositely, A does not return any money back to the bank upon the repayment due date, instead, he reduces the amount of 10,000 Yuan to his current account, then the whole current savings will be reduced by 10,000 Yuan.

(2) Through buying and selling bonds from individuals or enterprises to increase or decrease current savings. For example, a bank buys government bonds from an enterprise at the price of 10,000 (unit: Yuan; same as below). If this enterprise deposits the money into its account, its current saving will be increased by 10,000 Yuan; if the enterprise presents a check to another bank, the saving of that bank will be increased by 10,000. These two methods will generate the same result, increasing bank saving by 10,000 and money supply in the society will be expanded. On the contrary, current savings in banks will be reduced by 10,000 with the money supply decreasing accordingly.

The expansion of current savings cannot be achieved only with one bank. It is a result of the whole banking mechanism. Suppose bank A takes in 10,000 saving from a specific enterprise or individual, and leaves only 20% (i.e. 2,000) as reserve with the remaining 80% (i.e. 8,000) lent out or used for buying bonds, then money supply in the society will be increased by 8,000. This is to illustrate the relationship of a single bank and the society in relation to savings and currency supply. However, the amount of money created by banks is the multiple of the initial amount under the banking mechanism. That is, bank A takes in the initial deposit of 10,000 and withholds 20% as reserve and lends out 8,000, then, an enterprise or an individual who takes in the loan will deposits it into bank B. Bank B then leaves 20% of 8,000 (i.e. 1,600) as reserve and lends out the remaining amount of 6,400. This kind of cycle will keep on revolving until the total saving and loan amount reaches 50,000, which is 5 times of the original amount. This can be expressed in the following formula:

$$D = 1/r \times R \text{ or } D = R/r$$

. In which, D = the total amount of loan created by the banks; R = the original amount; r = deposit reserve rate, e.g.

    If R = 10,000, r = 20%, then D =20/R = 10,000/1/5 = 50,000

    If R = 10,000, r = 10%, then D = R/r = 10,000/ 1/10 = 100,000

When the deposit reserve rate is reduced from 20% to 10%, the initial deposit of 10,000 will become 100,000 through the creation power of credit activities of the banking mechanism. Hence, the inverse of the deposit reserve rate of r, i.e., 1/r, is the multiplier of banks, which has two functions: enlarging the amount of savings a few times or reducing it a few times. The process of saving expansion is the process of loan expansion and vice versa. During the money creation process, the process of increasing or decreasing savings will be quite similar.

However, the increase or decrease in currency will bring a significant impact to the economy and will intervene in the operation of social economic growth. In order to control the process to minimize the negative effect of money creation power on economic growth and maximize the positive effect, market economy countries have to adopt currency policies to a certain extent. Under a market economy, the management of currency by the central bank includes the management of coins, bills and current savings. For money supply, current savings takes up the greatest proportion, instead of coins and bills. Therefore, the central bank needs to monitor the current savings appropriately, the key point is to appropriately manage the reserve and to determine a deposit reserve rate.

Under normal situations, the policy used by the central bank in the management of the currency supply is "Against the Trend of the Economy". This is what Western economists call adopting appropriate monetary policy. When there is a deficiency of currency supply, employment and demand will not be sufficient for economic growth. When there will be an economic recession, the central bank will increase currency supply through lowering the reserve rate, and the multiplying effect of currency creation to stimulate the increase of current savings. With an increase in the currency supply and decrease in loan interest rates, banks will have enough money for investment activities. Economic growth and income expansion will come along with the multiplying effect. Increasing the reserve ratio and loan interest rates will achieve an opposite effect of tightening the economy. The two rates of monetary policy, i.e., reserve rate and interest rate, are used for adjusting the currency supply.

So, when adopting monetary policy with these two rates, what kind of tactics do we need to use?

A) Open market operation. When the central bank engages itself in the open market for buying or selling government bonds, this is actually a tactic to control the reserves of commercial banks. This method is commonly used by the central bank to stabilize the economy and is also flexible. When there is an indication of an economic recession without sufficient investments or employment, the central bank will buy the government bonds in hand to increase the reserves of the commercial banks. If the owners of the bonds are not commercial banks, they will deposit the money into the commercial bank accounts to increase the current savings, and their reserves. When the reserves of commercial banks are increased, the current savings will be multiplied a few times along with the increase in the currency supply. The interest rate in commercial banks will be lowered, which can stimulate investments and economic growth with better employment conditions. Oppositely, the central bank will sell government bonds to tighten the economy.

B) Discount rate change. Discounts are the loans the central bank lends to commercial banks and discount rates are the interest charged by the central bank for the discount. When there is a need for stimulating the economy through an input of currency, the discount rate will be lowered to increase the volume, so as to encourage commercial banks to issue loans and make investments; on the contrary, the discount rate will be increased to control the volume under the situation of price increase and "overheating". Simultaneously, the central bank will make use of reserves to lower or increase loan interests to expand or reduce credit loans.

C) Deposit reserve rate change. This is a ratio of banking reserve and deposit. As the reserve rate is a legal requirement, it is also called a legal reserve rate. The rate is determined by the nature of banks, types of deposits, terms and amount of deposits. Generally, the rate for banks in cities is higher than those in villages while the rate for current savings is higher than that of fixed deposits. There is also a maximum and a minimum regulatory reserve rate. The profit maximization principle requires commercial banks to keep a minimum reserve rate. The central bank is authorized to make changes on the reserve rate within a certain range for current savings in commercial banks to adjust the currency and credit loan supply. Under normal situations, the reserve percentage cannot be changed beyond a certain range without approval from an authorized organization. As mentioned before, changing the reserve rate is a kind of tactic to expand or tighten economic growth through increasing or decreasing of the reserve amount.

D) Moral guidance. This refers to the verbal or written advice the central bank gives to commercial banks to persuade them to loosen or tighten credit loans voluntary without any mandatory obligation. The precondition of using this kind of tactic is that the central bank possesses influential power to limit the actions of commercial banks.

E) Selective control or credit securities control. This is a partial control of securities credit under the market economy. It is different from comprehensive control. Comprehensive control is carried out by increasing or decreasing the amount of reserves and loosening or tightening credit loans. Selective control is only applied to some specific credit demands without impacting the currency or credit supply of the whole society. The way of implementing selective control is to fix the minimum cash repayment and the maximum cash repayment terms. Normally, the purpose of lowering the cash payment amount and lengthening the term is to loosen credit control, and vice versa.

F) Installment credit control and mortgage credit control. This is a control imposed by the central bank on the conditions of issuing installment credit loans and mortgage credit loans. Installment credit loan is a kind of service provided to consumers for buying durable goods, like automobiles, televisions, refrigerators, etc., or provided to enterprises for purchasing machinery. This can stimulate consumption and enhance production development and economic growth. Initially, mortgage credit loans were provided to housing purchasers with the house as a pledge, but now this kind of loan has developed as a means to ensure loan security, to control credit and to intervene in the economy.

Among these six tactics, the first three tactics, i.e., open market operation, discount rate change and reserve rate change, are used by the central bank as a main monetary policy tactic to adjust currency supply. They can be used together or independently. The integrated use of the open market and discount rate is mainly for adjusting macroeconomic activities. The reserve rate change is only used on special occasions. The remaining three tactics are complementary to support the first three tactics. This is a common situation found in countries all over the world under a market economy. However, one thing that needs to be paid attention to is that each country has its own conditions and stages of economic development, therefore, the monetary policy will be different in different countries. Along with economic and monetary development, countries and regions need to modify or increase their monetary adjustment tools and change their currency administrative policy according to their realistic local and international monetary development.

11.6 Income Allocation Policy and Economic Growth

The aforesaid monetary policy and financial policy are directly applied to social demands. Through the change of these demands, income level, price level, and other economic variables will be modified to actualize macro-level economic adjustment within policy systems under social economic growth. However, under a market economy, income, price and other variables are affected by not only total demands, but also spontaneous market forces. In order to actualize monetary policy and financial policy simultaneously with an effective control on the blind effect of market power, there is a need to choose, devise and implement policy of income allocation. During social production and re-production, the process of national income allocation is a middle stage with close connections to aggregate supply and demand, their structures, and social economic interests. Hence, income allocation policy is an important macro-level policy under the policy system to adjust conflicts among social demand, social supply and social benefit. It can be used together with other macro-level economic policies for better adjustment results.

So, how can income allocation policy adjust social supply and demand under national economic operation? And how can this adjustment process solve the conflicts between aggregate social supply and aggregate social demand? This links up to the function of income allocation policy and its relationship with economic growth which needs to be clarified. Under a market economy, aggregate social demand is determined by the currency income of economic entities such as the government, enterprises and individuals. The currency income of economic entities is finally determined by the volume and the structure of national income allocation. The function of income allocation policy in the interaction of three parties is to: enhance the formation of the structures of aggregate supply and aggregate demand to make them consistent with the volume and structure of the national income in order to solve the conflicts in volume and structure between aggregate supply and aggregate demand, through adjusting the volume and structure of the national currency income. This function can change the ultimate volume of the national income in the form of currency, to make the volume of the national income in the form of currency greater than, equal to or smaller than the actual volume of the national income. Finally, distributed currency from the national income produces different kinds of coordinated conditions between the total volume and structure of social demand and those of social supply. Hence, normally, there are three types of income allocation policies used by countries which can generate different levels of adjustments on the relationship between social aggregate supply and social aggregate demand.

Different effects of applying the three types of income allocation policies have been described as follows.

(1) "Surplus" income allocation policy or "Tight" policy. This kind of policy makes the ultimate distributed volume of the national income in the form of currency smaller than the actual volume of the national income. Different kinds of effects will be generated under different economic conditions: a) under the condition of social demand expansion, demand can be suppressed to a level equal to social supply; b) under the condition of the balance between social supply and demand, aggregate social demand from the distributed national income in currency form can be decreased to be less than the aggregate social supply, causing imbalance in the aggregate social demand and aggregate social supply; c) under the condition of insufficient aggregate social demand, a further suppression on aggregate social demand can lengthen its distance with aggregate social supply and make a further imbalance in demand and supply. The use of this income distribution policy is to further reduce aggregate social demand. This policy is suitable for a situation of a fast growth in aggregate social demand which exceeds that of aggregate social supply, Under the development of economic growth, if the growth rate of aggregate social demand outweighs the growth rate of aggregate social supply and even goes beyond the ability that the actual growth rate of aggregate social supply can bear, a country or region will usually adopt a "tight" income distribution policy. Otherwise, the "overheated"

demand cannot be suppressed; the rising price level cannot be curbed; aggregate social demand and supply cannot obtain a gradual balance; and social economy cannot have a stable and coordinated growth.

If aggregate social demand is growing slower than the aggregate social supply without exceeding the ability that the actual aggregate social supply can bear, the tight income distribution policy will normally not be used. Otherwise, two negative effects will appear: a) aggregate social demand formed from distributed national income in currency form is lower than the supply of products and services, then the value of some products and services would not be realized, which would lead to the waste of social resources and the lack of driving force for economic growth; b) the growth rate of social demand is far behind the actual growth rate of aggregate social supply, and then social supply would lack a driving force, and the growth of aggregate social supply would be suppressed. Hence, only under the condition of fast-growing aggregate demand which is beyond the actual ability of aggregate social supply, and when an expansionary demand is formed, will the execution of tight income distribution policy bring positive effects such as improving the economic environment and enhancing a stable and coordinated economic growth. Otherwise, there will be negative effects on total social demand and total social supply with a worsened economic situation and hindered economic growth.

(2) "Balanced" income allocation policy. This kind of policy will be adopted when the volume of ultimate distributed national income in currency form is almost the same as the actual volume of national income. Adopting this kind of policy can maintain a balance between total social demand and total social supply for an orderly economy and generate sufficient demand to motivate economic development and to maintain stable economic growth. However, when aggregate social demand is much greater or smaller than social supply, the use of this policy will bring negative results and enlarge the distance between total social demand and total social supply, which will affect the operation of a national economy and hinder the economic growth. This tells us that only under a quite balanced economic operation can adopting a "balanced" income allocation policy bring a positive effect; but when the economy is "overheated" or "overcooled", this policy is not appropriate.

(3) "Expansionary" income allocation policy. This kind of policy will be adopted when the volume of the ultimate distributed volume of national income in currency form is greater than the actual volume of national income, i.e., an aggressive national allocation policy. The result of the implementation of this policy is that, the volume of the ultimate distribution of national income would be greater than the total social supply within a specified period or be even greater than the accumulated total supply in the past years, and exceed the actual growth ability of total social supply. Hence, only under the condition of

insufficient total social demand or total social supply exceedingly greater than social demand, or when total social demand has already been greater than total social supply but within the actual growth ability of total supply, this policy can be used to generate positive results, such as to make the growth of social demand close to or be slightly over the level of social supply, and to speed up economic growth. If total social demand and supply are balanced, or the former is greater than the latter, adopting this policy would cause or worsen the imbalance between social demand and social supply. A deficiency of supply and high prices, along with financial pressures, will disturb the normal operation of the economy and hinder technological development and economic growth. Therefore, "expansionary" policy can only be used under the first two conditions. In the situation that aggregate social demand is greater than aggregate social supply but within its growth ability, application of "expansionary" policy can generate some positive effects for the development of productivity and macro-level economic coordination in a certain period of time, but this policy cannot be used for a long period of time. Once the total social demand gets close to the actual growth ability of total social supply, this policy has to be stopped.

Based on the aforesaid information, tight, expansionary and balanced income allocation policies have different effects on the formation of aggregate social demand and on the conflicts between aggregate social demand and aggregate social supply. On one hand, the common conflict found in developing countries and regions is a greater social demand then social supply. Hence, when getting ready for economic take-off, a tight income allocation policy should be considered to suppress the blindly expansionary demand instead of an expansionary income allocation policy.

On the other hand, the structure of income allocation policy has a strong effect on production and supply and it can determine the social demand structure to a certain extent. Therefore, income allocation policy has an important function in adjusting conflicts of the demand structure and supply structure. Effective adjustments on both sides can often be found. During the operation of a national economy, the national income is usually split between consumption and accumulation. Consumption refers to living expenses in a society which usually transforms into individual expenses. Accumulation refers to re-production accumulation in a society with a certain part, about 40%, however, it may be increased along with the level of economic performance, transforming into individual consumption during the process of the formation of accumulation while the rest turning into new fixed assets. In these two aspects of the national income, consumption has a shorter cycle of operation, while accumulation, has a longer cycle of operation. Hence, the adjustment function of income allocation policy on the national income distribution plays a role of structural adjustment on these two parts in short and long runs. The following is a description of the adjustment process and effects of these two areas.

First, make adjustments on total consumption fund volume and structure to influence the changes on demand structure to balance demand structure and supply structure. It is assumed that there will be an adjustment function on short term social demand. There are two ways to do this. A) To make changes on the demand structure through adjusting income. The structure of demand is mainly affected by the income structure. The increase in income usually stimulates people to make more consumption on a higher level of living needs after their fundamental living needs have been satisfied. This will make changes on the expenditure pattern of their income which will ultimately affect demand structure to obtain a balance between demand structure and supply structure. B) To adjust demand structure through price discrimination. Price discrimination is a re-allocation mechanism after national income. Prices are what drive people to make purchases in the market. Under the situation of price fluctuation, people will seek for substitute products to satisfy their needs, which will consequently affect the structure of demand. Surely, under a market economy, prices cannot be directly fixed by countries, hence, price discrimination will not be determined directly either. However, indirect methods can be used to adjust price differences so as to modify the structure of demand, reaching a coordinated balance between the demand structure and supply structure at the end.

Second, make adjustments on the total accumulation fund volume and structure, therefore, certain volumes of incremental capital will be formed in a long period to adjust the structure of the total supply so that it can meet the requirements of the demand structure. There are two ways to do this. A) To change the allocation proportions of accumulation funds in the different departments of a national economy in order to adjust the supply structure. That is to say, when the structure of new assets is changed, the existing assets will be restructured, so as to adjust the supply structure to make it consistent with the demand structure. This is the most important way for the income allocation policy to adjust the supply structure through changing the investment allocation structure. B) To change interest rates, tax rates, salaries and prices and use differentiated interest rates, differentiated tax rates, differentiated salaries and differentiated prices to adjust the allocation structures of fixed assets, labor, technology and other key elements in different industries. Thus making them transfer from long-term industrial departments into short-term industrial departments with deficient supply to enhance adjustment of supply structure aligned along with changes of demand structure.

Finally, the function of using income allocation policy to adjust conflicts in economic interests cannot be ignored as it affects economic growth.

Under a market economy, two situations cannot be avoided in national income distribution: 1) the enlargement of the income gap; 2) and the increase of non-labor income and objective differential income. The existence of these two situations is necessary with positive effects in developing countries and regions during the process of economic take-off. During national income distribution, the enlargement of the income gap has a positive impact of stimulating economic efficiency, promoting the development of social productivity, and increasing social wealth in an efficient way. The increase of non-labor income and objective differential income such as the increase of interest earned and stock dividends, can be helpful for savings and social capital accumulation to expand establishment capital, to motivate technological application and upgrading, and to enlarge the scale of production. However, some problems may come up. For example, social conflicts will become more serve with instability affecting stable social economic growth if the income gap keeps on enlarging under spontaneous adjustments from the market economy. If the proportion of non-labor income and objective differential income is too large, the economic effect will turn from positive into negative, creating an imbalance in the social benefit structure of which people may not be tolerant, and causing instability in the society which will affect economic growth. This kind of effect can be harmful in developing countries and regions with a market economy mechanism; hence, the negative effect in China with a socialist market economy mechanism cannot be ignored as its result conflicts with the principle of the common wealth under socialism. Therefore, in order to create and maintain a desirable economic environment under the process of economic take-off, it is necessary to choose, devise, and implement appropriate income allocation policy to fine-tune the allocation structure of national income, and to adjust the effects of the enlargement of the income gap and the increase of non-labor income and objective differential income. In social and economic activities, large income gaps should be avoided so that there will be a balanced interests structure and a stable material economic foundation in the society.

One thing that needs to be paid attention to is efficiency in the income allocation policy when fine tuning conflicts in economic interests. Under economic development, both the goal of income differences and that of preventing wide income gaps are to enhance labor productivity. These two scenarios have the same principle of emphasizing efficiency. The difference is that, the former is a micro-level adjustment in labor production while the latter is a macro-level adjustment by minimizing social conflicts and maintaining social stability. Without a firm upholding of this principle in national income distribution, there will result in existence of severe unfairness or absolute equality, the social benefit structure will be imbalanced, and will affect labor productivity and hinder economic growth. Hence, the priority of emphasizing efficiency should be considered in the making and implementation of the income distribution policy.

For socialist developing countries like China, their economic system and the goal of achieving common wealth determine that, they need to make the following differential adjustments on non-labor income and objective differential income. A) Savings and social capital accumulation as dividends of stocks and bonds, and interest earned. These kinds of income should be encouraged but with differentiation: the former should not be adjusted through taxes while the latter can be adjusted with a low tax rate. If the amount is not too large, tax is not needed. B) Non-labor income generated from circulation or other non-economic factors, in which non-labor income created by individuals or enterprises from strategies of differentiated prices, differentiated interest rates, differentiated tax rates, differentiated salaries is beneficial to the macro level of social adjustments. There is no need to adopt an income distribution policy to make stringent adjustments to this kind of income. However, for non-labor income formed by individuals or enterprises spontaneously from circulation of elements, like price and monopoly factors, a certain level of income allocation policy can be adopted to settle the conflicts in economic interests, to create a competitive economic environment, to motivate enthusiasm for production in individuals and enterprises, and to enhance economic growth and supply increase. C) Differential income generated from natural factors rather than subjective labor conditions. Countries can use income allocation policy to adjust certain kinds of income earned in this aspect in order to create a desirable production environment with equality, to protect and save resources in the processes of production and operation. 4) Non-labor income of private enterprises. Adjustment on this kind of income varies in developing countries and regions. For socialist developing countries, this belongs to a non-socialist economic category. This has to be monitored strictly by using income allocation policy to transfer part of it into national owned or collective owned, in order to prevent the occurrence of income disparity and social instability. For those non-socialist developing countries, a policy of income allocation is often used to adjust this kind of income, but may not be that severe as in socialist developing countries

11.7 Consumption Policy and Economic Growth

Consumption is a basic element in the process of social production and re-production. As Marx said, "no consumption, no production."[92] Under this process, consumption policy with its content of adjusting consumption activities, together with other related policies, especially investment combination policy, plays an important role as leverage in adjusting the structure of social demand and social supply and in the operation of a national economy. These policies and other macro-level economic policies construct the policy system which is the adjustment function in economic growth.

Consumption policy is crucial in a policy system and it has a close connection with other policies as well as relative independence, which reflects the basic economic relationship in consumption activities. From the perspective of a macro operation of the national economy, consumption has a structure with multi-level economic relations and is a process of economic activities during the distribution among different entities. During the process of social production and re-production, from the perspective consumption entities, consumption includes the government expenditure, organizational expenditure, enterprise expenditure, and individual expenditure. From the viewpoint of consumption, it covers several economic relationships. The first is the economic relationship within national income distribution. This relationship is formed from the initial distribution between enterprises and individuals within enterprises in the departments producing materials and services. It indicates the relationship among individual income, enterprise income and national tax income. Next is the economic relationship from the re-distribution of the national income in the society. In this re-distribution process, a new kind of distribution relationship is formed among individuals, enterprises, and the nation. Part of the individual income, enterprise income and national financial income will form a new distribution relationship through price mechanism, labor service charge, and national budget. Hence, under a market economy, distribution and re-distribution of national income involve the economic relationship among the government, enterprises and individuals. Every adjustment on volumes and structures is the adjustment on economic interests, therefore, new social consumption volumes and structures will be formed with impacts on social economic growth. This illustrates that consumption is an economic process which involves consumption activities of the government, organizations, enterprises and individuals with its scale and level directly determined by the volume and structure of national income distribution and re-distribution. Under a market economy, distribution and re-distribution of national income are greatly influenced and constrained by market mechanisms and administrative intervention by the government can only be actualized through tax collection and financial budgets. If the national income is determined totally by the market mechanism, income distribution will be out of control, possibly losing control of consumption as well. Surely, when the direction of consumption is out of control, national income distribution derived from consumption expectation will be out of control, which may lead to an imbalanced economic interest structure. If the imbalanced situation gets worse to a certain level, price soaring may appear which makes economic activities tense and influences the healthy development and stable growth of the national economy. Therefore, developing countries and regions have to consider clearly which consumption policy to choose and implement when actualization economic take-off, in order to make macro-level adjustments on income allocations and the total volume and structure of social consumption, so as to create a comparatively loose economic environment.

Besides, consumption policy is a reflection of the objective pattern of consumption activities in social production and re-production, showing the relationship between consumption and production as well as the basis of the impact of consumption policy on economic growth. According to the economic theory of Marx, production and consumption can be a unified system under social re-production, as they are consistently interdependent, interrelated, and inter-convertible under the certain conditions. However, they have their own unique positions and functions. Production is the staring part of the process of all economic activities and is an important element. It can create targets for consumption, the subjects of consumption and their consumption patterns. It determines the level and structure of consumption, limits consumption ability, and also determines the total volume and foundation of consumption. However, consumption is the ending part of direct production and it links with social re-production. Though it may be subject to production, it does not passively or negatively adapt to production. Under the developmental process of social production, it not only makes production finished and become actual products, but also has a rebounding effect on production (i.e., it may hinders or enhances the development of production and the whole social economy). The growth in consumption is actually the growth of social demand which will be a kind of new demand produced from social re-production for a new market to stimulate stronger economic growth. From this perspective, consumption determines production, and without consumption, no production will occur; without a continuous growth in consumption, there will not be a tremendous development in production or sustainable economic growth. Hence, adjusting the relationship between consumption and production is a critical issue in the development of production and the actualization of sustainable economic growth. If consumption is adjusted inappropriately, over consumption will appear and lead to excessive social demand and deficient social supply, or under consumption will appear and lead to a shrinking production. This is to show the leverage function of consumption policy in adjusting consumption. Because of its direct economic function, it can adjust the total volume and structure of consumption. If selection of consumption policy is inappropriate without a proper adjustment, or the adjustment goes out of control, aggregate demand and aggregate supply will not be balanced and there will be tension in economic activities and an economic recession.

So, what kind of consumption policy can developing countries and regions select to enhance sustainable and coordinated economic growth? Generally speaking, there are three kinds of consumption polices.

First, the under consumption policy, which is a kind of policy focusing on production and accumulation but not consumption. The key point of this policy is to focus on accumulation rather than consumption, and to emphasize expanding the production of production goods rather than the production of consumption goods; or only concentrating on satisfying a lower level of living needs for necessity products, instead of a higher level of needs for consumer products, without improving or upgrading the structure of consumption. As this kind of policy aims at limiting consumption rather than increasing consumption based on production development, this will hold back the growth rate of consumption to a point which is far below the growth rate of production and that of labor productivity, making social demand insufficient for economic growth. This kind of under consumption policy has been adopted by developing countries and regions for a long time to stimulate production. The result is generally undesirable. Under consumption appears without the actualization of economic take-off in economic growth; or there is little economic growth and the living standard of people has not been improved, which leads to dissatisfaction and may even cause undesirable political events such as in Russia or some other countries in Eastern Europe.

Second, the over consumption policy. In contrast with the first one, this policy emphasizes on stimulating a rapid increase in consumption with its rate higher than economic growth and labor productivity growth, and focuses on making currency earned by laborers and consumption expenditure outweigh the growth of consumer goods production. This is a policy inducing consumption. The direct results of this policy are: a) making saving reduced with insufficient capital, and making the expansion of re-production difficult; b) causing the unreasonable distribution of resources which excessively concentrates in the industries and enterprises producing existing consumer products and new consumer products. Hence, this policy cannot balance economic development but leads to economic imbalance and hinders economic growth.

Third, appropriate consumption policy. This policy aims at having consumption growth based on production development and enhancement in economic efficiency rather than deviate from production development and economic efficiency; make the growth rate a little lower than the growth of the national economy and labor productivity; guarantee a certain degree of accumulation for the benefit of enhancing economic development. Hence, this appropriate consumption policy is good for adjusting the relationship between consumption and production with a reasonable distance on the whole, so investment and economic growth will not be affected by the growth of consumption, affecting the enthusiasm and creativity of labor will not be affected by insufficient consumption, and the lack of initiative will not appear in social productivity development. This policy is undoubtedly more suitable for developing countries and regions as it can generate a more coordinated economic relationships among accumulation and consumption, production and living in the national economy, for maintaining balance in total volume and structure of aggregate social supply and aggregate total demand, for creating a more desirable economic environment for development, and for enhancing sustainable economic growth. The above analysis demonstrates that, the demerits of the first two policies, i.e., over consumption policy and under consumption policy, outweigh their merits, so they are not suitable for developing countries and regions. But appropriate consumption policy is a better policy for a coordinated operation of national economy and for economic growth. It is suitable for developing countries and regions to adjust economic activities, to enhance healthy economic development, and to obtain efficient growth.

Choosing consumption policy is only part of the issue. Its implementation and actualization of goals are also important. After determining an appropriate consumption policy, two elements need to be considered in the actual operation of the consumption policy.

First, keep a close watch on the initial allocation within enterprises and control impulsive consumption expansion in enterprises. The first or primary national income allocation is found in enterprises and plays an important role in the formation of the total volume and structure of the consumption fund. Under a market economy, developing socialist countries may suffer from having the initial income allocation out of control, as their interests conflict with state-owned and collective enterprises because of the consumption expansion impulse of their members and the short-term economic behaviors of their leaders. This can be found in non-socialist developing countries or regions. Though asset foundation and management systems in enterprises in non-socialist countries may be different, generally they are not national-owned with a company-based enterprise system, from that of socialist developing countries, there may also be consumption expansion in their initial national income allocation. Mobility of labor exists in enterprises. A worker usually stays in a certain enterprise for a very short period of time and the benefit from his accumulation can only be got very late, so enlarging accumulation affects not only the salaries of existing workers, but also the bonus payment of shareholders; hence, enterprises expect to have a benefit mechanism of more income allocation at a earlier day and through little accumulation. Representatives of long term benefits are the board of directors and key shareholders, but they may have to agree to distribute more income in immediate consumption and increase the consumption fund because of the above mentioned benefit mechanism. All these can demonstrate that one of the important problems that need to be solved in the consumption policy is to prevent control of the process of initial national income allocation among enterprises. It is also an important issue in actualizing appropriate consumption policy. Actually, it can only be solved by the mechanism of self-constraint on consumption expansion in enterprises themselves.

Second, keep a close watch on the re-allocation of national income to avoid the expansion of consumption caused by over allocation. Over allocation in national income is a critical issue causing the consumption fund to expand. Under normal conditions, over allocation in currency payment usually does not appear in the initial national income allocation in the economic cycle. It only occurs in the re-allocation of the national income under the administrative operation of the government. Over allocation of the national income in the form of currency needs to be based on the over issuance of currency. Initial national income allocation occurs in enterprises at the micro-level. As enterprises have no power to over issuance currency, over allocation in national income cannot be found at this level. However, the re-allocation process is different as the central government participates in this economic process. The central government has the authority to issue currency over a certain limit, like overdraft protection and issuance of currency in a non-economic ways when the situation of budget deficit occurs. These two methods may lead to the expansion of the consumption fund with "high-level consumption" or "overconsumption" in a society.

Therefore, it is an important step to control re-allocation of the national income, to prohibit the over issuance of currency, and to limit financial deficit through overdrafts from banks. Adopting an appropriate consumption policy can avoid an unreasonable expansion of social consumption.

Chapter Twelve

Economic System: Institutional Conditions for

Sustainable Economic Growth

As a development process of social productivity, modern economic growth is conducted under a concrete economic system which follows certain basic economic rules. Under this process, the contents of social economic growth include the development of social productivity, the spiral expansion of social production, and the increase of social wealth. The logics of social economic growth include relations among different groups of people (the economic subjects), and relations between human and production materials and the structure of interests formed in social production and social lives, and the social motive mechanism empowering them into social production. These two aspects are integrated during the growth of social economy as they are complementary to each other. Social economic growth cannot be separated from social economic mechanism. The function of social economic mechanism is to support economic growth. Hence, when analyzing social economic growth, its association with social economic mechanism and the impact of this association, the connection between the effects of social economic mechanism and practices of social entities, are not negligible.

12.1 The Meaning of Economic System and the Detrimental Factors for Selection

Economic system as the social formation of the economic growth process, which is with relative independence yet constraint from basic social economic institutions, is an institutional condition for social economic growth. We need to understand the meaning and selection of economic system about economic growth, linking it up with the actual basic social economic institutions. Karl Marx said: "The relations of production in their totality constitute what is called social relations, society, and, moreover, a society at a definite stage of historical development, a society with peculiar, distinctive characteristics."[93] This tells us that the social economic institutions are the totality of social production relations adapted with the social productivity at a certain historical stage, and form a kind of social-material relation existing in a certain society. The basic economic institution of a society, which matches with the level of social productivity development at a definite stage, is the social economic institution decided by the society's dominant production relation, and it also serves for this dominant production relation. What is called the economic system is decided by the basic social institution and reflects this institution. The economic system is a concrete social-economic form which responds more directly and flexibly to the requirements of social economic entities and the social economic process. Under the process of social economic growth actualization, an economic system mainly includes the following items: 1) Viewed from the phases of economic growth process, there are mechanisms of enterprise production and operation, price, product circulation, foreign trade, finance, tax and income allocation, etc.; 2) Viewed from the process control of national economy operation, there is an operation mechanism of national economy; 3) Viewed from the composing of productive relationship, there are a structure of production relations and a mechanism of assets management. Linking up these three areas, economic systems functions as a mechanism of integrated economic structure which constitute of economic structure, and social economic decision making and implementation, and are based on the social relations of ownership and identifiable by its national economy operation mechanism.

In an actual social economic life, the basic economic institution determines the economic system while the economic system illustrates the economic institution. However, there is some distance between the two. An economic system is relatively independent from an economic institution. Although it serves the institution, it does not directly reflect the social nature of the institution. This independency mainly is sourced from the economic system itself as a form of social links that occur during production. When the national economy operates, the establishment and development of an economic system are determined by the technical and artistic natures of production technology and the accumulations of technology and organizational management experience, rather than the replacement of authoritative organizations and the nature of social reforms. Thus an economic system can be historically continual at a definite stage of productivity development. When he analyzed the capitalist society in *Capital*, Karl Marx delivered the ownership and the allocation, as well as the production operation and organizational management. The basic economic institution constitutes a fundamental structure of a society and demonstrates this structure's social political-economic institution. It is a part of fundamental social institutions and its core issue centers around people's political-economic positions and their economic and political interests decided by their positions. Different from this, the economic system is a techno- organizational management structure which is constructed on the technique artistry of productivity. Its core is technical and organizational relations that occur when people are in social productions and social activities.

The so-called varied kinds of economic systems (or organizational operational system) are a reflection of the techno-organizational structure. If the basic social structure is to find out to whom it produces and to whom it works for – a beneficial scope with a strong sense of hierarchy and politics, then the scope of techno-organizational structure is about how to produce and how to work – a functional scope without a direct connection with hierarchy and politics. Because of this kind of relative independence in economic systems, countries implementing different kinds of social economic systems can choose a similar or the same kind of economic mechanisms at their own phases of development, while countries implementing the same kind of social economic systems can choose different kinds of social economic mechanisms at their different phases of economic development. Based on the situation of economic development in every country, socialist countries implement the same kind of socialist public ownership as their basic economic system, however, the selection of an economic mechanism in their phases of development are not the same. Some pick highly centered planned economic mechanisms, some choose an integrated economic mechanism of planned and market adjustment, some select the mechanism of a socialist market economy, etc. Capitalist countries carry out the mechanism of capitalism with private ownership. However, the selection of an economic mechanism in different stages or within the same stage of economic development varies. Some choose the traditional market economy mechanism, that is, a laissez-faire market economic mechanism (for example, Britain); some select free market economic mechanism (for example, America); some pick a planned adjustment market economic mechanism (for example, France); some choose a social market economic mechanism (for example, Germany); and some select welfare market economic mechanism (for example, Sweden), etc. Modernized socialist countries (like China which has been reformed) and capitalist countries have different mechanisms – the former with socialist public ownership economic mechanisms while the latter with capitalist private ownership economic mechanisms. However, both of them choose market economy mechanisms. This kind of universal basic social economic system and the diversified economic mechanisms illustrate that global basic economic systems can have a social nature, asset nature, and a communal nature. However, as economic mechanisms are relatively independent from social economic systems, the key characteristics do not include the issues of asset or community. Hence, Xiaoping Deng pointed out, "To be more oriented in a planned economy or in market economy is not the difference between the nature of socialism and that of capitalism. A planned economy does not mean socialism, as capitalism can have a planned economy. A market economy is not equal to capitalism, as socialism can have markets. Both plan and market is economics means."[94]

However, it cannot be concluded that a certain kind of economic mechanism can be established and work independently from the basic economic system. We must realize that, a certain kind of economic mechanism reflects the requirements of a certain kind of economic system, and the former is under the guidance of and serves the latter. In reality, though a lot of western countries and

China carry out a market economic system, they all choose the market mechanism as their basic way to allocate resources. But both of them cannot be disintegrated from each other. When establishing and implementing a socialist market economic mechanism in China, a public-owned foundation should be the subject matter of a socialist basic economic system, to serve under its direction, to reflect its needs, and to strengthen and develop services. Simultaneously, when western capitalist countries implement different kinds of market economy mechanisms, they need to stick with the basic economic systems of capitalism. No matter what kind of economic mechanism is implemented, like the highly centered planned economy mechanism implemented by Japan and Germany during the Second World War or the harmonious period after the Second World War with a variety of market economic mechanisms, their foundation was driven by the basic economic systems of capitalism that reflected the requirements of this system in order to strengthen and serve its development.

Due to its relative independency of economic mechanisms, if assumed that, economic mechanism can be isolated from basic economic system. This kind of thinking is not comprehensive, or might be wrong. The socialist market economic system established and implemented in China is quite similar (in terms of the basic way of resource allocation) to a variety of market economy mechanisms in western capitalist countries. However, the benefits and requirements that they have experienced are different. The socialist market economic mechanism in China reflects the benefits and requirements of the basic economic system of socialism while the various kinds of market economy mechanisms in western countries reflect the benefits and requirements of the basic economic system of capitalism. Therefore, although a market economy mechanism is implemented in both scenarios, the socialist market economic mechanism with Chinese characteristics is under the direction and constraints of the basic economic system of socialism, not allowing any utilization of a blind market economy mechanism. The blindness brought from a market economy mechanism is the negative effects in establishing an advanced material and spiritual civilization, and in developing a socialist economy. Because of the dual effects of the basic economic systems, which determine the reformation of economic mechanisms in countries, the nature of new mechanism will be the self-adjustment in the basic economics systems, taking over the old and inappropriate mechanism. The aim of the reform of the capitalist economic mechanism is to strengthen the basic economic systems in capitalism which should not be laid within a socialist realm. Similarly, the undergoing reformation and establishment of a socialist economic mechanism in China are aimed to enhance the development of the basic socialist economy systems by making use of the advantages of the basic economic systems in socialism, to make China a strong, prosperous, wealthy and civilized modernized socialist nation. Capitalism in the west should not hold any unrealistic illusion of this.

Under the process of social economic growth, the actualization of an economic mechanism is of the essence. Without a definite economic mechanism, social production and re-production cannot be executed. As described earlier, the nature of economic growth is the development of social productivity, is an enhancement of the scale and the level of social production, is an accumulation of social wealth and an advancement of social product quality, and is a process of improving the general living of a society. The nature of an economic mechanism is a social productive relationship which embeds a general form and dynamic elements of the basic economic systems. According to the historical materialism and economic theory of Marx, productivity determines productive relationship; productive relationship is an essential form for the survival and dynamic of social productivity; a definite productivity will lead to a similar kind of productive relationship. This is a fundamental pattern of social economic operation. Hence, the selection of a parallel economic system can help to achieve the growth targets of the economic process. Otherwise, without the support of a social economic form, the economic growth process cannot realize the allocation of resources efficiently, cannot integrate the main production elements into the production process with efforts of the entity, cannot establish a great motivation power for economic growth, and cannot realize economic goals.

So, in modernized economic growth, how to select an appropriate economic system for a country or a region? This is an issue that every country or region needs to be engaged in reformation with as it relates to economic development, prosperity, and the wealth of people. Exploration is required not only realistically, but also theoretically. From the reformation experience in China and countries under economic development in all over the world, the following factors need to be considered when choosing an economic system.

(1) The scale and level of social productivity of a nation or a region and the requirements for further development. Historically, this is a basic and ultimate determining factor when choosing an economic mechanism. Productivity determines a productive relationship. An economic mechanism is the survival and operational form of a productive relationship. The scale and level of the social productivity development of a country or a region reflect the level of social labor diversification and economic development within a certain phase of development. This is determined by material technology, including the level of productivity and the national economy in industrial departments, fields of industries, enterprises and distribution status in regions, directly determining the structure of production information; the scale of social productivity, the complexity of social production structure, immediately determining the complexity, form, transmission of information, strategic levels, management levels, and mobility levels of a macro level structure of national economy. Under a smaller scale with a lower level of social productivity, a highly centered economic mechanism can be chosen. This kind of system is suitable for a

simpler national economic structure and operational form to highly centralize and accumulate economic resources for speedy economic growth, and for maintaining a certain level of sustainable development. The Former Soviet Union is a representative for a series of socialist countries after the second war world for choosing a highly centered planned economy mechanism to suit their primary basic economic foundation under socialism with a low level social productivity, a small scale and a simple structure of national economy.

There was a tremendous positive function after the system had been implemented for a given period of time to enhance a speedy growth for their socialist economy; illustrating a profound impact on the basic economic systems in socialism and a planned economy mechanism. The Former Soviet Union was a particular example to establish its industrial system with a strong foundation of national economy under this kind of economic mechanism; it became the second largest economy in the 1960s. After that, this kind of highly centralized administrative management type of planned economic system turned from appropriate into inappropriate because of the enlargement of social productivity, the enhancement of economic level, and the complexity of its national economy. Hence, the development of social productivity and the sustainable economic growth pushed socialist countries to reform this out-of-date mechanism, and to choose and implement a market economy mechanism to utilize its functions. Evidence showed that, the former Soviet Union did not realize or implement a market economic system at an earlier time to transform the planned economy mechanism into market economy mechanism. The result was that, their economic growth slowed down and went even worse, and negative growth occurred, which ultimately made the country dissolve in the mid 1970s to early 1980s. The fundamental reason for the success of China with speedy economic growth after reformation is the implementation of the opening-up policy in line with the development of social productivity and the requirements of economic growth, the reform from the "Soviet mode" of planned economy mechanism, the establishment of the reformation goals to build a socialist market economy mechanism, together with the development of a socialist market economy mechanism during the reform. It is obvious that choosing and implementing the type of economy mechanism is not primarily based on the subjective willingness of people and the basic economic systems, but the conditions of social productivity development, and the objective requirements of continuous growth of the social economy itself.

(2) The size of the country or region and the demographic situation. Under a given level of social productivity development in a country or a region, the demographic situation and the size of its territory will affect the selection, establishment, and implementation of an economy mechanism. Normally, if a country is small with a scarce population, information network establishment can be easier, information transmission can be faster, and choosing a dispersed

economic mechanism does not hurt much; with greater flexibility in utilizing a market economic mechanism and a more systematic operation of a macro level adjustment in the national economy, hence, it can choose a freer market economic mechanism. Oppositely, if the country is large with a dense population, there will be a possibility or an essence of authority diversification. It is required to consider a more direct or indirect adjustment means to choose and implement a suitable economic mechanism for sustainable economic growth. Apart from the reason of implementing the basic economic systems in socialism, the selection of this type of socialist market economic mechanism also depends on the size of land, the population size and the diversified groups of people – utilizing the function of market mechanism and emphasizing the administrative power in adjusting a macro level of national economy under socialism.

(3) Economic growth strategy and external competitive strategy of a country or a region. This is the most important factor that affects the selection and implementation of an economic mechanism. An economic mechanism is a form to realize social economic growth and to serve the economic and social development of a country within a specified time. Hence, the internal environment and the associated economic development strategy, like external strategy for development at the developmental stage, greatly affect the selection of an economic mechanism. In the past, there was a lot of criticism on the long-implemented, highly centered planned economic mechanism of the Former Soviet Union. Criticism can also be found on the long-implemented planned economic mechanism copied from Soviet before the reformation in China. This is understandable. However, the basic problem still exists. We need to understand that countries implementing socialism in the 20th century are mostly relatively undeveloped countries, facing the problems of industrial actualization and establishment of a materialistic foundation. Moreover, they suffer the economical constrain from western capitalist countries and the attack of imperialism. Because of the international environment existed, every country needs to seek outlets for survival. In order to survive and develop, socialist countries like the Former Soviet Union, Eastern European countries, and China in Asia, promoted the development of heavy industrialization and extensive re-production as their economic development strategy after establishing their countries. The former Soviet Union was the first socialist country after the First World War during the time of weakened imperialism. Under the situation of not having any actual experience as reference and suffering from the great pressures of capitalism, the only way to centralize people, material and capital for the establishment of industry and to realize speedy economic growth, was to select a highly-centered planned economic mechanism. After that, socialist countries established after the World War II had a similar kind of problem as in the former Soviet Union – the hostile international environment, and the highly- centered planned economic mechanism. As the former Soviet Union achieved a great

success and a speedy economic growth within a given period of time, this kind of economic mechanism was copied by other socialist countries. Though the former Yugoslavia had its reform earlier, but adopted this basic kind of mechanism at first.

The process of formation and the development of the highly centered planned economic system had a positive historical impact. Its basic determining factors were the level of social productivity development, the internal and external conditions, the internal economic development strategy, and external development strategy. Reformation is the only way for survival. However, the formation and historical impact of the system are undeniable. This is the right attitude for the system when studying the idea of Marx's historical materialism.

To conclude, the selection and implementation of economic mechanism for economic growth and development in countries doesn't rely on the subjective intention of people, but the scale and level of social productivity development, the size of country, the density of population, the internal and external conditions (called "Guo Qing" in Chinese), internal and external economic development strategies, and a series of historical elements. After decades of a socialist establishment, productivity has been promoted to a certain level and scale, national economies have become more complex, the shortcomings of the highly centered planned economic mechanism have emerged and become hindrances for speedy economic growth and development, in addition to the mutual reliance and openness under globalization, determining the goal of economic mechanism to be socialist market economic mechanism. This is a requirement of the historical development and a wise choice of the Chinese communists and its people. The great achievement in economic social development of China after reformation gives us a prediction that the socialist market economic mechanism has been pushing the Chinese socialist economy to join the wave of global economic modernization, indicating the superiorities of socialism in China, leading socialist China to go into the world and the future, contributing to the worldwide socialist activities and to people of the entire world.

12.2 Basic Structure and Major Functions of Economic System

From a perspective ot historical materialism, social economic system is a structure of social economic relationship which is developed in line with the scale and the level of social productivity development, and with linkage to the basic social economic systems. Its major structure consists of the basic structure, i.e., social productivity and its associated basic economic systems, the subject structure the organizational structure and the normative systems, like regulations and policies. These four aspects are the basic structures which form the systems of information collection and handling, strategic decision-making, implementation, benefit mechanism and benefit structure, and motivational economic operational mechanism, and systems of motivation. All these make up a dynamic structure of economic mechanisms with a definite economic impact on economic growth activities and form the economic functions of a social economic mechanism.

So, what major kinds of economic functions can be found in a social economic system during economic growth?

First, the adjustment function of resources allocation. Under actual social production and economic living, a kind of mechanism or function that adjusts resource allocation exists in all kinds of social economic systems. The planned economic mechanism is based on administrative means and planned adjustment in allocating resources, while the market economic mechanism is based on price means and market adjustments in resources allocation. The adjustment level and its function in resources allocation determine the basic type of economic mechanism, making all kinds of economic mechanisms have a function of adjustment, i.e., the adjustment function of resource allocation. Based on the starting point and the process of economic growth, economic growth process is a process of installing and integrating resources. During this process, the scale, the structure, and the efficiency of adjusting and allocating resources determine the scale, the structure, and the efficiency of social production, which in turn determine the scale, the structure, the efficiency, and the speed of growth of the national economy. The adjustment function of an economic mechanism has a detrimental impact on the scale, the structure and the efficiency of resources allocation. If the adjustment function of the economic mechanism is reasonable with strength, there will be a strong adjustment power and allocation power in economic resources, resource allocation structure will be more reasonable with less wastage as there is a higher efficiency in utilization of resources, producing a greater output with a smaller amount of input to enhance a faster rate of social economic development. Oppositely, if the adjustment function of an economic mechanism is not strong enough to produce a desirable effect, resource mobility and allocation will be weakened with a weak resources allocation structure, which may create wastage in resources with low efficiency in resources utilization, and make a larger amount of input in producing a smaller amount of output, and hinder social economic development. The reason for a strong power to motivate economic growth is that the adjustment function of resources allocation has been improved and strengthened to enhance the efficiency of resource allocation and increase the efficiency of resources utilization and transformation.

Second, the motivation function of economic growth, which is a systematic economic function determined by the internal motivation of an economic mechanism. A definite social economic mechanism is a general social form for existing and acting of entities, and it has an mechanism of interests inside to allocate, adjust and actualize the interests by fulfilling and developing the needs of entities, creating a constraint in enthusiasm and innovation of social economic activities. Within social production and living, no one is isolated. No matter whether they are a laborer or an individual in society, they definitely have a certain relationship with social productivity and production. Besides, they are also linked up with political and theoretical relationships, in which the former is a material relationship while the latter is a spiritual relationship, forming spiritual benefits with motivational effects within an individual in a society. Surely, individuals are not simple "economic people" without any spiritual life or spiritual motivation. That's what Mao Zedong said, "men have to have some spiritual things." However, as beings in nature and society, people unavoidably have connections with materials. Enthusiasm of people cannot be stimulated without incentives of materials. Even though there is some short-lived motivation, it cannot be sustainable. Hence, material benefit relationship exists. Production information (e.g. all information, ownership of information, usage structure of information, and allocation structure of income) found within economic mechanisms should be linked up with the values of material benefit mechanisms, creating adjustment functions of the material benefit relationship of individuals in a society, affecting motivation and enthusiasm of laborers from a micro point of view, and combining enthusiasm and creativity of individuals from a macro perspective. This becomes a motivational mechanism for social economic growth.

Before the opening up policy executed in China, a highly centered planned economic mechanism was implemented with emphasis on unification and fairness rather than on differentiation and efficiency, depriving a direct benefit relationship from each laborer which neither helps to motivate enthusiasm and creativity of laborers nor helps to utilize the basic economic system of superiorities of public ownership in socialism. Moreover, it is not good for motivating economic activities in the root of a society for speedy social productivity development and economic growth. After the execution of the opening policy, there were a series of reforms in China in order to transform the planned economic mechanism into a socialist market economic mechanism and to establish a more flexible and direct benefit mechanism which supports differentiation and efficiency and laborer's individual material benefits and gives priority to efficiency with due consideration to fairness. These reforms enhance the enthusiasm and creativity of laborers, inject new vigor into the socialism public ownership, form a greater motivation for social economic development, and promote the growth of a socialist economy. This is to demonstrate that there is a motivational function of economic system. The dynamic process of reforming the economic system is a transformation of the motivation mechanism, creating synergy in the micro foundation of a national economy, strengthening social economic vigor, and promoting a stable, coordinative and speedy development process in a national economy.

Third, macro-level adjustments function of national economic growth. This is a crucial social economic function in an economic system for balancing and judging the suitability of social productivity development and growth of a social economy produced by a social economic mechanism. Under social production and living, the complex dynamic structure of the national economic growth process consists of a structural relationship between productivity and productive relations, a structural relationship among industrial departments associated with the first relationship, and some dynamic structural relationships that reflect the first relationship, such as the relations of accumulation and consumption, of central and local governments, of local and local governments, of present and future, and of individual and the society. Besides, it also includes a structural relationship between economic infrastructure and superstructure with a close link to the parts and the structures of superstructure. These kinds of relationships are embedded within the dynamic process and the structure of the basic economic systems under a socialist economic mechanism to reflect a positive function of these relationships. Hence, in the operational process of national economy, economic mechanisms place constraints on the motivation integration, the scale, structure, speed and quality of the economic growth. We consider this kind of constraint function to be an adjustment function of national economic growth.

Under the process of socialist economic growth, both highly-centered planned economic systems and socialist market economic systems enjoy a linkage of the basic economic systems of socialism, however, the macro level adjustment function on economic growth is different. The distinguishing feature of a planned economic mechanism is highly-centralized with administrative intervention as a main method to align with the idea of Marx, i.e., "manage the whole society as a huge factory",[95] with direct organization of production and operation in productive units, and with superstructures conducting strategic decisions on adjustment and organization of manpower, materials and capital, actualization of products, and even their allocation and consumption. Hence, under a planned economic mechanism, activities like composition of key production elements, operation of national economy, determination and execution of economic growth targets, and process of social economic living have marked with "commands" of the mechanism, thus the macro level adjustment function in national economic growth has been changed to a kind of political phenomenon, and the national economic growth process has been transformed into a non-economic process involved in the whole society with reliance on administrative tactics, in order to make economic growth become political campaigns and to make national economic life politicized.

Moving along with intensive reforms in the economic system in China, and with socialist market economic system established, the macro level adjustment function of economic mechanism on national economy has gradually reverted to its economic function, utilizing a great power on economic growth. Under the socialist market economic system, the functions of economic mechanism mainly fall on the diversified benefits of economic subjects and the multiple strategic levels of decision-making. These functions include: the market mechanism functions as a foundation, the economic leverage of adjustment functions as a tactic, the micro base of market economy -- the economic and technological connection among enterprises functions as a linkage, and the requirements of structural adjustment functions as guidance. All functions of economic mechanism work together to adjust production, products, technology, investments in social production and reproduction progress, to align investment amounts with volume and structure of demand and supply, to fine-tune motivations of economic subjects, and ultimately to actualize a macro level goals in national economy. Therefore, a socialist market economic system is more flexible than a highly-centered planned economic system and more suitable for a large scale and a more complex structure in economic operation with a better off in mobilizing fundamental production units and in motivating enthusiasm of general laborers. Holistic adjustment and integration functions of an economic mechanism are greatly utilized to enhance a faster development in social productivity with a faster growth in the national economy.

12.3 The Subject of Human and Functions of the Economic System

The above mentioned economic systems are analyzed from an objective and a possible way of their systematic functions, no matter under the conditions of capitalism or socialism, their actualization is relied on efforts of people in the process of economic growth. Under operation of national economy with high quality in entity, the practice of entity will be more active, more positive, more innovative and more appropriate, and the economic mechanism will have more motivation on economic development and economic growth which will then benefit economic growth and development. Oppositely, the motivational economic function will not be fully utilized. Looking back at the history of social development, especially after the birth of Marxism with practice of capitalism, the assumed production relationship in social productivity development has been maintained and created mysterious economic growth and development. One of the reasons for this is that, with a prerequisite of keeping private ownership as its basic economic system, the subjects of social economy, a nation or an enterprise, make some adjustments in an economic system, widen the economic motivational effect of an economic system, deepen the foundation of benefit mechanisms, and motivate certain enthusiasm and innovation of laborers. Under the condition of socialism, no matter whether it is a planned economic system or a market economic system, the superiorities and the economic motivational function of socialism rely on the enhancement of workers' quality in a society with enthusiasm and actualization of innovation. It is uncountable that mechanism reformation is required in the process of social economic development and survival cannot exist without reformation. However, if ignoring enhancement in quality of laborers and the utilization of entity mobility in reformation within production entity, even though mechanism has been reformed, systems have been changed, problems and conflicts in social productions and economic growth have been solved, speedy economic growth and healthy development have been realized, constraints in productive relationships are still not overcome, committing a mistake of "Worshipping A Mechanism". The importance of people in the economic system, and the unity between people and an economic system shall be realized with a new mindset of development under reformation. Without the existence of people as the subjects, material mobility and spiritual mobility will be lost in activities of economic system, losing the basic functions of economic system. Hence, under reformation of socialist economic system, people are the heart of having economic system reformed with self-enhancement in the process of reformation. Therefore, on one hand, people as the subject should reform the economic system; on the other hand, with the transition of the old mechanism, changes of social conditions require the subjects to change themselves, i.e., to update their concepts, and to know and adapt to the new structure of benefits consciously, and to enhance their capability of adapting to and mastering the new mechanism. Otherwise, the newly established mechanism cannot utilize its motivational function in economic growth efficiently, and it may face a risk of regression. This is a profound issue that needs to be solved during the transformation of a highly centered planned economic mechanism into a socialist market economic mechanism. It is also a fundamental problem associated with speeding up economic growth, actualizing economic prosperity and undergoing modernization.

It is clear that tremendous utilization of people as the subject under an economic mechanism for economic growth is determined by the social meaning and the dynamics of people in the society. An impressive idea of Marx is to observe the role people in economic activities and economic relationships while enhancing people's cognitive competence for understanding economic activities and economic relationships. There is a further interpretation for this profound idea – "people themselves are the foundation of their own materialistic production, which is also a basis for undergoing other kinds of productions. Hence, anything related to people in production, more or less, will change the extent of functions and activities, and change the role of people in functions, in activities of materialistic wealth, and in production innovation. Based on this rationale, it has been proved that anything related to relationships and functions will have a certain impact on materialistic production with a detrimental function in the occurrence of materialistic production, no matter what format it is and where it appears.[96] This tells us that people of an entity are man-kind found in a society who are linked up with materialistic productivity, production relationships and superstructures; production relationships can function as motivational factors of economic systems and economic mechanisms in social productivity development and economic growth, with people, especially laborers as the subjects in production process. Therefore, people are a dynamic medium and a responsible party for the structural relationship under economic mechanisms; they are the subjects of undergoing economic activities within economic mechanisms, and they maintain new mechanisms or reform old mechanisms, make full use of the motivational functions of a reasonable mechanism on social economic growth, with the great passion generated from fulfilling their needs and actualizing their own benefits.

So, by what kinds of channels or power to realize the role of people in economic mechanisms for economic growth?

First, the quality of the people themselves. This refers to quality of mindset and ability. Parallel to the reformation of the old mechanism for establishing socialist market economic mechanism and developing socialist market economy, something needs to be done for these two aspects on entity itself. As you can see, reformation is a self-enhancement for socialist mechanism with a holistic and integrated social reformation process. The main goal of the reformation is not only to have a breakthrough of the old mechanism that hinders the development of the economic development mechanism, but also to establish a motivational mechanism for speeding up economic development and social improvement. The ultimate aim of reformation is to renew social life comprehensively, including quality of belief and the ability of people to fully utilize their capability, creativity and talent exploration with the unique characteristics of socialism in China together with the advanced and modernized socialist economic mechanism in the organizational form of socialism. This relies on the function of continuous improvement and quality of people. Besides, the aim of reformation is to realize the final destination of the impact of the new socialist market economy mechanism. Hence, the fundamental meaning is that reformation includes upgrading and entire utilization of personal capabilities of each member in a society to complete tasks of reformation and to establish a socialist market economic mechanism by utilizing its superiorities in conditions, in foundation, in tactics and in its final goals. Only with fully utilization of each member's enthusiasm and innovation in enhancing his quality comprehensively, a human-based socialist market economic mechanism can then be established with a great motivational function of market economic mechanism on economic growth and development. In realistic economic life, even though the same mechanism is implemented within the same unit in the same place, the impact of leadership in production development and in its associated economic outputs will not be the same. This is to show a detrimental effect of entity in utilization of the functions in mechanisms. Reformation of an entity in every country or every region, including China cannot only focus on objective peripherals, as self-enhancement and improvement of quality should also be emphasized. Without following this regularity, reformation cannot be intensified with the foundation of the new mechanism for its survival, development and improvement.

Second, to enhance the quality of people during the actualization of reformation and to transform it into force for motivating economic growth. From a philosophical point of view to interpret development of social production and economic growth, it is a process of practice in nature with the natural ability of people, the full utilization of the ability and quality in practice. Marx pointed out that, "philosophers use different methods to explain the world. However, the problem is to change the world."[97] A newly established socialist market economic system with Chinese characteristics is a result of realizing and getting hold of the regularity of modern economy by all communist comrades and all social members who act as the subjects of reform. It is also an outcome of having the reform done correctly under this regularity by the Chinese government and the whole Chinese people. However, as Marx said, the problem is to change the world. This means reforming the lagging economic situation in China with realization of modernization. This has to change the reformation of economic subjects into actualization of production improvement for economic development under the new mechanism. Therefore, Marx has made some wise comments that the consistency between changes in the environment and activities of people should be considered and interpreted as actions of reformation.[98] In order to utilize the motivational effect of the new socialist market economic mechanism, the idea of reformation should be converted to the execution of social production, and the improvement of people's quality should be emphasized by enhancing people's production capability. The appropriateness of the policy depends on this fundamental point.

Based on the aforesaid, a further conclusion can be made that, from the view point of the human factors and the utilization of economic mechanism, there are two criteria for judging the appropriateness of the new mechanism: whether it would be beneficial to enhancing the quality and ability of workers or people's competence; whether it would be beneficial to transmitting the production ability of people into production, or in another word, whether it would be beneficial to the utilization of human productivity in social production and economic growth in order to create more social wealth. Therefore, we can understand that, during the process of intensifying reform and promoting the socialist market economic system, we need to enhance human as the economic subjects and foster a new proper work force to manipulate market economic mechanisms, so as to utilize economic functions of the new mechanism and achieve the strategic goals of speeding up economic development through continuous reform.

Chapter Thirteen

Value Systems: Social Spiritual Conditions for

Sustainable Economic Growth

Values are a key component in social ideology and a concept system reflecting the deep structure of a society. On one hand, they change along with the evolvement of the economic foundation. On the other hand, they have a tremendous impact on economic foundation. Economic growth in developing countries and regions reflects the transformation process from an agriculture-based traditional economy into an industrial and information-based modern economy. This inevitably brings changes to social economic structure and social economic living along with the changes to people's values. They will break with the old values of an agriculture based economy and adopt a new set of values associated with a modernized industry information-based economy. In this process, we not only need to see that the changes in economic foundation and economic growth determine and promote the enhancement of the formation and development of the new value system but also need to see the formation and development of the new value system promote the initiative and creativity of people as well as stimulate people's enthusiasm and passion in economic activities, which in turn becomes a great social spiritual force that stimulates economic growth and economic modernization in developing countries. Hence, to analyze the issue of economic growth from the perspective of people as an economic subject and to explore the social spiritual conditions of values for economic growth are indeed very necessary.

13.1 The Meaning, Transformation and Choice of Values

Values reflect the relationship between the environment of certain values and the values found in an environment that reflect the attitudes and intentions of people. Values mean the perspectives of people in relation to social phenomenon, with a stable and intensifying viewpoint with a systematized structural mechanism for choice of values. It is a set of integrated concepts with world outlook, criteria for values and value criticism of thinking. To put it simple, a value system is a mechanism with a scope of criteria for commenting on values, guiding people's activities from a world outlook with methodology and principle of thinking. As there are material needs and spiritual needs in people's activities, executing activities is actually an activity of values. Through repetitive activities of values, people will have basic concepts of advantage and disadvantage, goodness and evil, kindness and awfulness, good luck and bad luck, beauty and ugliness, and other concepts of values. The most fundamental, most stable and most deep parts of all these concepts are the concepts of values. Hence, the sense of values are the summation of value concepts, which have abstract meaning and crystallizing values to reflect the nature and essence of the concepts of values in relation to a world outlook and methodology in the intangible world. The macro meaning of a value system is a mechanism with a summation of concepts to comment values in a generic sense, including a long list of economics, politics, culture and other phenomena involved with values, which are long enough to write a book. However, since we only focus on economics in this book, we study and observe the values issue from the perspective of the relationship between economic growth and values of the entity. As the process of economic growth involved with the entity itself – fulfilling the entity's needs and actualizing the entity's self-development for production and re-production, this process is also one of the activities of values. During this process, issues of value judgment are involved in the following situations: in the determination of economic strategic goals, establishment of economic order, choice of individual behavior, treatment and adjustment on the relationship of people and economic growth, establishment and adjustment of human relationships within in a society. All these are linked to the guidance of values. Economic culture refers to the impact and function of a culture on an economy, with a value system as its core element. Hence, if we consider the process of economic growth as a process of movement of values, then values—as we said—can be viewed as the combination of value concepts and a system of value criterion for judging economic growth.

Simultaneously, the sense of values does not refer to the unique value system of each individual but to a whole value system generally agreed to by all people in the whole society and performs a leading function in economic growth. Only with this kind of value system, can an ideal of values be established during the process of economic growth in the whole society, providing a scope of desirable goals and behaviors for people and giving a kind of generally accepted criteria for value judgment in economic activities.

The above has illustrated the meaning of a value system. Then, how can we deal with the changing values along with economic growth and development as well as changes of social economic structure and living style? What are the highest criterion for judging and choosing appropriate value systems that aligns with social economic growth and development?

First, we should note that a social value system is also the value system of history which cannot remain intact. Actually, it changes along with social productivity development, social economic growth, social economic relationships reform, social economic systems and mechanism changes. Engels claimed that, "along with tremendous historical changes in social systems people's values also change."[99] Historical materialism claims that economic foundation determines the establishment of superstructure and social ideology. A value system is regarded as a summation of value concepts though a certain kind of independency and historical inertia may be found. A value system is built upon social concepts and political system. Comparing to economic foundation of a society, social concepts and political system play a passive role, because the latter is determined by the former, and the latter act on the former. Once there are changes in the social economic foundation, the value system will undergo changes sooner or later with old values being discarded and new values coming in – a reformation of values. Since the existence of human society, the stage of economic development will affect the shape of social formation. Moving along with the development of productivity, social economic system changed from a primitive publicly-owned property into a system of property owned by slave landlords, which had social value systems experienced reformation. Therefore, Engels said, "If our concepts of law, philosophy and religion are branches of economic relationships in a society, then all these concepts will consequently be influenced by the changes in economic relationships."[100]

History has proved the change of value systems in the past, from the value system of landlord ownership over slaves in the early days of civilization to the value systems of feudalism, capitalism and individualism. To put it another way, change in economic foundation has a decisive function. The value concept of "putting agriculture ahead of commerce" could not live long under the influence of product economy; the value concept of "Confucius- obtaining balance, ignoring extremity" (Absolute Middle Way, or the "Confucian Mean") could not withstand the competitive and explorative trend in modernized social economy; the value concept of "pursue moral perfection, abandon human desire" (Doctrine of Song Dynasty) could not exist any longer under the temptation of materialistic lives and dream for a better life in a modern civilization.

In the contemporary history of China, people have undergone transition from old values to new values based on principle of science and democracy ever since the "May Fourth Movement" (1919). However, due to the insufficient transition of economic relationships, this revolution of values system was not complete. After founding of the People's Republic of China, especially since the reform and opening-up policy (1978). Which brought about profound changes in China's social and economic foundation, the nation was ready for a thorough values reform. Though there has been a difficult historical transition period to transform old values into new ones, the process already began, and we are faced with an age of new value system with great innovation. We need to get hold of two main issues during the process for realizing the changes and for obtaining gorgeous accomplishments. (1) Critical thoughts on existing values system. Innovation and in-depth analysis on the traditional values to reflect nature, characteristics, process, development and the kinds of emerging formats, investigate its merits and demerits, point out the conflicts that barriers economic prosperity and modernization, advocate new values and promote the transition between old and new values. (2) Practical criticism – encourage people to be dedicated in reform and opening up and modernization, creating social economic condition for the formation and development of new values, improve oneself through discarding the old values and establishing the new values, promote value reform in society.

Second, although the sense of values is relatively independent, it can only lag behind or go beyond economic foundation for a short period of time. We can find plenty of examples in the history of economic development and value evolution. Normally, new values might not be able to replace the old ones immediately after the economy has developed and economic foundations have been modified. Or, under the situation in which social economic foundation has not yet changed, new values have already emerged from advanced scholars in a society. For example, new value systems of "denying individual benefits", "large in size and collective in nature", and "equalitarianism" emerged in the initial stage of socialism. However, as the scale and development of social productivity and associated social wealth at that stage has not yet been advanced enough to make people ignore the development of their individual benefits, values system of socialism have been discarded by people after a certain period of time. They transform those values into new ones, which incorporated individual benefits into socialist modernization with communal benefits, balancing efficiency with fairness, recognizing individual differences, and encouraging some people to become rich first. Another example is that "tradition is a great hindrance with historical inactivity,"[101] though there have been great changes in China's social economic structure after reform and opening up, some traditional ideas still stay in the minds of people, like emphasizing on collectivity rather than individual, focusing on agriculture rather than commerce. These ideas hinder the actual practice of people and make economic foundation slack. To go parallel with continuous revolution of open up and modernization of social economy, people need to have a breakthrough of the old value systems with new value systems to replace them. One more example to support this is found in the revolution in the event of "May Fourth Movement" at the beginning of the 20th century. At that time, with appreciation of science and democracy, some intellectual have severely criticized the old values, and began to advocate new values such as freedom, equality and individual emancipation. However, since the new economic foundation had not been established yet, the revolution did not last long. This demonstrates that the transition of the old values into new values has to be aligned with a corresponding economic foundation, with requirements of economic growth, as well as with changes in economic foundation.

Finally, we need to realize that productivity development, sustainable economic growth, and improvement in society are the highest standards for the choice and establishment of new value systems during value revolution. Social value change is a complex historical process in the dynamics of social economic structure. The replacement of old values by the new ones, and the new direction of values is not only subject to historical traditions, but also to the influences of geographical locations of a country or a region, the long-stayed psychological characteristics, socio-political issues, and cultural atmosphere. However, the most influential factors are the objective requirements of productivity development, sustainable economic growth, and improvement in society. In developing countries and regions, realization of speedy economic growth, economic take-off as well as enhancement of the change to modernize its economy should all go along with the reform in values system. If there is no change on values, social economic growth will be easily affected and even meet failure in social economic modernization. During the change of values, the highest criteria for determining and judging values lie on the benefits of emancipating the thinking and productivity of individuals in a society, and on the benefits for social productivity development and speedy stable economic growth. China is a developing country which is undergoing its economic growth and economic modernization process. A comprehensive change on values system is inevitable. Among the traditional values, some possess our privileged advantages which need to be retained for actualization of modernization. This is the so-called "Virtues of the East". Examples are: unyielding enterprising spirit, being upright and with noble spirit, modest and courtesy- these are our invaluable spiritual wealth which need to be carry forward.

However, some other old values were developed from the social economic structure; which might not align with the changes in economic structure, social productivity development and economic living pattern after the reform and opening up. For instance, the concept of "Iron Bowl– seek for stability and scare of change", collectivity over individual, focusing on agriculture rather than commerce, emphasizing on absolute ethics and neglect profits, Engaged Confucianism, letting things take their own course (a Taoist concept of human conduct), etc. These values may not adapt to the reform and opening up, economic take-off and social modernization in China. This kind of traditional ideas concentrate in blind worship of the classics while boycott the reform and opening up; promote collectivism while ignore individualism by denying the idea of reasonable competitiveness; advocate "being absolute middle way" while being scared of innovation , of being a pioneer in competition, and of taking risk with aggressive exploration; worship authoritarian while ignore the use of knowledge and talents without emphasizing on scientific technology and productive labor; pursue perfect virtue while suppressing necessary needs, regard human desire as the source of evil rather than a kind of historical motivation by denying the value of life; promote being content rather than striving for further development, etc. The core idea of all these values is taking the merits of morals to replace the demerits of technology, focusing on ethic while neglecting technology, economics, and productivity development.

Emphasizing on ethic is correct. However, it is not correct to disregard the development of technology, economics and productivity development. This is contradict with the idea of reform and opening up, establishment of socialism market economic mechanism, development of socialism market economy, acceleration of global economic development, and socialist modernization. Under modernized global economic development, should a country and region intends to develop productivity and actualize economic take-off, they need to arouse the awareness of all people to compete positively, to explore for improvement with a never-satisfied heart to utilize the value of life with encouragement of innovation, with enthusiasm for developing personal productivity so as to promote social productivity and help the society enter into a new era. Hence, if taking the highest criteria of developing productivity, economic growth and social improvement to judge the foresaid traditional value systems, they become a "tremendous conservative power" (by Marx) for undergoing revolution for open up and "a great force of hindrance" for socialist modernization" (by Engels). So, we need to adapt to the requirements of socialist modernization, build on new value systems and discard the outdated traditional values system for innovation. Meanwhile, we need to emancipate our thinking for creativity and competition, and to become pioneer, to respect knowledge, talents and value of life, strive for people's happiness and social progress, and to seek for new values to reach new level of life.

13.2 The Structure of Value System and Its Functions in Economic Growth

As described above, values are the combination of evaluation criteria system and different concepts. This is a static definition of values system from philosophical perspectives. In order to further analyze the relationship between value system and economic growth, it is necessary to probe into the structure of values in a dynamic manner so as to get a comprehensive understanding. This part also studies the functions of values in economic growth.

Concerning modernized economic growth, as for developing countries and regions, especially for a developing country like China, value systems are actually a dynamic structural system composed with different elements analyzed vertically with different levels or horizontally with different processes of developments. Only this kind of dynamic value systems can be adaptable to the fast changing needs of a diversified society with a social structure in the process of economic growth.

During the transition of social economic growth from a traditional economy to a modernized economy, there are three basic characteristics in its structure.

(1) The diversification. From a social values perspective of human subject, there are personal values, organizational values and social values. From a global perspective of object, there are materialistic and spiritual values. In the past, because of the requirement of maintaining a single unified communal system and a highly planned economic mechanism, we have not paid attention to the

levels and requirements of productivity development, neither did we emphasized on individual value and material value. We segregated social value systems with "spiritual capability". Moving along with the development in the reform and opening-up, aligning with our multi-levels economic structure and with the requirements of transition of social modernized economy, there is a need to reassess and refresh the past value systems so that we could identify the gap existing in the single-layer value system which is contradictory to our situation of social productivity development, and to the objective requirements of economic growth. In this way, we could facilitate the re-structuring of social values built on actual economic foundation, recognize individual values while maintaining collective value, and recognize material value while maintaining spiritual value. The restructuring of the value system in the initial stage of socialism should include multi-layered values such as individualism, collectivism, social values, materialistic values, spiritual values etc.

(2) The multi-levels. At present, we must advocate and insist on equality in socialism. We need to realize that the role of each individual in the present social structure is different. Therefore, the needs based on this foundation, and the requirements for fulfilling those needs are also different. Varied existing conditions determine that people choose different goal, direction, and standard to fulfill their needs. And these choices are then reflected in levels of value activities. As the saying going, "vicious men live on greed, noble men live on need". For instance, some pursue material things for survival while some others more spiritual things for appreciation; some seeks for individual benefits while some others for fame and social status; some pursues personal accomplishment while some others group achievement with collective strategies, etc. All these pursuits demonstrate different levels of value activities in value structure. The multi-layers of need of each person has resulted in their pursuit. In society, individual needs would form their own levels of value structure in certain stage of economic growth and development.

(3)   The process or periodic nature. In the developmental process of social productivity and economic growth, mode of production evolves from low level to high level in accordance to human evolution. This low to high level stage of development is also applied to the value systems of people. During the process, people are the entity of values with changes in their values and thinking. People continuously reform themselves with intensifying cognitive power to pursue the meaning of life in a profound way, to ultimately change their value systems and make their value systems bear different kinds of characteristics in different historical stages with levels of proliferation. There are different levels of productivity development in history during different social structures with social value systems performing leading roles. The content and format of values may be different even within the same social structure of different stages with similar

leading social value systems. This is what we call historical nature, stage nature or process nature of value performance. In the process of social and economic transforming from an agriculture-based traditional society to a modernized society, inevitable changes in value systems from old ones into socialist modernized new ones. This kind of value system is suitable for the needs of modernized economic growth, for reform and opening up, which can provide guidance to people involve in creativity activities for socialist modernization,. Meanwhile, as a great ambition, modernization stimulates the spirit of exploration, diligence and innovation.

Following is the functions of value systems from the perspective of economic growth.

First, realization. As previously mentioned, value systems is a kind of global outlook and methodology about value phenomena. As we know, what surrounds us is a universe made up of a world of nature, of human, of values. The world of nature is a material world which externally exists without relying on people. The world of human is about human activities, which is the combination of production relationships and interpersonal relations. As for the world of value, it is a world of "meaning". That is to say only when the world could satisfy human need can it be valuable, and in turn stimulate people to set up goals and make choices. Value system, a kind of global outlook and methodology about value phenomena, has its function in guiding people's value activities and provide people with the method to understand the relations between economic activities and fulfillment of human need. In this way, value system helps to set up principles for goal-setting, choice-making and judgment. With the principles, people are more likely to make right decision based on their own knowledge of the importance of economic growth as a kind of value activity. Hence, the first thing is to realize relationships between subject and objective issues in economic growth process with for the sake of strategic decision-making, devising strategic goals, determining strategic points and implementing strategies. Values guides people in their value activities to judge economic growth, or to understand the important role played by economic growth, its scale, speed and quality. If there is no referential value system, people would find it difficult to make judgments when confronted with different kinds of indicators in economic growth, in establishment and modifications of economic relationships, etc.

Second, stimulation. Value system reflects the relationship of the subject and the objective, acting as lighthouse for people's thinking and behavior, realizing the benefits deriving from objective issues for making a right decision under a guidance principle. In the process of social productivity development and economic growth, value systems facilitate people to understand the beneficial relationship between economic activities and themselves, stimulate them to satisfy their needs, and to motivate them to participate in economic activities in a positive way so as to promote economic growth. This is the motivational effect of value systems in the process of economic growth, namely, function of stimulation. The reason for having support and participation of enthusiastic people from the base of the society is the encouragement from the value of socialist modernization for pursuing the meaning of life. This can be shown in the revolution of the old planned economic mechanism for establishing a new socialist market economic mechanism when developing market economy, for speeding up economic growth, making the twenty years after revolution a speedy economic growth. This is actually encouraged by the value system of socialist modernization for people to pursue values of life, to forge ahead and to innovate. Meanwhile, another stimulation function of values is to prevent the occurrence of negative effect from economic growth. During the process of economic development and the reform and opening up, some people may be reluctant to changes and stick to stability rather than seek for exploration, initiatives, or innovation. This is because of the burden of old value systems, which blinded them from realized the impact of the value activities on themselves. As a result, people were afraid of releasing themselves from stereotype thinking to make new judgment and establish new value targets. Hence, they would prefer to go for the old ways rather than establish new values during reform and opening-up and the process of developing social productivity and accelerating economic growth. What is worse, they dare not insist on their rights, neither would they make any contribution. These phenomena can be regarded as historical lag of old value system.

Third, adjustment. Regulation of value is also a major component of value system. Guided by certain value goals, standards and principles, peoples' regulation and adjustment of value activities is a reflection of subjective initiative, intention and wisdom building on knowledge of value activities and benefit relationships. Benefit relationships can be found in many layers of social production and re-production, such as accumulation and consumption, production and allocation, scale and speed, speed and efficiency, as well as short-run and long-run, regional and central, even among regions and departments. The ways of interpreting and handling these beneficial relationships are actually value activities. A direct decisive function is found in practice – using the kind of values as a guiding reference, the way of knowing the benefit relationship, and the way of handling them properly. It is assumed that time and place of conflicts are related to value systems all the time. Adjusting and upgrading people's value systems, adjusting value goals of people and choices of value orientations are necessary in sorting out the thinking of people when handling conflicts. This can help people make right value judgment and choose value systems.

Obviously, value system is, on the one hand, constrained by economic growth, and on the other, imposes significant impact on economic growth. Therefore, while development economic growth and strengthening material culture, we should also emphasize on spiritual culture and the value reform among people. Moreover, great attentions should also be given to the establishment of modern social value systems that is in accordance with the speedy economic growth so as to provide the society with spiritual motivation and conditions.

13.3 Channels for Value Systems to Affect Economic Growth

While value systems falls into the category of conceptual belief, economic growth is a process which witnesses the increase of social materialistic and cultural wealth and development of social productivity and re-production. In the transformation from spiritual factor into an action power for enhancing economic growth, value system needs to go through a series of steps. Without these procedures, value systems could only remain as static spiritual factors without motivating economic growth or realizing its function in economic growth.

First, only through practice can value system be transmitted into a real power, and function for economic growth. The three functions of realization, stimulation and adjustment in economic growth remain a conceptual power until values are channeled into people's value activities. Only through practice can values stimulate people's need, so as to motivate or hinder people to integrate production factors and turn them into social productivity in a larger or in a smaller scale. Value activities in the process of economic growth are in fact an integration of knowledge and practice. To be specific, realizing the rationale of the process is the value of knowledge, and development in productivity and economic growth is the value of practice. In this process, action is the foundation, motivation and source of realization, and also the basis for value systems to turn into a dynamic power for historical activities. Realization, conceptual thinking, rational thinking, including value systems are all built on the foundation of actions, which then transmitted into materialistic power that motivates or hinders economic growth. During the development of socialist market economy in our county, functions of stimulation and motivation are derived from modernized value systems of exploration, enthusiasm and innovation. However, if only stay in the stage of investigating value systems without putting into actions such as reforming the old mechanisms, creating new enterprises, exploring and producing new products, studying new markets, enlarging the volume of national income, or increasing the level of national economy, these values will only remain as concepts, instead of a consequence of economic growth. Hence, no matter what kind of value system it is, no matter what function it has, only people's practice can make things happen. Therefore, action is the only channel to turn value systems into economic growth.

Second, there is a certain distance between value systems and actions. The transformation from values to actions must undergo a series of intermittent process. (1) Recognition and judgment of values. This means people's reorganization and judgment towards economic growth and beneficial relationships in production activities. In this process, people are the entity of value judgment and entity of economic activity benefits. Based on their own value judgment, people would understanding the meaning and benefit of economic growth to them. Then they form their own needs for these benefits, and the desire to participate in value activities. This is a starting point of converting value systems into value of actions. (2) Goal of values. This means ideals and life pattern, guidance for people's value activities. In economic growth process, it guide people in devising strategic growth targets, determining the key areas of strategy, stages of strategy and choosing the principles for implementation of the strategies. (3) Choice of values. This refers to the choice of value targets, value environment, value direction, and value principle. For value targets, it means the subject and object of values. This is determined by the needs of value targets and the attributes of objective values. Value environment refers to the environment which has relations to values. Only under a desirable environment, entity will put into efforts in value activities to create more values. Value direction means the focus of perspective, labeling a leading direction of entity's choice of value. Value principle means the generic ways that entity follows in realizing their value targets. Applying into economic growth process, value choice is actually the choice and creation of a certain production environment of an entity under the guiding principle of value targets - leading industry, leading fields of work, leading products, producing what you are capable of, and creating increasing wealth for production. (4) Monitoring and evaluation of value activities. This is the last and the highest level of realizing conceptual values into actions. Conceptual values have been transmitted into action-based values in this stage, changing from a spiritual power into a material power with adjustments made from collection of information in the process. The process of economic growth has been demonstrated through growth strategy, plan change and the growth process of social production and national economy, and adjustments on national economy from the government. Hence, we can see that people's value activities consist of four basic elements so as to convert conceptual values into action values. In fact, it is a integrated process of value recognition and application

To sum up, value systems can be transformed into an influential power only through actions of the four basic stages mentioned above. Otherwise, value systems cannot be changed into actual power to affect social economic growth. Admittedly, the reform and upgrading of value systems are crucial to developing countries and regions. However, more attention shall be paid to the four elements of "conversion" so as to give a full play to modern value systems in promoting economic growth. In the meantime, the interchange stage of the four elements in the conversion period shall be monitored closely for the sake of overcoming hindrance from traditional value systems and preventing the outdated value systems from transmitting into value-based activities.

Chapter Fourteen

Conclusion: All-around Individual

Development is the Highest Objective of

Economic Development

This is the concluding chapter of the book. The main theme of this chapter is to illustrate that the ultimate aim of economic growth is the integrated development of individuals, and to display the historical logic that social economic growth is a historical process, which is consistent with the theoretical logic of the humanistic economic development theory.

Social economic growth is driven by the demand of people. It is a process of recognizing and transforming the natural world and the society, as well as a process of social reproduction and the increase of social wealth. Marx once said, "production starts from need; new need and consumption come from production."[102] The history of economic development proves that the idea of Marx is definitely right. Under social production and re-production, people are the center of national development. On one hand, the needs of people are the starting point and mutative power of reproduction and the enhancement of economic growth; On the other hand, the satisfaction of people's needs, the improvement of themselves, and the generation of new needs, are the ending point and outcome of reproduction and economic growth, and also the ultimate aim of value activities, and at the same time the beginning of new economic growth in social reproduction. Hence, from the perspective of production and re-production, social economic growth is a process of generating social wealth, improving oneself and creating new subjects in order to the fulfill one's needs for survival and development. From the perspective of consumption, social economic growth is a process of absorbing labor and productive materials, and a process when human subject continuously take in all kinds of social wealth for consumption, for enhancement of facilities, and for self-development. From the perspective of value activities, it is a process where human beings strive for living, life enjoyment and self-development. Therefore, the integrated individual (i.e., the subject) development is the most important target for economic growth, from both the perspective of value objectives and the perspective of value activities. This is not only a reflection of people's status in economic growth but also the outcome of the regularity of the economic growth process.

From a historical point of view, the developmental process of people as social entities and the economic growth process as the development of social production and productivity are united in the process of social progress. However, the united process of social progress is realized in conflicts. In a certain period of history, the abilities of humanity are realized through economic growth, which is the development of social productivity. The sacrifice of certain individuals cannot be avoided during this kind of development, which has been mentioned by Marx as part of the conflicts of humanity and individuals. Marx said, "although it is necessary to sacrifice individuals or the whole class of people at the beginning of the development of humanity, the conflicts will finally be solved and the development of humanity will be in line with that of individuals".[103] When these two kinds of development are in line with each other, the developmental process of people as social entities will be consistent with the economic growth process as the development of social production and productivity, and the highest level of communism can be realized.

The reason why we cannot avoid the occurrence of conflicts between humanity and individuals in certain historical periods, and then why the economic growth is at the price of sacrifice of some individuals, is that the process of social evolution relies on the objective pattern of social production development. History is created by humans; however, logic exists among their productive and creative activities and the synergy formed by all these activities, and logic does not change with the subjective willingness of people. The objective logic is that, as long as the level of productivity stays in the stage of hand tools, social division of labor (starting from division of mental labor and physical labor) is the main motivator for economic growth. As mentioned before, according to a rough estimation by economists, in the Stone Age when there was no such social division the level of labor productivity increased by 1-2 % every 10,000 years.

After the emergence of social division in the Iron Age, the level of labor productivity increased by 4% every 100 years. This shows that traditional division (mental and physical division) has a certain impact on labor productivity. Traditional division is linked up to the stratification of social classes and the lopsided development of human beings, which is illustrated in slavery, agricultural labor and workers who specialize in physically intensive work but are deprived of the right of mental development. Only when people enter into the age of intelligence beyond the age of machinery production, will their free time (leisure time) be increased, and the time spent on making a living decreased and traditional social divisions then completely disappear. When these happen, the conflicts of humanity and individuals as mentioned by Marx will come to an end, and it will be time for the unification of social economic growth and free and integrated development of individuals.

In the evolution of human society, from the perspective of the connection between social economy and individuals, the historical process centered by the development of individuals can be divided into the following stages.

The first stage is primitive economic growth. At this stage, people are separated from the nature as subject of the world (considering the natural as object). Individual productivity and social productivity were very low, and the social economy was based on primitive agriculture and animal husbandry. The social economic growth was small scale and low level, and the world population "remained around 5 to 10 million"[104] At this stage, there were almost no surplus products left for labors. The fundamental aim of social economic growth is to satisfy the needs of every member in the society and to create labor for future development. Marx claimed that this was a natural economic stage as the survival and development of people relied on the natural world and the very nature of individuals. People needed to stay together to fight against nature in order to obtain food for survival. If people separated themselves from the group, they would lose their ability to survive. Hence, judging from value objectives, in the stage of primitive economic growth, the satisfaction level of people's needs by economic growth was also at the initial stage of human social development.

The second stage is economic growth in the age of civilization. This stage started from the time when people began to create and use iron tools, private ownership and the age of civilization were born, to the time when the traditional agricultural economy was transformed to the modern industrial economy. It went through the Slave Society, Feudalist Society and early Capitalist society before the first Industrial Revolution. There were two economic forms during this stage, i.e., natural economy and commercial economy. The pre-capitalist society in the age of civilization (i.e., from when Primitive Society clasped to Slave Society and Feudalist Society) was dominated by natural economy with few commodity productions.

The exploitation of surplus value based on natural economy could only be realized through enforcement. The basic feature of social relationships was the "interdependence of human beings". In other words, individuals could not be independent. In the primitive period, an individual could not survive without their tribe members. Later on, in class society, the interdependence relationship was displayed on one hand as the dependence of every individual on his class or the governing class, on the other hand as the personal bondage of individuals to the exploited class or to slave owners or feudal lords. This kind of dependent relations guaranteed that these types of societies could get surplus from labors and that a social economy could develop. However, in these societies, the dependent relations harmed the incentives of labors. Hence, in this stage, the development of social productivity was low speed, small scale and low level, and so was the development of social economy.

The emergence of capitalist societies marked the transformation from the traditional agriculture age to the industrial age. Societies that once depended on natural connections turned into ones that depend on social and historical connections. Commercial and monetary relations became dominant, and even labors became goods. The relations among people displayed as the exchanges of goods and interests. Since the exchange of goods is in essence the exchange of equal quantities of abstract labor at the free will of owners, the owners of goods are equal and free. In other words, individuals start to become independent and free employees replace slaves. However, both employers and employees rely on markets and commodity-money relationship. What employers produce are commodities rather than simple products, so the market plays a leading role in determining their fates. Employees have nothing but their labor; therefore, they make a living by selling their own labor. In a commodity economic society, all people depend on commercial and monetary relations, with the special feature of the dependence of people on goods.

From the perspective of the independent development of people, the change from the dependence among people to that of people on goods means that, people become independent, and laborers start to have equal rights and freedom. This transformation is a great breakthrough in the history of mankind, and it marks the jump of productivity. The secret lies in the governance of commodity-money relationship. As we all know, commodities and money are subject to the law of value, and the mechanism of the latter is competition. Competition stimulates the greatest potential out of each employee. Marx describes the stimulation of the law of value as, "this law pulls capitalist production out of its original track over and over again, and forces capital to improve labor productivity as it did before. This law does not allow capital to stop and keeps saying: Forward! Forward!"[105]

However, people that depend on "goods" are not comprehensively developed. The transformation from people's lopsided development to all-around development finishes in the third period in human social development.

The third stage is modern economic growth. This stage paves the direct way to the future ideal society based on highly advanced social productivity, highly developed social economy and abundant social wealth.

Marx regards communist society as "a social form based on the principles of integration and the free development of each human being."[106] The free, all-around development of each human being has always been an ideal of many scholars and great poets. Schiller, a German classical philosopher, expressed his support for the comprehensive and free development of individuals. "It is wrong to develop one kind of ability of an individual at the cost of his overall interest." He disagreed with Kant, who disregarded individuality and supported lopsided development. On one hand, he cheered for the great development of all of mankind in the 19th century; on the other hand, he was not satisfied with the lopsided development of human beings, and was sad that the progress of mankind was at the price of lopsided development of individuals. He said: "our athletes run faster than winners in the ancient Olympics, and our mathematicians calculate more accurately than Archimedes. But can we find a modern man who is an outstanding politician, historian, philosopher, strategist, elocutionist and priest? Can modern people compete with the Greeks one-to-one in an all-round competition?" However, Schiller, as a poet and philosopher, did not have the scientific vision to find a realistic way for human beings to solve this problem. Marx was the one to complete the task through his historical materialism.

According to historical materialism, when productivity is low, most people have to devote all of their energy to earning a living to ensure that the few individuals or exploiters can take the mental work with all their time in science, art, etc. As a result, human beings live in a world of natural inevitability, which means that, with low productivity people are subject to the need for living, and they have to devote most of their time to the necessary labor for survival, so it's impossible to develop comprehensive. Marx described the workers in 19th Century as follows, "time is the space for the development of human beings. If a man has no free time, and he has to serve capitalists all his life except for breaks caused by physiological needs such as sleeping and eating, then he is just a machine making wealth for others, which is less meaningful than a draught animal."[107] Only when social productivity is greatly developed will people be able to get rid of the exploitation of capitalism and the blind slavery of production relations, as well as make a living for themselves with labor productivity greatly improved by science and technology, and have the free time to develop themselves. Free time begins from the end of labor for living, so the key lies in the reduction of working time. The key to shortened work time is the replacement of human labor by machines in production. A hundred years ago Marx predicted that, with the help of science and technology, people "could be freed from tedious labor that can be replaced by machine", "labor would be no longer like before which was included within production; rather than, labor will be more like supervision and coordination instead of making production, and workers will become monitors and supervisors."[108] The popularization of machinery helps to achieve such a vision. Ever since the 1980s, some western industrial countries adopted new machinery systems which needed few workers for production and reduced labors by 80% and production cost by 50%, and still maintained the same quality of goods. Without the popularization of intelligent machines, it is impossible to prepare material technological foundation for an ideal future society.

The fourth stage is the all-around development of individuals with the preconditions of rapid economic development. During this period, productivity and individual capability will be highly and efficiently developed. Dependence of people on goods will be replaced by harmonious relations among human beings, as the economy develops into product economy, liberal economy and time economy. Under these social economic conditions, the major and ultimate goal for production and economic growth of the whole society will not be survival but happiness and the all-around development of human beings. People will not only possess great material wealth and good eco-economical conditions but also create and possess unprecedented spiritual wealth and excellent spiritual conditions. Only in this stage can people fully develop themselves and have spiritual qualities for development. These qualities include: noble ideals, a lofty moral character, good education, comprehensive knowledge, extensive interpersonal relationships, sound personalities, a strong will, a perfect inner world of oneself, and practical and creative abilities. Only in this stage can the all-round development of social individuals be the highest priority for economic development.

From the above mentioned points, we can conclude that the all-around development of individuals, as the ultimate goal of economic development, is a historical process of economic and human development. The beginning and ending of economic growth are also the beginning and ending of the economic theories in this book. In such a new era when human society is culturally advanced with a highly developed modern economy, developing countries, especially socialist developing countries, should have new views of economic growth and development, put the demands of people at the center, and regard the comprehensive development of social individuals as the highest goal of economic growth. This is the objective requirement of modern economic growth. At the same time, they should adopt the view of economic growth centered on people's needs to analyze and study modern economic growth issues, and to measure the degree of modern economic growth. When developing countries quicken the steps of economic development and modernization, they should follow three golden standards: first, to develop productivity; second, to increase social wealth and to satisfy individual needs; third, to fully develop social individuals and enhance their productivity.

Last but not least, in order to achieve the ultimate goal of economic growth, we should work joint-handedly and bravely to build a highly developed and highly civilized modern society with the all-around development of individuals as its ultimate goal!

Notes

Chapter One

1. Marx, K., *German Ideology*. In *Selected Works of Marx and Engels*, Vol. 1, p. 32. Beijing: People's Publishing House, 1972. (In Chinese)
2. Apostol, G. P. (Romania), *Modern Capitalism* (p. 345). Beijing: People's Publishing House, 1979. (In Chinese)
3. Marx, K., & Engels, F., *Selected Works of Marx and Engels*, Vol. 2, p. 91. Beijing: People's Publishing House, 1972. (In Chinese)
4. Marx, K., *Preface*. In *The Critique of Political Economics* (p. 14). Beijing: People's Publishing House, 1971. (In Chinese)
5. Marx, K., *Collection of All Works by Karl Marx and Frederick Engels,* Vol. 12, p. 740. Beijing: People's Publishing House, 1962. (In Chinese)
6. Engel Index = Food Expenses / Consumption Expenditure...(Referred to Chinese literature)
7. Hofmann Index = Net Output Value of Light Industries / Net Output Value of Heavy Industries...(Referred to Chinese literature)
8. Gou, D. Z., *Chinese Economy at the Stage of High Growth* (p. 6). Chendu: Sichuan People's Publishing House, 1993; Fang, J., *Research on Industrial Structure,* Chapter 21. Beijing: China Renmin University Press, 1997. (In Chinese)
9. Marx, K., *The Outline of the Critique of Political Economy*, Vol.3, p.168. Beijing: People's Publishing House. 1978. (In Chinese)
10. Marx, K., *Capital*. Vol. 1, p. 649. Beijing: People's Publishing Press, 1975. (In Chinese)
11. Lenin, V. I., Collection of *All Works by Lenin,* Vol. 1. p. 89. Beijing: People's Publishing Press, 1961. (In Chinese)

Chapter Two

12. Adam Smith, a founder of classical economics. His epochal book *The Wealth of Nations* was published in 1776, which indicated the start of the classical economics of British capitalism. He discussed the growth problem of national wealth in this book. As the earliest discussion about economic growth, this book is considered as the original form of economic growth theory. (Referred to Chinese literature)
13. Liszt F., *The National System of Political Economy* (p. 118). Shanghai: The Commercial Press, 1961. (In Chinese)
14. Marx, K., *Selected Works of Marx and Engels,* Vol. 4, p. 320. Beijing:

People's Publishing House, 1972. (In Chinese)

15. Marx K., *Selected Works of Marx and Engels*, Vol. 4, p. 321. People's Publishing House, 1972. (In Chinese)
16. Marx K., *The Outline of the Critique of Political Economy*, Vol. 1, p. 112. Beijing: People's Publishing House, 1977. (In Chinese)
17. Bach, G. L., *Economics*. 1966, p. 228. (Referred to Chinese literature)
18. Domar, E. D., *Collected Works of Economic Growth Theories*. 1957, p. 18. (Referred to Chinese literature)
19. *Economic Research References*. 1986, Vol. 124, pp. 12-13. (In Chinese)
20. Zhou, L., & Zhang, Z., *Economic Policies*. Sichuan: Chongqing Press, 1991, 79. (In Chinese)
21. Xiong, Y., *An Introduction to Productive Economics,* Section 7.2. Harbin: Heilongjiang People's Publishing House, 1983. (In Chinese)
22. Xue, M., *A Research on Socialist Economic Problems in China* (p. 157). Beijing: People's Publishing House, 1979. (In Chinese)
23. Quesnay (France). *About Handcraft Industry Labor*. In *Selected Works of Quesnay* (Translated by Wu F., & Zhang C.), p. 372. Shanghai: Commercial Press, 1979. (In Chinese)
24. Marx, K., & Engels, F., Collection of All Works by *Karl Marx and Frederick Engels*, Vol. 49, p. 98. Beijing: People's Publishing House, 1972. (In Chinese)
25. *Allison, L., Global Economic War* (p. 2). Beijing: Chinese Friendship Press, 1985. (In Chinese)
26. Zhang, D., *Productivity*, Chapter 9. Beijing: People's Publishing House, 1993,(In Chinese)
27. Zhang, D., *Productivity*, Chapter 9. Beijing: People's Publishing House, 1993. (In Chinese)
28. Zhang D., *Productivity* (p. 303). Beijing: People's Publishing House, 1993. (In Chinese)

Chapter Three
29. Marx, K., *Capital*, Vol. 1, p. 560. Beijing: People's Publishing House, 1975. (In Chinese)
30. Leontief, W., *Future of Global Economy* (p. 100). An UN Research Report (monograph). (In Chinese)
31. Marx, K., *Capital*, Vol. 1, p. 53. Beijing: People's Publishing House, 1967. (In Chinese)

Chapter Four
32. Deng, X., *Selected Works of Deng Xiaoping,* Vol. 3, pp. 224-225. Beijing: People's Publishing House, 1993. (In Chinese)
33. Debt-paying Ratio refers to the ratio between the sum of principal and interest of foreign debt and the export revenue of goods and services. It's an

indicator for the repaying capability of a certain country in the current year. (Referred to Chinese literature)

34. Ma, H., & Sun, S., A *Research on Chinese Economic Structure* (p. 304). Beijing: China Social Sciences Press, 1984. (In Chinese)

35. *People's Daily,* 1993, Nov. (12), International Supplementary (2). (In Chinese)

Chapter Five

36. Marx, K., & Engels, F., *Selected Works of Marx and Engels*, Vol. 1, p. 277. People's Publishing House, 1995. (In Chinese)

37. Fan, Y., *Investment of Japan and the Rise of Asia,* p. 4, 5, 69. Shanghai Sanlian Press, 1991. (In Chinese)

38. Deng, X., *Selected Works of Deng Xiaoping,* Vol. 3, p. 383. Beijing: People's Publishing House, 1993. (In Chinese)

39. Deng, X., *Selected Works of Deng Xiaoping,* Vol. 3, p. 377. Beijing: People's Publishing House, 1993. (In Chinese)

40. Deng, X., *Selected Works of Deng Xiaoping,* Vol. 3, p. 64. Beijing: People's Publishing House, 1993. (In Chinese)

41. *Economic Daily,* Dec. 28th, 1993, p. 4. (In Chinese)

42. Chen, L., *Global Economy towards 2000* (p. 386). Beijing: China Foreign Trade Press, 1990. (In Chinese)

Chapter Six

43. Marx, K., *Capital,* Vol. 2, p. 393. Beijing: People's Publishing House, 1987. (In Chinese)

44. Lewis, W. A., *Economic Growth Theory* (p. 283). Shanghai Sanlian Press, 1990. (In Chinese)

45. The concept of "primitive accumulation of socialism" was first raised in 1920's by Pulieaobularensiky E. A., a Soviet famous economist in former Soviet Union. Please refer to Chapter 2 in his book *New Economics* published by Shanghai Sanlian Press in 1984. (In Chinese)

46. Yang, M., A *Research on Industrial Policy* (p. 289). Shanghai Sanlian Press, 1989. (In Chinese)

47. *Economic Research*, Vol. 1. 1990, p. 21. (In Chinese)

Chapter Seven

48. Ji, Z., *An Introduction to Global Economy* (p. 236). People's Publishing House, 2003. (In Chinese)

49. Ji, Z., *An Introduction to Global Economy* (p. 236). People's Publishing House, 2003. (In Chinese)

Chapter Eight

50. The development of world economy post-W. W. II showed that, the

tertiary-industry greatly developed in developed countries after they entered the post-industrial society. For example, in 1952, the employment of tertiary-industry represented more than half (52%) of the total employment in USA. (Referred to Chinese literature)

51. Kuznets, S., *National Economic Growth* (pp.42-44). Shanghai: Commercial Press, 1985. (In Chinese)
52. Qiu, Y., *World Economy at the Turn of the Century* (p. 237). Beijing: China Social Sciences Academic Press, 1992. (In Chinese)
53. Zhu, J., The Basic Structure of National Economy. *Encyclopedic Knowledge*, 1982, No. 3, p. 4. (In Chinese)
54. *People's Daily*, Apr. 10th, 1992, p. 7. (In Chinese)
55. The backward effect hereby refers to the influence of leading industries on production suppliers; the forward effect refers to the influence of leading industry on new industries, new technologies, new materials, and new energies; side effect refers to the influence of leading industries on other industries in the nation or region. Such effects can be shown in the following graph.

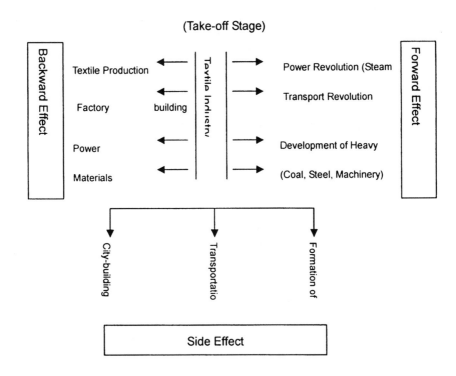

56. Marx, K., Theory of Surplus Value, in Collection of All Works by *Karl Marx and Frederick Engels*, Vol. 26, p. 23. Beijing: People's Publishing House, 1968. (In Chinese)

57. *Chinese Electronic Newspaper*, Mar. 13th, Apr. 7th, 1991. (In Chinese)

58. Thirlwall, A. D., *Growth and Development* (p.112). Beijing: People's Publishing House, 1992. (In Chinese)

59. Zhang, B., *Technology Education and Technology Advance*, p. 19. Beijing: Guangming Daily Press, 1987. (In Chinese)

Chapter Nine

60. Schumpeler, J. A. (Germany). *The Theory of Economic Development* (p.73). Shanghai: Commercial Press, 1990. (In Chinese)

61. Williams, T. (ed), *A History of Technology*, Vol. 6, Part 1. Oxford: Clarendor Press, 1978, p. 462.

62. *A Research on Productivity Rules* (p.198). Beijing: The Publishing House of Economic Science, 1985. (In Chinese)

63. Liu, Y., *Technological Innovation Economics* (p.145). Beijing: China Economy Press, 1994 (In Chinese)

64. Gu, S., *The General Theory of Socialist Economics* (pp.682-683). Shanghai People's Publishing House, 1991. (In Chinese)

65. Chen, C., Science and its Position and Role in Social History, in *The Principles of Historical Materialism* (Edited by Xiao Q., Li X., & Wang Y.), p. 326. Beijing: People's Publishing House, 1983. (In Chinese)

66. In this formula, Y refers to the output level of a country; Q refers to the diffusion level of foreign knowledge; T refers to knowledge innovation of a country; C refers to the ability of knowledge utilization; Z is a constant. (In Chinese)

67. Liu, Y., *Technology Innovation Economics*, Section 7.4. Beijing: China Economy Press, 1993. (In Chinese)

68. Liu, Y., *Technology Innovation Economics* (p.147). China Economy Press, 1993. (In Chinese).

69. In the Table, Team A includes the countries with high productivity and high level of technological activities, such as Switzerland, USA, Germany, Sweden, etc.; Team B includes the countries with medium productivity and medium level of technological activities, such as France, UK, Netherlands, Austria, Finland, New Zealand, Italy; Team C includes the countries with high productivity and low level of technological activities, such as Norway, Belgium, Canada, Australia, Denmark; Team D includes the countries or regions with low productivity and a semi-industrialized level, such as Spain, Ireland, Greece, Hong Kong, Argentina, Mexico, Korea, and Taiwan.

70. Temple, R. G., The West's Debt to China. *Philosophy Translations*, 1992(3): 71. (In Chinese)

71. Temple, R. G.., The West's Debt to China. *Philosophy Translations*,

1992(3): 70-71. (In Chinese)

72. *A Report on Global Science and Technology Development in 2004* (pp. 3-4), Beijing: Science Press, 2005. (In Chinese)

73. Lewis H., & Allison D., *Global Economic War* (p.2). China Friendship Publishing House, 1985. (In Chinese)

74. Peng, J., Challenge from Japan and Adjustment of Relationship between Japan and USA. *Global Economy,* 1987(9): 8. (In Chinese)

75. Deng, X., *Selected Works of Deng Xiaoping,* Vol.3, p.279. Beijing: People's Publishing Press, 1993. (In Chinese)

76. Naisbitt, J., & Aburdene P., *The Big Trend of Year 2000* (p.36). Beijing: The Central Party School Press, 1990. (In Chinese)

77. Thurow, L. C., *The Competition of 21st Century* (p.4). China Social Sciences Press, 1994. (In Chinese)

78. Thurow, L. C., *The Competition of 21st Century* (p.4). China Social Sciences Press, 1994. (In Chinese)

79. Bell, D., *The Arrival of Post-Industrial Society* (p.272). Commercial Press, 1986. (In Chinese)

80. National Statistics Bureau of China, *The Statistical Bulletin of National Economy and Social Development in 1991.* (In Chinese)

Chapter Ten

81. Engels, F., Cited from *International Business Newspaper,* June 14th , 1994, p.1. (In Chinese)

82. Temple, R. G.. The West's Debt to China. *Philosophy Translations,* 1992(3): 71-72. (In Chinese)

83. A comparison of economic growth in different regions: during 1960-1980, the annual economic growth rate was 3.5% in USA, 4.5% in Western Europe, and 7.5% in Asia. Since the late 1970's, the Western Countries' economy has almost entered into stagnation and crisis, but Asian economy including China's economy has still kept a high growth rate. (In Chinese)

84. Kravis, I. B., Trade as the Handmaiden of Economic Growth. *Economic Journal,* Dec., 1970.

85. *People's Daily,* Jan.13th, 1995, p.1. (In Chinese)

86. Asia Economic Research Institute, *A Report on Technological Trade Conflicts between Japan and Developing Countries and the International Division of Labor in the Future,* 1986, p.24. (In Chinese)

87. *The World of Information: Asia & Pacific Review,* 1993/1994 edition, p. 59. (In Chinese)

88. Robertson, D. H., Future of International Trade (1937 edition). In *Essay Collection on International Trade,* 1949. (In Chinese)

89. Mantoux, P. (France), *The Industrial Revolution in the Eighteenth Century* (translated by Yang R.), p.79. Shanghai: Commercial Press, 1983. (In Chinese)

90. Yao, Z., *International Trade* (p.32). Beijing: People's Publishing Press, 1987. (In Chinese)
91. Eebee, S., The *Economic History of the United States in the Last One Hundred Years* (p. 214-217). Beijing: China Social Sciences Press, 1983. (In Chinese)

Chapter Eleven
92. Tinbergen, J. (Netherlands), *Economic Policy: Theory and Design* (pp. 48-49). Shanghai: Commercial Press, 1988. (In Chinese)
93. Marx, K., *Preface and Introduction to the Critique of Political Economy* (p. 14). Beijing: People's Publishing House, 1971. (In Chinese)

Chapter Twelve
94. Marx, K., *Employed Labor and Capital* (p.26). Beijing: People's Publishing House, 1971. (In Chinese)
95. Deng, X., *Selected Works of Deng Xiaoping,* Vol.3, p.372. Beijing: People's Publishing House, 1993. (In Chinese)
96. Marx, K., *Capital*, Vol. 1, p.395. Beijing: People's Publishing House, 1987. (In Chinese)
97. Marx, K., *Collection of All Works by Karl Marx and Frederick Engels*, Vol. 26, p. 300.   Beijing: People's Publishing House, 1962. (In Chinese)
98. Marx, K., Engels, F., *Selected Works of Marx and Engels*, Vol. 3. p.19. Beijing: People's Publishing House, 1972. (In Chinese)
99. Engels, F., *Selected Works of Marx and Engels*, Vol.3. p.17. Beijing: People's Publishing House, 1972. (In Chinese)

Chapter Thirteen
100. Engels, F., *Collection of All Works by Karl Marx and Frederick Engels*, Vol. 7, p. 240. Beijing: People's Publishing House, 1962. (In Chinese)
101. Engels, F., Engels, F., *Selected Works of Marx and Engels*, Vol. 3. p. 402. Beijing: People's Publishing House, 1972. (In Chinese)
102. Engels, F., *Selected Works of Marx and Engels*, Vol. 3. p.402. Beijing: People's Publishing House, 1972. (In Chinese)

Chapter Fourteen
103. Marx, K.. *Preface and Introduction to the Critique of Political Economy* (p. 14). Beijing: People's Publishing House, 1971. (In Chinese)
104. Marx, K., *Collection of All Works by Karl Marx and Frederick Engels*, Vol. 26, pp. 124-125. Beijing: People's Publishing House, 1962. (In Chinese)
105. Cipolla, C. M. (Italy), *The Economic History of World Population*. Shanghai: Commercial Press, 1993, P. 84. (In Chinese)
106. Marx, K., *Selected Works of Marx and Engels,* Vol.1, p.375. Beijing: People's Publishing House, 1972. (In Chinese)

107. Marx, K., *Capital*, Vol.1, p.1987. Beijing: People's Publishing House, 1987. (In Chinese)
108. Marx, K., *Selected Works of Marx and Engels,* Vol.2, pp.195-196. People's Publishing House, 1972. (In Chinese)
109. Marx, K., *Collection of All works by Marx and Engels,* Vol. 46 (I), p. 287 & Vol. 46 (II), p. 218. Beijing: People's Publishing House, 1962. (In Chinese)

Index

Breinigsville, PA USA
21 October 2010

247840BV00001B/6/P